D1169530

Celebrating Brain Science in Canada
Mary V. Seeman & Neil Seeman

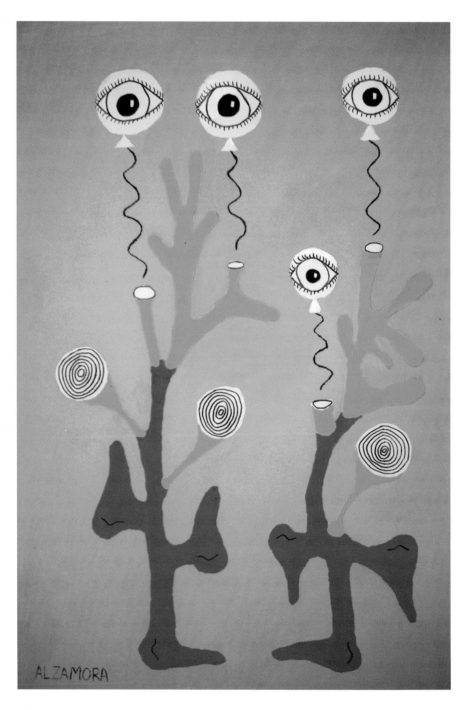

"Light Headed Dancers" by Michael Alzamora. 2003. Acrylic on canvas.

Psyche in the Lab

Celebrating Brain Science in Canada

Mary V. Seeman & Neil Seeman

HOGREFE

Library of Congress Cataloging in Publication

is available via the Library of Congress Marc Database under the
LC Control Number 2006922642

Library and Archives Canada Cataloguing in Publication

Seeman, M. V. (Mary Violette), 1935-
Psyche in the lab : celebrating brain science in Canada / Mary V. Seeman & Neil Seeman.

Includes bibliographical references.
ISBN 0-88937-304-3

1. Psychiatry--Canada. 2. Psychiatry--Research--Canada. I. Seeman, Neil II. Title.

RC447.S42 2006   616.89'0072'071   C2006-901102-8

© 2006 by Hogrefe & Huber Publishers

Cover picture "Let Sleeping Psychiatrists Lie" by Renée Claire Marier. 2006. Watercolor and ink.

PUBLISHING OFFICES
USA: Hogrefe & Huber Publishers, 875 Massachusetts Avenue, 7th Floor,
                Cambridge, MA 02139
                Phone (866) 823-4726, Fax (617) 354-6875; E-mail info@hhpub.com
EUROPE: Hogrefe & Huber Publishers, Rohnsweg 25, 37085 Göttingen, Germany
                Phone +49 551 49609-0, Fax +49 551 49609-88, E-mail hh@hhpub.com

SALES & DISTRIBUTION
USA: Hogrefe & Huber Publishers, Customer Services Department,
                30 Amberwood Parkway, Ashland, OH 44805
                Phone (800) 228-3749, Fax (419) 281-6883, E-mail custserv@hhpub.com
EUROPE: Hogrefe & Huber Publishers, Rohnsweg 25, 37085 Göttingen, Germany
                Phone +49 551 49609-0, Fax +49 551 49609-88, E-mail hh@hhpub.com

OTHER OFFICES
CANADA: Hogrefe & Huber Publishers, 1543 Bayview Avenue, Toronto,
                Ontario M4G 3B5
SWITZERLAND: Hogrefe & Huber Publishers, Länggass-Strasse 76, CH-3000 Bern 9

Hogrefe & Huber Publishers
Incorporated and registered in the State of Washington, USA, and in Göttingen, Lower Saxony,
Germany

Printed and bound in the USA
ISBN 0-88937-304-3

Table of Contents

Section I: Research and Researchers

Foreword

' "Mental illness affects one in every five people… Every family copes with one mental illness or another. Those who say there is no mental illness in the family haven't inquired too deeply into the well being of their relatives" '
(P. Seeman, p. 94).

Stigma can be thought of as made up of one part fear, and one part separateness. If I tell myself the lie that we are disconnected from one another, then I can engage in any behaviour, be it altruistic or destructive. Either way, I will believe it has no effect on others. This belief system will also allow me to view the experience of others as fundamentally dissimilar from mine. It will enable me to believe in the possibility that there are "crazy people out there", and that those people could not be anything like me. Because they are nothing like me, I will not understand them, and therefore I will fear them.

This belief system provides the conditions for stigma to thrive.

If I believe that people are connected to one another through their shared experience of a planet, a country, a time in history, a community, a neighbourhood, and a family, then I will also agree that my actions have a tremendous impact on others. I will be aware that like physical illness, mental illness arises blamelessly, and sometimes without warning, and I will readily be able to recall friends, colleagues, and families I know of who have struggled with mental health issues at some point in their lives. I will have no need to fear mental illness, because I will know it socially, and sometimes personally.

This belief system, coupled with a desire to help as well as to expand the existing knowledge of causes and treatments for various mental illnesses, unites the collective efforts of this text's expert contributors in Section 1. Their remarkable knowledge base is as palpable as their humanity.

This text contains multi-disciplinary contributions from researchers, funding agencies, and those whose lives have been changed through the experience of mental illness. Each contribution is dissimilar from the others, allowing for a breadth of topic areas to be summarized within one volume. The research questions at the heart of each summary in Section 1 are very specific, but the narrative surrounding each contribution provides both a personal and professional context, allowing the individual scientist or practitioner to become visible. The gift to the reader, then, becomes a glimpse of the contributors as whole people – a struggling graduate student, ambivalent about the erosion of his family life should he take on a research (in addition to clinical) position; a researcher who was told by a granting agency she was "delusional" for proposing a progressive vision. The contributors' resilience in the face of rejection, lack of funding, glass ceilings and other politically-based oppressive experiences are not hidden from the reader. However, the impression of mental health practice and research that is formed as a result of reading this book is one of astonishment, excitement, curiosity, and deep respect.

Section 2 is devoted to Benefactors and Beneficiaries. It comprises the experiences of leaders in high-powered funding positions, as well as recipients of mental health services, and their families. Similar to Section 1, the contributors in Section 2 are revealed within their social and emotional contexts, so that the image of a full human being is present within each chapter. Incredible curiosity, crushing sadness, a sense of celebration for triumph despite adversity, as well as continued understanding of mental health and illness in Canada – these are the gifts of the second part of this book.

Taken together, the compilation of these essential contributions will surely spark the interest of Canadian youth, to whom it is dedicated, should they themselves be grappling with mental health issues, or discovering a desire to become mental health professionals. For those who both suffer and aspire, these pages contain much hope for the future, based on the efforts of those who have given so generously of their work, ideas, and experiences.

May the future for Canadians be a healthy one – one without stigma.

LGen The Hon Roméo Dallaire, Senator
Sophie Hyman, Doctoral Student in Clinical Psychology
The Senate, Ottawa
March 2006

Preface

This book commemorates the 25th anniversary of the Canadian Psychiatric Research Foundation (CPRF) by celebrating the science of the mind. The book draws on the experience not only of researchers but also of those who struggle with mental illness and those who, through the contribution of time, energy, and resources, make research possible. The stories of the philanthropists we interview shed light on the roots of altruism, without which research would stagnate. Many research donors, not surprisingly, are themselves expert in this area in that they have had family experience with mental illness. Tapping into this variety of knowledge, *Psyche in the Lab* explores the motives of those who dedicate their lives to the alleviation of mental illness. By profiling these extraordinary individuals, the authors' aim is to encourage and expand Canadian neuroscience. An additional goal is to answer a policy question: What are the impediments to more and better science research in Canada? How can we speed the march of Canadian research into mental illness?

The book is based on a series of interviews with Canadians who have contributed significantly to contemporary advances in mental illness research. The scientists selected for interview are stars but have, in addition, instructive personal stories to tell, stories of hardship, ambition, competition, struggle, heartbreak, and (sometimes) triumph. The strategy that we used to select interviewees is called criterion-based selection. We established a set of standards that potential interviewees needed to meet (outstanding in distinctive fields of psychiatric science, working in varied geographic locations, representing a mix of women and men of diverse cultural backgrounds, associated with the Canadian Psychiatric Research Foundation or with the Canadian Institutes of Health Research). We were assisted in this process by what health services researchers call a "modified Delphi panel": Canadian experts across a variety of fields of philanthropy and science helped us to identify the required criteria and helped direct us to individuals who best demonstrated those attributes. This "snowball" approach to interview selection gives the authors confidence that what we have presented, though not perfect, is a representative portrait of Canadian researchers and philanthropists and service users working together to solve the mind's great mysteries.

The interviews were based on a semi-structured guide, with open-ended questions that encouraged individuals to reflect on their experience and allowed the interviewer to follow their lead. The guide covered a checklist of topics but the interviewer adapted the questions and their sequence to the specific respondent. The interviewees were often asked to tell their life story. In this open-ended way, the person was given the opportunity, undisturbed, to talk about whatever he or she saw as relevant.

The Canadian Psychiatric Research Foundation is a member of the Canadian Alliance on Mental Illness and Mental Health (CAMIMH). This 15 member organization includes Autism Society of Canada, Canadian Association for Suicide Prevention, Canadian Association of Occupational Therapists, Canadian Association of Social Workers, Canadian Coalition for Seniors' Mental Health, Canadian Medical Association, Canadian Mental Health Association, Canadian Psychiatric Association, Canadian Psychiatric Research Foundation, Canadian Psychological Association, Mood Disorders Society of Canada, National Network for Mental Health, Native Mental Health Association of Canada, Registered Psychiatric Nurses of Canada, Schizophrenia Society of Canada. In response to lobbying from this umbrella organization, the Honourable Ujjal Dosanjh, Health Minister for Canada, stated publicly in February 2005 that mental health is a top Canadian priority, recognizing the need for increased research in the area of mental illness. Currently, funds for research related to mental illness comprise only a small fraction of the total research expenditure for health, whereas mental illnesses affect disproportionate numbers of people and the costs of treatment amount to almost 15% of all health care expenditures. According to 2005 data from the Canadian Institute for Health Information (CIHI), one in seven hospitalizations in Canada now involves patients diagnosed with mental illness. Patients diagnosed with a mental illness remain in the hospital more than twice as long, on average, as other patients. Such hospital admissions tend to occur during the prime working years of a person's life. From this, the reader will appreciate how damaging the costs of mental illness are to Canada.

By highlighting the individual stories of researchers, private and public funders, and those who suffer, we hope that *Psyche in the Lab* will inspire young people to enter the mental health professions as both clinicians and scientists. We hope to lift the veil of secrecy that still surrounds mental health problems and make the public aware of the important achievements of Canadian scientists. We also hope to encourage support for research because much remains to be learned.

We are grateful to Alex Lowy whose brainchild this project is. It was his idea, prescient in retrospect, to celebrate the 25th anniversary of the Canadian Psychiatric Research Foundation with a book about Canadian psychiatric research. We thank Judy Hills, Paul K. Bates, Kevin McNeil and the Board of the Canadian Psychiatric Research Foundation, for supporting the idea and making it possible. We thank David M. Campbell, Joey and Toby Tanenbaum, and the Institute of Neurosciences, Mental Health and Addiction for their invaluable contributions. We thank the scientists, mental health service consumers, family members, philanthropists, and policy makers who agreed to be interviewed, who tolerated personal questions, who gave their time so generously and were so candid. We thank David Gentili, the amazing young man who conducted all the interviews, transcribed them, and criss-crossed the country on a busy schedule so that the book could be completed on time. We are especially grateful for the editing and morale-raising skills of Doris Sommer-Rotenberg who helped to edit almost all the chapters. We thank the many whose thoughts we have borrowed (see bibliography) and whose wisdom we sought.

The book is dedicated to the youth of Canada. We hope it will inspire them to deepen their knowledge about mental illnesses and to contribute to the easing of the pain that these illnesses bring. We hope some who read this book will devote themselves to mental health research, some to philanthropy, some to policy change, some to the care and support of those who hurt. Most of all, we hope that this book leads to a larger acceptance of the reality that mental illnesses are pervasive, that we are all vulnerable, that – unless treated – mental illnesses lead to distress and disability, that research clears misunderstandings, reduces stigma, and spirits the development of improved treatments.

Neil Seeman   Mary V. Seeman

Both authors are affiliated with the Faculty of Medicine, University of Toronto. Mary Seeman is a Professor of Psychiatry. Neil Seeman is a Toronto healthcare consultant and lawyer in the Department of Health Policy, Management and Evaluation and teaches health law at Ryerson University.

References

Atkinson M, el-Guebaly N. Research productivity among PhD faculty members and affiliates responding to the Canadian Association of Professors of Psychiatry and Canadian Psychiatric Association survey. Can J Psychiatry. 1996;41:509–512.

Burke JD Jr, Pincus HA, Pardes H. The clinician-researcher in psychiatry. Am J Psychiatry. 1986;143:968–975.

Cleghorn RA. The development of psychiatric research in Canada up to 1964. Can J Psychiatry. 1984;29:189–197.

de Groot JM, Kennedy SH. Integrating clinical and research psychiatry. J Psychiatry Neurosci. 1995;20:150–154.

el-Guebaly N, Atkinson M. Research training and productivity among faculty: the Canadian Association of Professors of Psychiatry and the Canadian Psychiatric Association Survey. Can J Psychiatry. 1996;41:144–149.

el-Guebaly N, Atkinson M. Physician resource variables and their impact on the future pool of research expertise among psychiatrists: the Canadian Association of Professors of Psychiatry and Canadian Psychiatric Association Survey. Can J Psychiatry. 1996;41:150–155.

Fang D, Meyer RE. PhD faculty in clinical departments of U.S. medical schools, 1981–1999: their widening presence and roles in research. Acad Med. 2003;78:167–176.

Garfinkel PE, Goldbloom DS, Kaplan AS, Kennedy SH. The clinician-investigator interface in psychiatry I: Values and problems. Can J Psychiatry. 1989;34:361–363.

Guelich JM, Singer BH, Castro MC, Rosenberg LE. A gender gap in the next generation of physician-scientists: medical student interest and participation in research. J Investig Med. 2002;50:412–418.

Honer WG, Linseman MA. The physician-scientist in Canadian psychiatry. J Psychiatry Neurosci. 2004;29:49–56.

Kates N, Blum HM, Keegan D. The teaching of psychiatric epidemiology in Canadian psychiatry residency programs. Can J Psychiatry. 1988;33:25–27.

Kupfer DJ, Hyman SE, Schatzberg AF, Pincus HA, Reynolds CF 3rd. Recruiting and retaining future generations of physician scientists in mental health. Arch Gen Psychiatry. 2002;59:657–660.

Lam RW, el-Guebaly N. Research funding of psychiatric disorders in Canada: a snapshot, 1990–1991. Can J Psychiatry. 1994;39:141–146.

Leibenluft E, Dial TH, Haviland MG, Pincus HA. Sex differences in rank attainment and research activities among academic psychiatrists. Arch Gen Psychiatry. 1993;50:896–904.

Mark AL, Kelch RP. Clinician scientist training program: a proposal for training medical students in clinical research. J Investig Med. 2001;49:486–490.

Nemeroff CB. How will we solve the critical shortage of clinician-scientists in psychiatry? CNS Spectr. 2001;6:889.

Pardes H, Freedman AM, Reus V. Research training in psychiatry. Am J Psychiatry. 1977;134 Suppl l:S24–128.

Pincus HA, Dial TH, Haviland MG. Research activities of full-time faculty in academic departments of psychiatry. Arch Gen Psychiatry. 1993;50:657–664.

Pincus HA, Haviland MG, Dial TH, Hendryx MS. The relationship of postdoctoral research training to current research activities of faculty in academic departments of psychiatry. Am J Psychiatry. 1995;152:596–601.

Reiser LW, Sledge WH, Fenton W, Leaf P. Beginning careers in academic psychiatry for women – "Bermuda Triangle"? Am J Psychiatry. 1993;150:1392–1397.

Shapiro T, Mrazek D, Pincus HA. Current status of research activity in American child and adolescent psychiatry: Part I. J Am Acad Child Adolesc Psychiatry. 1991;30:443–448.

Stephens T, Joubert N. The economic burden of mental health problems in Canada. Chronic Dis Can. 2001;22:18–23.

Sutton J, Killian CD. The MD-PhD researcher: what species of investigator? Acad Med. 1996;71:454–459.

Swenson JR, Lam RW, Morehouse RL. A psychiatric fellowship in the United States. Can J Psychiatry. 1990;35:243–247.

Introduction

According to the World Health Organization, four of the 10 leading causes of disability in developed countries are mental disorders such as major depression, bipolar disorder, and schizophrenia. In any one year, approximately 23% of adults fulfill the diagnostic criteria of a mental disorder.

To support research into psychiatric disorder, Dr. Harvey C. Stancer in 1980 established the Canadian Psychiatric Research Foundation (CPRF), a national non-profit organization. Harvey Stancer graduated from Medicine (University of Toronto) in 1957, trained in psychiatry, and obtained his PhD in biochemistry, one of the first psychiatrists in Canada to obtain a PhD degree. For many years, he was Director of Research at the Clarke Institute of Psychiatry. In his honor, the University of Toronto's Department of Psychiatry Research Day is appropriately called Stancer Day.

The aim of CPRF is to raise and distribute funds for research to Canadian universities and teaching hospitals. It operates with a very lean staff, a volunteer Professional Advisory Board and a volunteer Board of Directors. To date, CPRF has provided more than $10 million in support to over 300 researchers for work in child and adolescent mental health, mood disorders, addictions, and schizophrenia. The Foundation specifically targets young researchers at the threshold of their careers.

Few young scientists, however, are featured in this book. This is because youth is the promise of tomorrow – today, the stars among young scientists are difficult to identify while the achievements of their seniors, with the passage of time, are easier to spot. Science is a young person's sport, it is said, but Galileo was 52 when he discovered that the rate of fall does not depend on weight; Roentgen was 50 when he stumbled upon X-rays. Pasteur made his most significant contributions to science between the ages of 55 and 58. In today's technological world, scientific experiments require expensive equipment and a large network of collaborators. This is a problem for the young. That being said, young scientists play a crucial role in the future of science. They continue to produce the most original ideas; unless Canada invests in them – there will be no scientists, young or old, tomorrow.

Psyche in the Lab is about the achievements of psychiatric research. The treatment of Alzheimer's disease and memory deficits and mood disorders, the understanding of genetic variation, cognitive therapies, schizophrenia, anxiety disorders and stress, sleep, child and forensic psychiatry, developmental disabilities, substance abuse, family dysfunction, and end-of-life distress would be lacking without the scientific advances of the Canadian scientists chronicled in this book. The reader will be exposed to information about molecular neuroscience, neuroimaging, bedside studies, population genetics, and classical epidemiology, techniques used to explore the mind and its many complexities.

The reader will also meet individuals who are not scientists but who have furthered the cause of psychiatric research in other ways. Those with experience of mental illness, family members, private donors, and policy makers have contributed their time and their money in the hope of solving the riddles of complex diseases of the mind. Each chapter acquaints the reader with current day understanding of disorders of the psyche in order to inform and to encourage more young people to enter a field of science that melds biology and culture, experience and experiment, nurturance and nature.

"The search for the truth is more precious than its possession."

Alfred Einstein

In writing this book, we learned what the scientific method was – an original idea, a hypothesis, leading to experiments intended to prove the hypothesis wrong. Good scientists, we came to realize, always try to disprove their hunches. They may not ever prove their discoveries to be right but they continue to conduct more and more experiments to try to prove them wrong. Competing scientists, of course, also try to prove them wrong. Eventually, one way of interpreting clinical observations is accepted as probably correct. Little by little, opposing hypotheses are discarded. That is how scientific breakthroughs are born, through this very gradual testing and retesting of possible mechanisms in an effort to explain observable facts.

There is a second way of doing science, a "neutral" way. Many experimentalists may start with no hypothesis at all. They accumulate data and make correlations; evidence emerges. While doing away with bias, this method makes it difficult to ascertain cause and effect. For instance, a positive correlation between happiness and the state of being married can mean that marriage leads to happiness, but it can also mean that happy people are more likely than grouches to get married in the first place. Another possibility is that the two factors that correlate with each other are both due to a latent variable, a third factor that no one has considered. An instance of this is the correlation between television viewing in children and their subsequent inclination to aggression. Both, from what we know at present, probably result from a third independent factor, i.e., parental neglect.

Preparing biographical sketches for the chapters in this book bears an analogy to the two research methods described above. At times, we had a starting premise about the importance of the work of a particular scientist and the interviewer made sure to explore that premise. At other times, the interview was conducted with no preconceived ideas. The narrative unfolded by itself.

We wanted to capture the experience as well as the experiment. We wanted to understand the impact of psychiatric disorders on individuals and their motivation for participating in a book about research. We knew that psychiatric illnesses caused not only subjective distress but often also lowered educational attainment, contributed to marital instability, aggravated difficulties with parenting, lessened job satisfaction and reduced income. We also knew that psychiatric illnesses took their toll on caregivers, emotionally, socially, and economically. What we learned from psychiatric patients and families made us realize something new. Yes, the toll is sometimes great, but so is the joy of recovery, the growing confidence when a challenge is overcome and help can be offered others in return for help received.

In writing this book about the achievements of psychiatric science, we were also aware that there is much to criticize about psychiatry. Mistakes have been made in Canada, as elsewhere, under the guise of psychiatric scholarship. There was the era when the world believed in eugenics and two Canadian provinces, Alberta and British Columbia, passed legislation to allow involuntary sterilization of mentally retarded and psychiatrically ill adults (1928–1972). Dr. Joseph Berg of Toronto, who has studied the figures carefully, reports that 2,800 adults were sterilized in Alberta alone during this period. Prominent Canadian psychiatrists were proponents of eugenics, believing that some people were inherently more worthy of survival than others.

> As late as 1920, Dr. C.K. Clarke [1857–1957], Canada's leading psychiatrist at the time, argued strenuously against allowing the immigration of refugee Jewish children from the Ukrainian famine on the grounds that they " .... belonged to a very neurotic race."
>
> From Gerald Tulchinsky Taking Root:
> The Origins of the Canadian Jewish Community

The general public knows about these mistakes and is quick to ferret out scandal. Some are of the opinion that psychiatry is not to be trusted, that it advances its own agenda, which is to pathologize the problems of everyday life by, for instance, giving *worry* the official label of anxiety disorder and calling *grief* depression.

Who are psychiatrists, the critics ask, to determine what is a disorder, to decide what is or is not within "normal" range? Some think that too much money is being spent (wasted in their view) on psychiatric research. They cannot see how studying the brains of laboratory animals, which is what some psychiatric researchers do, is relevant to human health. They even question the peer review system (the way decisions are made about what research proposals are funded); they think there is something wrong when researchers who sit on peer review committees receive funds from the very committees to which they belong. They feel that there is not enough accountability and oversight. Chapter 31 on the protections accorded to psychiatric research participants addresses several of these issues.

Under Further Reading (below) the reader will find references to Canadian psychiatric scandals (C.K. Clarke's eugenic convictions – he thought "mental defectives" should not only be kept out of the country but, if already in Canada, sterilized, D. Ewen

Cameron's (1901–1967) psychic driving and LSD experiments, and David Healy's recent (and strongly denied) assertions that the Centre for Addiction and Mental Health, Canada's foremost psychiatric research institute, is "in the pocket" of pharmaceutical companies). But there is much more to psychiatry than scandal, real or imagined. This book illustrates how much the academic and private sector of a community can accomplish for humanity when they join forces and work together, and how important it is that they do so. We hope that everyone who reads *Psyche in the Lab*, including psychiatry's critics, is lured by the sheer excitement of the quest into the often mysterious workings of the human mind.

Further Reading

Cameron DE. Psychic driving. Am J Psychiatry. 1956;112:502–509.

Cameron DE. Psychic driving: dynamic implant. Psychiatr Q. 1957;31:703–712.

Collins A. In the sleep room: The story of the CIA brainwashing experiments in Canada. Toronto: Lester & Orpen Dennys; 1988.

Dowbiggin IR. Keeping America sane: Psychiatry and eugenics in the United States and Canada, 1880–1940, Ithaca (NY): Cornell University Press; 1997.

Farrar CB. I remember C.K. Clarke, 1857–1957. Am J Psychiatry. 1957;114:368–370.

Gillmor D. I swear by Apollo: Dr. Ewen Cameron and the CIA-brainwashing experiments. Montreal: Eden Press; 1987.

Greenland C. C.K. Clarke: a founder of Canadian psychiatry. Can Med Assoc J. 1966;95:155–160.

Healy D. Psychopharmacology and the government of the self. Available at: http://www.pharmapolitics.com/feb2healy.html

Hyde C. Abuse of trust: The career of Dr. James Tyhurst. Vancouver: Douglas & McIntyre; 1991.

Joint Statement of Dr. David Healy, The Centre for Addiction and Mental Health and the University of Toronto http://www2.camh.net/press_releases/healy_camh_uoft_statement.html

Rakoff VM, Stancer HC, Kedward HB, editors. Psychiatric diagnosis. New York: Brunner/Mazel; 1977.

Wray KB, Middle-aged scientists are most potent. The Scientist, 2004;18(22):6.

Section I

Research and Researchers

Chapter 1

Alzheimer's Disease:
Pat and Edie McGeer and the
Inflamed Brain

*"That is the essence of science: Ask an impertinent question, and you are
on the way to a pertinent answer."*
Jacob Bronowski

Alzheimer's disease is both commonplace and mysterious. A few genes have been
found that contribute to individual risk but much about this dementing illness remains unknown. Vancouver neuroscientists Patrick and Edith McGeer have worked
as a team for half a century; their pioneering discoveries point to the role of inflam-
mation in the Alzheimer brain.

This first section of *Psyche in the Lab* pays tribute to Canadian psychiatric scientists, alphabetically, by the name of the disease to which they have committed their lives. This chapter describes research into Alzheimer's disease pioneered by husband and wife team, Patrick and Edith McGeer. The work of the McGeers at the University of British Columbia has brought renewed hope to the 14 million people around the world who suffer from Alzheimer's disease. This is a disease that, as we grow older as a population, affects more and more of us. It is diagnosed in three percent of the population aged 65 to 75, in 19% of those 75 to 85, and in 47% of those 85 and older. With Canada's average lifespan hovering around 82 – and rising – solving the riddle of Alzheimer's will emerge in the coming decades as health priority #1. Nursing home care for an Alzheimer's sufferer costs between $30,000–$50,000 yearly. Cutting the incidence of this disease by half could save Canada at least $3.5 billion yearly.

Patrick Lucey McGeer, the youngest of three children, was born in Vancouver in 1927 to James, a county court judge, and Ada, the first female CBC producer in British Columbia. Young Pat grew tall and soon became a southpaw basketball star, a forward for Ryerson United Church, the team that won the 1941–42, 1942–43, and 1943–44 junior B.C. championships. Pat left the team in 1944 to study chemistry at the University of British Columbia and did not make the Varsity team, the Thunderbirds, so played instead for a commercial team called Laurie's Pie-Rates, managed by a local pie-maker.

He made the Thunderbirds squad the following season, and remembers 1945–46 as the pinnacle of his sports career. On January 11, 1946 at the Varsity Gym, the Thunderbirds took on the spectacular Harlem Globetrotters. The University of British Columbia newspaper covered the game. Would-be spectators had to climb to the roof of the packed gym to get a glimpse of the play. After missing several shots during the first quarter and giving the New Yorkers the lead, the 'Birds gained a seven-point lead by the end of the second quarter. "Harlem crept within four points in the third quarter… until McGeer sank his southpaw flips from all over the court in the final frame… Harlem pulled within four points again in the fourth quarter … but McGeer was equal to the occasion… The 'Birds held a 42–38 lead all the way to the final whistle."

Within a week, they beat the top-ranking Oregon Webfoots twice, and ultimately won the U.S. Conference title. Pat McGeer's shining moment came in 1948, when the Thunderbirds took the Canadian Championship and represented Canada in the Olympic Games in London. (They didn't win that one). Instead of going on to play with the Vancouver Hornets, Pat visited his elder brother Peter who was finishing up his PhD in chemistry at Princeton. Going mostly on Peter's reputation, Dean Hugh Taylor offered Pat a scholarship on the spot. "We are really scraping the bottom of the barrel this year," he purportedly said to Pat.

Princeton University was populated with legendary, awe-inspiring scientific figures such as Albert Einstein and John Von Neumann, and this couldn't help but rub off on Pat. He graduated with a PhD in physical chemistry in 1951 and joined DuPont's Experimental Station in Wilmington, Delaware to work in high polymer research, the dawning of the plastics revolution. By the standards of the day, the salary was generous, so Pat promptly invested in a second-hand car and part ownership in a boat. When he visited Princeton, his former supervisor remarked: "Well, Pat, you have lots of transportation, but where are you going?"

E.I. duPont de Nemours stood at the pinnacle of industrial chemistry in the early postwar years. The company was hiring one-half of all chemistry PhD graduates in the United States. Its sprawling new Experimental Station in Wilmington looked like a large university campus with nothing but chemistry buildings. During the 1930s, the company's organic chemists had worked out the basic principles of high polymer chemistry. Nylon was the crown jewel, inspiring the company slogan "Better things for better living – through chemistry." Scientists working at DuPont were made to feel like family. Bordering the Experimental Station was the DuPont Country Club complete with tennis courts and 36 holes of golf, a fringe benefit provided to DuPont workers at low cost.

On the distaff side, Edith Graef was born in New York, the youngest child of Dr. Charles Graef, an eye, ear, nose and throat specialist, and Charlotte Graef (née Ruhl), a housewife from a German family where all the men for the last two generations had been physicians. Edie attended a small private school in New York and then Swarthmore College on an Open Scholarship. She had a traumatic introduction to Swarthmore: when she went to get her course card signed by the Professor and Head of the Chemistry Department, he gave her a half hour lecture on how she was wasting her time and, more importantly, *his* time because women could not fathom chemistry! The younger staff were more supportive and even the Professor thawed a little when the male students were called out in 1943 to join the war effort and he had to turn to Edie for help assisting in the freshman laboratory.

Edie was not as athletic as Pat but did manage to acquire her letters in both golf and badminton. She left Swarthmore in 1944 and moved on to graduate work at the University of Virginia where she tried to synthesize antitubercular agents. Edie had been so well trained at Swarthmore that she left Virginia two years later, in September of 1946, with a PhD in organic chemistry to take up a position with the DuPont Company. Edie chose DuPont because she appreciated honesty. Several other companies that offered her a job had said she would receive equal treatment with the men, but none could point to any woman in a supervisory role. The DuPont representative said Edie would receive equal treatment as far as pay and bonuses went but would not be moved into the managerial stream because there was no guarantee that she would not get married and leave.

Edie worked in the Intelligence Division of the Chemicals Department, which provided basic research for new lines of chemicals. Her major achievement during those years was suggesting a synthetic route to tetracyanoethylene, which ultimately led to a whole new branch of organic chemistry. It meant patents and citations from the American Chemical Society for both DuPont and for Edie.

Pat had been with DuPont for more than two years before crossing paths with Edie. One of Pat's bachelor pals approached him one evening asking if he wanted to buy a plane. "Yes, of course," Pat replied, not knowing how to fly. So he and two others bought a small Aeronca for the princely sum of $750. On their first flight they ran out of gas. Word quickly spread around the Experimental Station that these three mavericks were best to avoid. But chance dictated otherwise for Edie. She moved into a new apartment building only to find that Pat and a roommate lived across the hall. It took Pat just a few weeks to realize he was on the wrong side of the hall. And so they married, Pat moved across the hall, and a lifelong collaboration began.

Edie remembers the week in February when they got engaged. She wrote her Mother, then in Florida: "Last week was quite a good week. I won the DuPont women's ping pong tournament on Sunday, my partner and I won the duplicate bridge match on Tuesday, and I got engaged on Thursday."

Pat had applied to medical school at the University of British Columbia before he met Edie and had been accepted for the fall of 1954. Edie felt Pat would not be happy unless he had a chance to pursue his ambition. So they moved to Vancouver in June and got settled before medical school opened in the fall of 1954. The field of neuroscience had not yet been born. Watson and Crick had just discovered the structure of DNA.

At this time, Dr. William C. Gibson established a neurological research unit at the University of British Columbia, with a special interest in mental disease. Gibson had been a student of Wilder Penfield at the Montreal Neurological Institute. Penfield had sent him to work with Sir Charles Sherrington in Oxford where he developed silver staining methods for the boutons terminaux of presynaptic neurons. He then went to Madrid to study under Del Rio Hortega but this was short-lived due to the outbreak of the Spanish Civil War. At UBC he set about to apply chemical techniques toward attaining an understanding of psychiatric problems and, due to Edie and Pat's background in chemistry, they fitted well into his plans. Pat started working in his laboratory during the summers of medical school. Pat and Edie's first child, a daughter, died shortly after birth. This was a painful period but it led to Edie volunteering part-time in the Gibson laboratory. Son Rick (now a computer scientist) was born in 1957, Tad (an aeronautical engineer) in 1958, and daughter Tori (a philosopher) two years later.

Pat graduated in 1958 and assumed leadership of the neurological lab in 1961 but Edie did a lot of the work because, in 1962, at the age of 35, Pat won a Liberal seat in the B.C. legislature. He came from a political family. His uncle, Gerry McGeer, was a mayor of Vancouver, a Liberal MP, and a senator.

In October of 1968, Pat was voted leader of the B.C. Liberal party. "This is a whale of a party and a whale of a province," he told cheering delegates. Whales had been an interest of his since 1964 when he was a member of a Vancouver Aquarium scientific expedition that captured the first killer whale.

Pat disliked UBC premier's Dave Barrett's socialism so much that he and two other Liberals joined the Socred party for the 1975 provincial election. Under the leadership of Bill Bennett, the Socreds ended the three-year administration of Dave Barrett and Pat McGeer was appointed to cabinet, where he held a variety of portfolios. During his long tenure, he was responsible for launching B.C.'s Open Learning Institute and the Knowledge Network. He assisted Edie in the laboratory during evenings and weekends.

The McGeers began researching Alzheimer's disease in 1982, pressed by Phyllis Forsyth who subsequently started the Alzheimer Society of British Columbia. Mrs. Forsyth's husband, Quintin, suffered from Alzheimer's. Pat was able to obtain funds from BC's Minister of Health to establish an Alzheimer disease Clinic at the University of British Columbia.

In 1984, the McGeers thought they saw viral particles in brain samples taken from Alzheimer's victims. Because viral infections would naturally induce an immunological response, they began to search for evidence of an immune reaction in Alzheimer brains. One grant proposal after another was rejected because the work was thought to be too "innovative." As a result, they looked for funding from private institutions and from private donors. An important early supporter was Guy Mills from Hudson's Hope who had made money in the Toronto real estate market, had heard Pat McGeer speak on the radio, and was inspired to give the husband and wife team an initial $150,000 gift. Mr. Mills' mother had died in 1974 of a degenerative brain disease, amyotrophic lateral sclerosis.

Pat McGeer's political career ended in 1986. At the age of 61, he returned full time to what was now UBC's Kinsmen Laboratory of Neurological Research, set on finding a cure for Alzheimer's disease. Because of the generosity of Mr. Mills and other private donors, the McGeers were able to discover that brain cells called astrocytes and microglia surround the amyloid plaques in the brains they were studying (a core feature of Alzheimer's disease). The McGeers found that these cells were particularly active in Alzheimer's brains. In their attempt to destroy the amyloid plaques, these cells secreted toxic proteins that damaged and eventually killed nearby neurons. With time, more and more microglia surround the plaques and, the more there are, the more healthy neurons die. Once started, this became a self-perpetuating process. Twenty years of work on this problem has convinced the McGeers that inflammatory processes contribute to cell death. They call this inflammatory process autotoxicity to distinguish it from autoimmunity.

Because they could see an inflammatory process at work, Pat got the idea that anti-inflammatory drugs could be used for prevention. If this were true, he reasoned, people with rheumatoid arthritis would be less likely to have Alzheimer disease than the general population. Statistics Canada data and the records of arthritis clinics confirmed that the numbers of those suffering from both diseases simultaneously were unusually low. In 1992, in the journal, *Lancet*, the McGeers published their data on the low prevalence of Alzheimer's disease in those with rheumatoid arthritis. They suggested that the long-term use of anti-inflammatory drugs could be one of four possible explanations for the finding.

On a visit to Japan, a psychiatrist told Pat and Edie that leprosy patients never got dementia. They visited a leper colony on a Japanese island where most of the patients were over 65. Younger cases were rare because Dapsone, an effective treatment for leprosy, had been introduced in Japan in the late 1940s. Patients on the island lived in separate cottages and were followed weekly in the hospital clinic. There was no way that a developing dementia could be missed and yet none of them had been so diagnosed. Could Dapsone, which was known to have anti-inflammatory properties, be responsible? A Japanese study from 1992 had shown that the prevalence of dementia in leprosy patients taking Dapsone was 2.9% compared to 6.25% in those who did not take it, the latter percentage being almost identical to that of the general Japanese population. When patients were taken off the drug, they became as vulnerable to dementia as anyone else. Studies in the McGeer laboratory have since shown that Dapsone is effective in delaying the onset of memory loss.

Alzheimer's disease is not the only kind of dementia that afflicts human beings but it is the most common, accounting for at least 50–60% of the dementias. Precise diagnosis could, in the past, only be made on autopsy but, currently, clinical diagnosis aided by laboratory and imaging techniques is 80% accurate. Vascular dementia, Lewy body dementia, and frontotemporal dementias have to be ruled out, although the different types of dementia often overlap. Vascular risk factors, for instance, increase the likelihood of Alzheimer's. Important other illnesses to exclude when making a diagnosis include delirium, depression, Vitamin B12/folate deficiency, hypothyroidism, and the normal aging process.

Alzheimer's is a complex genetic disease, much like the other diseases described in this book. When Alzheimer's starts before age 50, there appear to be three causative genes (called beta-amyloid precursor protein (APP) and presenilin-1 (PSEN1) and presenilin-2 (PSEN2) that account for about half the cases. These genes are transmitted in an autosomal dominant fashion, meaning that half the offspring of an affected person will eventually develop Alzheimer's. With respect to late onset disease (symptoms beginning after age 70) about 50% of afflicted people carry the apolopoprotein E (APOE)-epsilon 4 form of the gene, which may bring forward the onset of disease by several years. Studies on the effects of mutations in the four known genes seem to point to the conclusion that they all cause dysregulation of the protein that leads to the accumulation of amyloid plaques in the brain. This, in turn, leads to problems with intracellular tau protein. Renowned Canadian Alzheimer researcher Rémi Quirion (see Chapter 12) has said that those who study Alzheimer's can be divided into Popists (followers of APOE), Baptists (followers of beta-amyloid peptide), and Taoists (followers of the tau protein). In line with these divisions, the McGeers, who study inflammatory processes, could well be called Infidels. Nevertheless, all researchers agree that a cascade of errors ultimately causes nerve dysfunction and nerve death, leading somewhat mysteriously to the neuropathology and clinical expression of Alzheimer's disease.

It is thought that dementia can be delayed or prevented not only with anti-inflammatory agents but also with prompt treatment of hypertension and the use of lipid-lowering agents. It is important to maintain control of diabetes, not smoke, avoid head injury, lose weight, and treat all possible sources of blood clot to the brain. Intake of

Vitamin E, green tea, red wine, and Ginkgo biloba has sometimes been reported to lower the risk of Alzheimer's disease. There is an inverse correlation between years of education and age at onset of Alzheimer's, but this does not mean that education prevents dementia from setting in. It could mean that a factor associated with duration of education (such as socioeconomics, good health, or good nutrition) is preventive or it could mean that those destined to develop early Alzheimer's are already affected in a subtle way in youth, causing them to abandon educational pursuits. Nevertheless, continued participation in educational and cultural activities in older age is helpful.

For their achievements in neuroscience, in May 1995, Edie and Pat McGeer were inducted together as Officers of the Order of Canada. Were they the first husband and wife team to be so recognized? Yes and No. A husband and wife team had previously been honored but, before the award was conferred, they had a fight, divorced, and refused to take part in the same ceremony. The two McGeers were jointly named fellows of the Royal Society of Canada in 2002 and this was a definite first for the Society. The recently established Henry Wisniewski Award was bestowed on Pat at the ninth International Conference on Alzheimer's Disease and Related Dementias held in Philadelphia in 2004. Pat said to reporters, "it's nice to be rated by your peers as number one, but they picked the wrong McGeer."

The involvement of immune mechanisms in Alzheimer's, a novel idea when first proposed by the McGeers, is gaining scientific ground. It has recently been discovered, for instance, that Alzheimer's patients produce an antibody response to proteins found in neuronal plaques at three to four times the rate of non-Alzheimer's patients, even though the actual blood levels of such proteins do not differ. This finding could lead to a blood test for Alzheimer's. The McGeers, now approaching their 80s, take anti-inflammatory drugs themselves, though they show no sign of cognitive slowing. Aside from the occasional day skiing, they continue to work seven days a week in the laboratory.

Further Reading

Kar S, Quirion R. Amyloid beta peptides and central cholinergic neurons: functional interrelationship and relevance to Alzheimer's disease pathology. Prog Brain Res. 2004;145:261–274.

McGeer PL, Harada N, Kimura H, McGeer EG, Schulzer M. Prevalence of dementia amongst elderly Japanese with leprosy: apparent effect of chronic drug therapy. Dementia. 1992;3:146–149.

McGeer PL, Rogers J, McGeer EG, Sibley J. Does anti-inflammatory treatment protect against Alzheimer disease? Lancet. 1990;335:1037.

McGeer PL, Rogers J. Medical hypothesis: anti-inflammatory agents as a therapeutic approach to Alzheimer's disease. Neurology. 1992;42:447–450.

McGeer PL, Schulzer M, McGeer EG, Arthritis and anti-inflammatory agents as negative risk factors for Alzheimer disease: A review of seventeen epidemiological studies, Neurology. 1996;47:425–432.

Poirier J, Delisle MC, Quirion R, Aubert I, Farlow M, Lahiri D, Hui S, Bertrand P, Nalbantoglu J, Gilfix BM, Gauthier S. Apolipoprotein E4 allele as a predictor of cholinergic deficits and treatment outcome in Alzheimer disease. Proc Natl Acad Sci USA. 1995;92:12260–12264.

St George-Hyslop PH, Petit A. Molecular biology and genetics of Alzheimer's disease. C R Biol. 2005;328:119–130.

Chapter 2

Anxiety Disorders:
Richard Swinson Quells Disquiet

"We deem those happy who from the experience of life have learnt to bear its ills without being overcome by them."

Carl Gustav Jung

Anxiety disorders are the most widespread and potentially disabling of mental disorders. This chapter focuses on the work of Hamilton psychiatrist Richard Swinson who has demonstrated that behavioral techniques are superior to drugs in the treatment of anxiety.

Canada's 10 millionth official immigrant, Dr. Richard Swinson, arrived in Canada with his family on May 27th, 1972. He had completed a psychiatry residency and doctoral work in the U.K., studied psychopathology at the University of Liverpool with Frank Fish and behavior therapy with Philip Ley. Appointed staff psychiatrist at St. Michael's Hospital in Toronto, Swinson and his colleague, Klaus Kuch, established a behavior therapy clinic. That first initiative was a bit of a disaster "because referring sources kept sending us clients who wouldn't behave," while the referrals they were seeking, of course, were people who were anxious. Anxiety disorders, though some of the most common and potentially disabling of psychiatric conditions, are eminently treatable with behavior therapy.

One in four individuals in Canada has experienced at least one of the many forms of anxiety disorder. While feeling anxious is not an illness, it becomes one if it is excessive and if it persists when there is nothing, objectively, to worry about. Anxiety can, at those times, become so pervasive that it interferes with daily functioning. People can, for instance, feel worried and stressed about everything, a condition called generalized anxiety disorder (GAD). GAD affects from 4% to 8% of all people at some time in their lives. The worry is persistent and uncontrollable; muscles feel tense and mental focus is lost. When the worry is mostly about health, the condition is popularly referred to as hypochondriasis. Anxiety can also take the form of episodes of terror, as in panic disorder. Aberrant electrical firing in specific brain regions, notably the region called the amygdala, has been implicated in panic disorder. Yet another form of anxiety is known as obsessive-compulsive disorder, characterized by repetitive ruminations and behaviors – constant hand washing for instance, or repeated checking to see if the stove is on.

Post-traumatic stress disorder (PTSD) is also included among the anxiety disorders. It refers to long-lasting distress after a traumatic life event such as a natural catastrophe – war, rape, or child abuse. Because memories of past threats can be rekindled even by harmless events that have some similarity to the initial triggering event, a person who suffers from PTSD often responds with fear or with a tendency to startle in circumstances that appear, to others, to be risk-free. Phobias, another form of anxiety, are fears that are seemingly unreasonable accompanied by the avoidance of common objects or situations. Social phobia, also known as social anxiety disorder, is a persistent fear of being observed and negatively evaluated in social situations. Individuals with this phobia too often feel humiliated or embarrassed. The mere anticipation of a social obligation can cause them intense anxiety.

Others notice social phobia because there are outward signs: inaudible voice, averted eyes, blushing, sweating, stuttering, and trembling. Such reactions can be pervasive but, more often, are limited to specific performance settings such as public speaking. Anxiety reactions are so common in human beings that they almost certainly have served an evolutionary purpose. It has been hypothesized that avoiding eye contact or blushing or speaking in a low voice may be analogues of what, in other primates, are called appeasement displays; they signal submission to someone higher up in the dominance hierarchy. Appeasement prevents warfare or other types of attack and, thus, has definite survival advantages for the human race. But for the individual doing the appeasing, feelings of intimidation can be excruciatingly painful and can lead to other health problems including substance abuse when alcohol or drugs are used in an effort to quell anxiety.

It is all these kinds of anxiety disorders that Dr. Swinson had been studying in England and continued to study in Canada. In England, he had trained as an addictions specialist. He had had experience with anxious patients not only because they so often turn to drink for comfort but also because withdrawal from an addicting substance such as alcohol brings about a severe anxiety state.

Naturally occurring anxiety states are thought to result from both familial predisposition and childhood experiences. Rather than attempting to uncover the initial causes (which was proving not to be an effective approach to treatment), Dr. Swinson focused on specific behavioral steps a person can take to reduce anxiety and prevent its return. Behavior treatments in his clinic included a variety of techniques such as relaxation, biofeedback, meditation exercises, systematic desensitization, exposure, and flooding. Sometimes these strategies were used in conjunction with drug therapy.

Newer forms of behavioral treatment called cognitive behavioral therapy (CBT) target specific ways of thinking that are known to perpetuate anxiety. For instance, anxious individuals often think there is nothing they can do to control a potential danger. In co-operation with the patient, the cognitive therapist challenges this belief. Anxious individuals are often intolerant of uncertainty. Behavioral techniques help them gradually tolerate larger and larger doses of uncertainty. In hypochondriasis or health anxiety, sufferers are taught to become more at ease with innocent bodily sensations and so not to catastrophize about what these sensations might mean. For panic disorders, sufferers can be trained in deep breathing techniques. Virtual reality therapy (VRT) represents a new software tool for gradually exposing social phobics to social situations.

Drug therapy may work faster than behavioral psychotherapy; drugs are more widely available, easier to administer, and cost less initially. Taking pills is easier for most patients than regularly visiting a therapist. But drugs are less effective than CBT in stopping people from avoiding anxiety-provoking situations. CBT techniques have no side effects and they promote active coping rather than the more passive dependence on medications. Discontinuing either drugs or CBT can lead anxious people to relapse. However, CBT offers greater protection against relapse than do drugs.

There may be arguments about the most effective form of therapy but there is no question that childhood experiences do shape the expression of later symptoms and behaviors. They can also prove pivotal in shaping a career. Richard Swinson's father had been involved in the development of techniques to treat burn victims during World War II and, as a child, Richard studied the before-and-after pictures. This made him more and more determined that, when he grew up, he would try to alleviate suffering. Then he himself had a back injury at age 16 that put him in a body cast for 14 weeks. The doctor who treated him was a significant influence in Richard's decision to apply to medical school. At age 17, he went straight into second year Medicine (because he had already done the course content for Year One in High School). His decision to pursue psychiatric medicine was based on his admiration of the physicians he met during his psychiatry elective time in medical school.

A tragedy shaped forever the course of Richard Swinson's life. On Feb 12, 1993, his eldest son, Rob, was killed at the age of 27. He was driving home from buying his girlfriend a Valentine gift when his car was hit by a driver whose alcohol level was two-and-a-half times the legal limit. This tragedy contributed to major changes in priorities. It led Richard's wife, Carolyn, to join MADD (Mothers Against Drunk Drivers), an organization that promotes awareness of drunk driving and supports families of victims killed by impaired drivers. She became the National President of MADD and received a Governor General's Caring Canadians award for her work with the organization.

Loss, such as that experienced by Richard's family, leads inevitably to a reappraisal of career goals and an assessment of what is important. One of the most sustaining factors for the family was the strong support from Richard's colleagues and friends. The processes involved in the emotional and legal consequences of such a loss are draining and seemingly endless. At that time Richard decided to return to clinical research and reduce his administrative load. He focused his energies on OCD, obsessive-compulsive disorder, whose lifetime prevalence is 1–2%.

Many people with OCD believe that they have the power to either provoke or prevent crucial negative events. Although officially classified as an anxiety disorder, OCD can also be considered a belief disorder because the obsessions about responsibility, cleanliness and sin often become so huge that they appear delusional. Such ideas, secondarily, trigger anxiety. OCD is also, at times, associated with a movement disorder because some people with this diagnosis suffer from tics and repeated movements such as hair pulling (trichotillomania) or nail biting or skin picking.

> "And when I heard this thing, I rent my garment and my mantle,
> and plucked off the hair of my head and of my beard."
> Book of Ezra, verse 9:3

OCD can also be thought of as an impulse disorder because some people with this condition act or fear they will act impulsively. Dr. Swinson has studied the different ways that symptoms of OCD can be expressed. They fall into several categories:
1. Contamination obsessions and cleaning compulsions
2. Sexual/religious/somatic obsessions and checking
3. Fearfulness and checking
4. Impulses and fear of loss of control
5. Need for symmetry and exactness, and ordering and counting compulsions
6. Ruminations.

It is significant that a biological cause has been proposed for some (rare) childhood onset cases of this disorder. The immune reaction to a streptococcal bacterial infection can sometimes lead to the development of crippling obsessions and compulsions called Pediatric Autoimmune Neuropsychiatric Disorders Associated with Streptococcal Infections (PANDAS). The symptoms have been reported to disappear with antibiotic treatment and to recur with subsequent streptococcal infection. It is hoped that knowing what areas of the brain are affected by the immune response to streptococcal infection will lead to a better understanding of the site of brain impairments in the more common forms of OCD.

The selective serotonin reuptake inhibitors (SSRIs) are today considered the front line medications for this disorder but 30–40% of OCD sufferers do not respond to SSRIs and another 40% to 60% achieve a partial remission only. Combining SSRIs with low dose atypical antipsychotic agents has, more recently, been found to work in about 50% of initial non-responders.

One hypothesis for the activity in the brain of OCD sufferers is that the successful completion of an act is not sufficiently rewarded, as it should be, by a surge of pleasurable chemicals in the brain. Without that signal, OCD sufferers need to go on repeating the act. This hypothesis has led to clinical trials of tramadol, a drug with some serotonin and norepinephrine reuptake properties. Electroconvulsive therapy (ECT) may also be effective in nonresponse. Another new treatment, repetitive transcranial electromagnetic stimulation (rTMS), also shows promise.

While anxiety disorders are prevalent in all countries and cultures, interesting differences exist around the world. These differences may point the way to new understandings and, perhaps, new treatments. For instance, in cultures that emphasize interdependency, personal traits such as humility and social inhibition are seen as promoting group cohesion and are therefore not pathologized. Anxiety is viewed as a positive social force because it draws people together in mutual support.

Considerable work is being done in Canada in tracing the brain circuits involved in anxiety. One of these circuits is subcortical, operating below the level of awareness. It serves to warn immediately the amygdala part of the brain that a potential threat is nearby. A second neural pathway connects the amygdala to the cortex and brings thinking, reasoning, evaluation, and consciousness into play. There are also inputs from the hippocampus, the seat of memory, allowing previous memories to modulate the initial response to a threat. In addition, the sensory brain (which is receiving information from eyes, ears, nose, and skin) informs the amygdala about the potential danger of any incoming stimulus. A complex array of neural connections to different regions of the hypothalamus in turn activates the sympathetic nervous system and causes the release of brain stress hormones that subsequently bring about a whole body hormonal cascade. The sum total is called the fight or flight response to fear, named by Hans Selye the general adaptation syndrome. (Please refer also to Chapter 15 on stress disorders).

If I may venture a prediction, I would like to reiterate my opinion that research on stress will be most fruitful if it is guided by the principle that we must learn to imitate – and if necessary to correct and complement – the body's own auto-pharmacologic efforts to combat the stress factor in disease.

Selye H., Stress and Disease, *Science*, 1955; 122:625

With respect to genetic contributions to anxiety disorders, it has been proposed that what is inherited is not one or another of the clinical forms of anxiety described earlier but, rather, inhibited temperament or a tendency to harm avoidance in response to a novel or threatening stimulus. Approximately 10–15% of young children show fearfulness and shyness when faced with unfamiliar people, objects, or situations. Twin and adoption studies have shown that shyness, introversion, and behavioral inhibition are among the most heritable of personality traits. Genetic factors appear to account for about 50% of the variance in behavioral inhibition during childhood; the rest is learned.

Richard Swinson wishes he had more time for research these days, especially as his field, anxiety disorders, is so rapidly changing. As the Morgan Firestone Chair (please also see Chapter 10) of Psychiatry and Behavioral Neurosciences at McMaster University in Hamilton, his research currently involves many collaborative projects. He enjoys all facets of psychiatry – management, teaching, clinical service, research. He has just completed his sixth book (listed below) and, as of this year, will assume the chairmanship of the Professional Advisory Board of the Canadian Psychiatric Research Foundation. Just as Frank Fish and Philip Ley once boasted about the achievements of young Richard Swinson, the now older Swinson takes justifiable pride in the successes of those who have learned from him.

Further Reading

Fish F, Hamilton M. Outline of psychiatry for students and practitioners. London: Butterworth and Heineman; 1984.

Krijn M, Emmelkamp PMG, Olafsson RP, Biemond R. Virtual reality exposure of anxiety disorders: a review. Clin Psychol Rev. 2004;24:259–281.

Ley P. Communicating with patients. London: Chapman and Hall; 1988.

Selye H. The stress of life. New York: McGraw Hill; 1956.

Selye H. The stress of my life: a scientist's memory. New York: Van Nostrand Reinhold; 1979.

Summerfeldt LJ, Kloosterman PH, Antony MM, Richter MA, Swinson RP. The relationship between miscellaneous symptoms and major symptom factors in obsessive-compulsive disorder. Behav Res Ther. 2004;42:1453–1467.

Swedo SE, Grant PJ. Annotation: PANDAS: a model for human autoimmune disease. J Child Psychol Psychiatry. 2005;46:227–234.

Swinson RP, Eaves D. Alcoholism and addiction. London: Woburn Press; 1978.

Swinson RP. Obsessive-compulsive disorder: theory, research, and treatment. New York: Guilford Publications; 1998.

Swinson RP. Obsessive-compulsive disorder: theory, research, and treatment. New York: Guilford Publications; 2001.

Swinson RP, Antony MM. When perfect isn't good enough: strategies for coping with perfectionism. Oakland, CA: New Harbinger Publications; 1998.

Swinson RP, Antony MM. Phobic disorders and panic in adults: a guide to assessment and treatment. Washington DC: American Psychological Association; 2000.

Swinson RP, Antony MM. The shyness & social anxiety workbook: proven techniques for overcoming your fears. Oakland, CA: New Harbinger Publications, 2000.

Chapter 3

Autism:
Jeanette Holden Searches
for Elusive Genes

"There is continuing speculation that geniuses such as Glenn Gould, Nikola Tesla, Albert Einstein and Isaac Newton were affected by Asperger's syndrome because they all showed intense interest in specific, relatively narrow subjects."
(See BBC News, Einstein and Newton "Had Autism", 30 April 2003).

Developmental disorders take an especially heavy toll on families. The life and career of Kingston geneticist Jeanette Holden illustrate how a family problem can spur scientific curiosity.

Jeanette Jeltje Anne Holden was seven or eight when she first realized that something was wrong with her younger brother, Jim. "My whole life has been geared toward researching what he has," she said in an interview for this book. Autism is Dr. Holden's major research focus. She is the program director for a large international Autism Spectrum Disorders Canadian-American Research Consortium (ASD-CARC) funded by the Canadian Institutes for Health Research. She wants to discover more about the inheritance patterns of these conditions and uses cytogenetic and molecular genetic approaches to identify and characterize potential genes. Because the genes for autism spectrum disorders (ASD) have proven to be elusive, this research consortium is using an assortment of techniques to try to identify them. By tracing the pathways of *known* genes for rare autistic syndromes such as Rett's syndrome and fragile X syndrome (located on the X chromosome in both cases), researchers hope to better understand the more common autistic syndromes whose genetic underpinning remains unknown. Other strategies are to look for clues by separating genes that are inherited through the father from those inherited through the mother. Another method is to study ASD in relatively isolated populations that have intermarried for generations. There are several such populations in Canada.

Jeanette Holden is well acquainted with all these methods. Born in Vancouver shortly after the end of World War II, she knew, from an early age, that she wanted to work in genetics. It was in a high school biology class that she learned the electrifying news that the genetic code had been deciphered. This was in the mid-1960s. In 1953, Watson, Crick and Franklin had discovered that the DNA in chromosomes came in a paired helical structure. Organic chemist Har Gobind Khorana was working at the University of British Columbia at the time. He went on to show that every three nucleotides constitute the coding region of amino acids and that some of these triplets or codons signal the start or stop of protein synthesis. With Holley and Niremberg, Khorana was awarded the Nobel Prize in 1968 for discovering how a DNA message is translated into a protein.

While still an undergraduate at the University of British Columbia, Jeanette began working in the laboratory of David Suzuki and did her PhD under his supervision, intent on finding the genetic causes of mental retardation. After her PhD and travel abroad, Jeanette came to Queen's University in 1978 as the director of the Cytogenetics Service Lab at Kingston General Hospital. Her first genetic target was fragile X syndrome.

Dr. Holden was not the first woman attracted to the mysteries of this disorder. The Fragile X syndrome was formerly known as the Martin-Bell syndrome. Bell stands for Julia Bell (1879–1979). Bell graduated in mathematics at Trinity College, Dublin, investigated solar parallax at the Cambridge Observatory and worked initially as a statistician. At the age of 35, she changed fields, and received a medical degree in 1920. She went on to pioneer the documentation of familial disease patterns. In 1937, she wrote a classic article with JBS Haldane on the linkage of the genes for color blindness with those of haemophilia. At age 80, she wrote a paper on the risks of rubella during pregnancy. She "retired" at the age of 86, but stayed intellectually active until her death at age 100.

The Fragile X syndrome is the second commonest cause of learning disability after Down syndrome, and the most common inherited cause. It results from the absence in brain neurons of the FMR protein (FMRP). This occurs when the FMR-1 gene on the long arm of chromosome X ceases to work, and that happens when a small part of its DNA sequences goes out of control and begins to repeat itself over and over, producing an expanded (and useless) form of the gene.

FMRP normally shuttles genetic information from the nucleus of nerve cells to their branches, a process that is essential to the manufacture of synapses. Synapses are the specialized connections between neurons that permit the passage of chemical substances (neurotransmitters) from one neuron to the next. Girls are relatively protected from Fragile X syndrome because the healthy gene on their second X chromosome takes over and produces the needed protein. The syndrome affects between 1 in 1,250 to 1 in 2,000 males and about half as many females. Approximately 2% of all children diagnosed with autism carry the expanded form of the FMR-1 gene.

Dr. Holden knew that a career in medical genetics was an uncommon choice for women in the 1970s but she never realized that there would be difficulty. "I never imagined there would be any barriers. I never realized that I was going to run into trouble as a woman, but that happened many times."

Throughout Jeanette's training, she only had two female professors. She concluded that women could not "do it all": practice science, teach, tend to a home, and raise a family. She believes that still, in 2005, it is hard for women researchers. A year of pregnancy leave, intended to help, does not make it any easier. "Taking a year off from science puts women at a disadvantage when they return. You cannot leave basic science and come back. This type of research is so fast paced, the whole methodology would have changed within a year." Because it is hard to be the caregiver for aging parents and to look after children and other family members while staying ahead in a highly competitive field, Jeanette made a decision to forego a family of her own. Does she regret it? "If I had to do it differently? I would have liked to have had a family, I miss that."

By 1973, the Holden family had come to realize that Jim's developmental problems were attributable to autism. Autism is a lifelong disability affecting from 15 to 40 people per 10,000. Family members remain lifelong caregivers; they can never retire. Dr. Holden, for instance, never takes holidays. She travels for study and for conference presentations but she does not know how to take a holiday because, in her family, no one ever did. Jeanette's mother, now 83, is only beginning to catch up on activities she had always wanted to do. And that is because, more recently, Jim is able to do more on his own. A big change took place when the family realized that Jim's hearing was impaired. They hadn't at first understood that he was unable to speak clearly because he couldn't hear clearly. Now that Jim can hear better, with the help of a small FM hearing aid that filters out background noise, he is starting to learn new skills, such as typing words on a computer. Jim, Jeanette, and their mother live together, supporting one another. Jeanette and her mother are in the process of teaching Jim how to read and write with the aid of a one-to-one attendant and specialized computer software.

Jeanette does not hesitate when asked who her hero is. It is her mother. Her mother's character and the devotion she has shown to her family have influenced Jeanette more than anything else in life. Her mother is her model; her brother Jim is her inspiration.

"I've had bad times at work, I don't even want to think about them – they were really not that pleasant," says Dr. Holden. She didn't like the competitiveness of genetic research. She didn't like the lack of generosity she often saw and the dishonesty she sometimes saw, including reviewers taking their cue from results in a submitted manuscript, repeating the experiments, and rapidly publishing them. Science can be cutthroat, but the atmosphere has improved in Canada since the advent of the Canadian Institutes of Health Research.

> The best thing to happen to basic sciences is the CIHR. I think that the scientific directors of each Institute are incredible. They are bright, insightful, and generous. They have great vision. They are not doing this for their own personal benefit. Instead, they support innovative researchers and innovative approaches to science.

Leo Kanner first described the syndrome of autism in 1943 but it only became clear recently that autism was a developmental disorder of the early fetal brain. Recent imaging studies show that, in children with autism, abnormal brain overgrowth occurs during the first two years of life. By two to four years of age, overgrowth can be seen clearly with magnetic resonance imaging, particularly in cerebral, cerebellar, and limbic parts of the brain. This is followed by abnormally slow or arrested growth just at the time when neural circuits are forming, rendering brain connections dysfunctional. While the estimated prevalence of pure autism is 15–40 per 10,000 children, autistic spectrum disorders are present in about six per 1000, with a male to female ratio of 4:1. The male to female ratio of Asperger's syndrome (a high IQ form of autism with normal language development but impaired social interaction and narrow interests) is greater, 10–20:1. This skewed gender ratio remains unexplained.

Male-to-male transmission (father to son) does occur and, thus, rules out X-linkage as the prevailing mode of inheritance of most autistic syndromes. There is a three to six percent risk of autism in siblings of autistic children, considerably above that of the general population. There is a 60–90% concordance rate in identical twins, depending on how concordance is defined. The prevalence of autism has increased dramatically (an apparent increase of 4 to 10 fold from the 1980s to the late 1990s), probably (but not necessarily) owing to the loosening of diagnostic criteria and, more importantly, to better identification. But environmental causes for the increased rates cannot be altogether ruled out. The syndrome is not only genetic. Epidemiologic studies indicate that factors such as toxic exposures, teratogens, perinatal insults, and prenatal infections such as rubella and cytomegalovirus account for some cases. Rigorous studies have failed to support the fear that immunizations with the measles-mumps-rubella (MMR) vaccine are responsible for the surge in autism, but the potential role of thimerosal, a mercury-based preservative used in some vaccines (not MMR), is less clear.

There are impairments in three behavioral domains in autism spectrum conditions: 1) social interaction, 2) language, communication, and imaginative play, and 3) range of interests and activities. These impairments usually appear by the age of three (often earlier) and interfere with a child's ability to communicate and interact with others. Autistic children might not respond to their names or even look at other people. Social and communication skills and the ability to put oneself into other people's shoes and empathize with them are difficult tasks for autistic children. But these children show specific strengths as well as deficits. They are good at detail and they are usually especially good at something that interests them. These narrow interests are called "islets of ability." Family members often show similar strengths. Treatments such as early intensive behavioral interventions and changes in diet can improve behavior. Autistic children are teachable and can learn, through appropriate education, to communicate with and enjoy the company of others.

The genetic contribution to autism is probably attributable to the combined small effects of ten or more genetic loci. In some cases, there may be a major responsible gene that runs in a family. A region that is thought to mediate speech and language on the long arm of chromosome 7 has been linked to autism. Other candidate genes have been examined in nearby regions with varying results. Cytogenetic abnormalities on the long arm of chromosome 15 and the short arm of chromosome X have also been found in people with autism. Variants of the serotonin transporter gene are said to be more frequent in individuals with autism than in nonautistic populations. At the time of writing, these findings are among the most replicated in autism gene research. In addition, animal models and linkage information from genome screens have implicated the oxytocin receptor on chromosome 3. Though not all researchers agree with one another on details, they all concur that science is on the brink of exciting discoveries in the molecular genetic underpinnings of autism spectrum disorder.

One form of ASD occurring almost exclusively in girls is the scientifically intriguing but debilitating neurodevelopmental disorder known as Rett syndrome (RTT). Girls with RTT develop normally for the first year or two, and then regress. They lose the social skills they had mastered, lose their ability to maintain eye contact with others, and begin to show a general lack of interest in most activities. Most of the affected children develop seizures, wring their hands repetitively, show developmental delays, motor-control problems, and autistic tendencies. Rett syndrome is believed to affect one in 10,000 females. The genetic causes of RTT are mutations in the MECP2 gene on the X chromosome, a gene that probably influences synaptic plasticity. Male fetuses with this genetic anomaly do not survive to birth. Females, with their extra X chromosome, not only survive but fare well until the first year of life. Rett syndrome is caused by defects in a protein involved in DNA methylation of chromatin. Current progress in the decipherment of the causative chain that culminates in this syndrome is likely to lead to a better understanding of a growing number of human genetic disorders.

In the interview for this chapter, Dr. Holden said:

> I always thought that, once we understood autism, we would understand much about other human conditions such as schizophrenia, Tourette syndrome, and other neuropsychiatric and neurodevelopmental disorders. The more I learn about what is known about autism, the more I realize how little we know and how wrong we have been in what we thought we knew. Many of the behaviors that are associated with autism – the tantrums and the withdrawal into one's own world – are really no more than frustration at not being understood by others, and not understanding why one is not being understood. Take the example of my brother. Jim's behaviors when he was young were typical of classical autism. Only when he was 47 did we learn that he had moderate hearing loss and probably always has had. Can you imagine what it must have been like for him to repeat what he heard (aang, ahhuh, etc) and not be understood? He was learning our language (what he heard of it), yet when he repeated what he heard, we did not understand him. If only we had known he was hearing impaired…. When we know someone has a hearing impairment, we adjust our speech and enunciation. When we don't know someone has a hearing impairment, we cannot make adjustments. Jim wasn't tested before because he already had a diagnosis – when he was young, the diagnosis was mental retardation; when he was older, the official diagnosis was autism. But just like everyone else, a diagnosis of vision or mobility impairment, for example, does not preclude other medical conditions. Adjusting for Jim's hearing impairment has given Jim a second chance, which he has readily taken up. Fifteen months ago, he did not know a single letter of the alphabet. Now he is writing sentences – words are all committed to memory, since he cannot hear the sounds of all words, and phonics, therefore, is difficult. He has always wanted to tell us things and now he can. His speech has improved with his introduction to literacy.
>
> Jim gave the first public demonstration of what he now can do at the Canadian-American Disabilities Meeting at Queen's. More than 100 people attended. He really enjoyed it and next year wants to do it again and to speak more! He demonstrated how he learned to spell words and how he is now writing short (and some not so short) sentences. He was a hit!
>
> I don't believe that individuals with autism want to be in their own world. I believe they don't know how to be a part of ours. We have to give them choices for communication so that they can share their needs and dreams with us, making it a world that we can share.

Further Reading

Bell J. On rubella in pregnancy. Br Med J. 1959;15:686–688.

Courchesne E. Brain development in autism: early overgrowth followed by premature arrest of growth. Ment Retard Dev Disabil Res Rev. 2004;10:106–111.

Boddaert N, Belin P, Chabane N, Poline J-B, Barthélémy C, Mouren-Simeoni M-C, Brunelle F, Samson Y, Zilbovicius M. Perception of complex sounds: abnormal pattern of cortical activation in autism. Am J Psychiatry 2003;160:2057–2060.

Glaze DG. Rett syndrome: of girls and mice–Lessons for regression in autism. Ment Retard Dev Disabil Res Rev. 2004;10:154–158.

Grandin T. Autism first-hand: an expert interview with Temple Grandin, PhD. http://www.medscape.com/viewarticle/498153

Holden JJ, Wang HS, White BN. The fragile-X syndrome IV: progress towards the identification of linked restriction fragment length variants (RFLVs). Am J Med Genet. 1984;17:259–273.

Kirby D. Evidence of harm. Mercury in vaccines and the autism epidemic: a medical controversy. NYC: St. Martin's Press; 2005.

Kremer EJ, Pritchard M, Lynch M, Yu S, Holman K, Baker E, Warren ST, Schlessinger D, Sutherland GR, Richards RI. Mapping of DNA instability at the fragile X to a trinucleotide repeat sequence p(CCG)n. Science. 1991;252:1711–1714.

Mulligan LM, Phillips MA, Forster-Gibson CJ, Beckett J, Partington MW, Simpson NE, Holden JJ, White BN. Genetic mapping of DNA segments relative to the locus for the fragile-X syndrome at Xq27.3. Am J Hum Genet. 1985;37:463–472.

Ozonoff S, Rogers SJ, Hendren RL. Autism spectrum disorders: a research review for practitioners. Arlington, VA: Am Psychiatric Publishing Inc; 2003.

Stanford A. Asperger syndrome and long-term relationships. Philadelphia: Jessica Kingsley Pub; 2003.

Stone JL, Merriman B, Cantor RM, Yonan AL, Gilliam TC, Geschwind DH, Nelson SF. Evidence for sex-specific risk alleles in autism spectrum disorder. Am J Hum Genet. 2004;75:1117–1123.

Veenstra-Vanderweele J, Christian SL, Cook Jr EH. Autism as a paradigmatic complex genetic disorder. Annu Rev Genomics Hum Genet. 2004;5:379–405.

Volkmar FR, Lord C, Bailey A, Schultz RT, Klin A. Autism and pervasive developmental disorders. J Child Psychol Psychiatry. 2004; 45:1–36.

Chapter 4

Bipolar Disorder: Martin Alda and the Genes of Mood

"If a man loves the labour of his trade, apart from any question of success or fame, the gods have called him."

Robert Louis Stevenson

Bipolar disorders exact a price in creativity squandered and lives lost. This interview with Martin Alda at Dalhousie (he has since moved to McGill) shows how free ranging intellectual inquisitiveness leads to good science.

Martin Alda is a twin and he is a geneticist…. a linked fact because twinship necessarily leads to questions about heredity. He and his brother, an architect, were born in what was once northeastern Czechoslovakia. Their father was a mathematician; their mother a computer technologist. Education, intellect, and creative work were long held in high esteem in the Alda family but Martin was the first to show an interest in medicine. He was also interested in history, biology, mathematics – a diversification of curiosity that made it difficult to decide on any specific vocation.

Martin and his father spent time together discussing the nature of mathematics and, as they talked, Martin began to wonder about the nature of mind. He thought that mental illness might be "the royal road" to the deciphering of the mysteries of the mind. In physics, to analyze the properties of a particle, standard procedure was to perturb the system. By analogy, a naturally "disturbed" mind might prove the key to understanding fundamental properties of mind.

> If you think of the brain as a black box, you have difficulty piercing through it all, but maybe if something is disturbed, you can open the door a little bit and understand what is going on.

Through dint of a brilliant mind and very hard work, Martin was accepted into the prestigious Charles University in Prague. In the absence of the political pull that was often needed in Communist-run Czechoslovakia, his intelligence and industriousness were his tickets to entry. After an M.D. with distinction, he specialized in psychiatry. When his psychiatry training was complete, he went back to study more mathematics; he realized he would need it to try to conceptualize the brain, a very complicated organ. His father, an expert in abstract concepts, played a major role in his intellectual development and he was also influenced by Dr. Filip, his psychopharmacology and statistics mentor, and Dr. Zvolsky, one of the first persons in Europe to work in the area of psychiatric genetics.

Alda was particularly interested in genetics because it was a mathematical science. Consider this: the DNA sequences of any two unrelated humans vary at millions of locations. Most individuals differ from each other at about 4 million DNA sites. Variations at these sites are called single-nucleotide polymorphisms (SNPs), markers of biologic diversity that are useful in gene discovery because of their potential proximity to disease-producing genes. Physical proximity means that, despite the 5,000 generations of genetic recombinations that the human race has passed through over the course of evolution, a marker and a gene may have been inseparably inherited together. In the language of genetics, they are said to be in linkage disequilibrium with each other. Haplotypes are longer sequences of nucleotides, averaging about 25,000, that tend to be jointly inherited. SNPs and haplotypes are the key to association studies of complex diseases such as psychiatric disorders, i.e., the comparison of the genes of persons with an illness to those without the illness.

Fortuitously for Martin Alda, Dr. Paul Grof, from Hamilton, Ontario became a friend and mentor. Grof had been investigating the families of bipolar patients treated with lithium and had found that some patients responded well while others did not. He wondered why. In 1985, Alda visited Grof in Hamilton and, before long, Martin received a job offer to come to Canada. But Czechoslovakia was under Communist rule and it was not easy to obtain the necessary papers. He finally managed to come in 1988, assuming that he would be away from home for a maximum of two years. Luckily, the political situation changed, and he stayed permanently. He had to redo part of his psychiatric residency to obtain his Canadian credentials, which he finally completed in 1992. The attraction of Canada was its excellent tradition of neuroscience and there was an additional major plus: extensive family pedigrees, all willing to participate in research.

The Canadian Psychiatric Foundation (CPRF) proved a godsend to Martin Alda by awarding him his first Canadian research grant. "The first grant is always the most difficult." It put him on the right track and he has not looked back.

Martin Alda has become one of Canada's top psychiatric geneticists in the area of bipolar illness (manic depression). This quite common disorder is marked by recurrent periods of depression and euphoria. Lifetime prevalence rates are estimated to be in the vicinity of 0.4% to 1.6%, meaning that, among any 100 people, one to two on average will suffer from a form of bipolar disorder. Bipolar disorder ranks among the world's leading causes of disability in young adults (please see Chapters 20, 29, and 30).

The clusters of symptoms that characterize the disease vary among patients and Dr. Alda believes that recognizing these clinical subtypes will provide important clues to the genes that contribute to susceptibility. One such clue, for example, is the response to treatment: He has found that two commonly used mood stabilizers – lithium and lamotrigine – are effective in very different groups of patients. Lithium works in the more typical presentation of bipolar disorder. Lamotrogine works for those with rapid cycling, those with co-occurring anxiety and those who have a family history of panic disorder. Dr. Alda is interested in comparing these two distinct groups on further variables. As a recent Canada Research Chair, Dr. Alda investigates the effects of bipolar drugs on gene function. His ultimate goal is to discover the susceptibility genes leading to bipolar disorder and to study their interplay with external factors such as stressful life experiences.

Like many colleagues, Alda believes that nonpsychiatric areas of medical research are preferentially funded, that a stigma continues to exist when it comes to psychiatry. Furthermore, within psychiatry, he finds that research is often considered less important than clinical practice.

> "CPRF has done a great job trying to educate the public about psychiatric research. Individuals who are willing to go public about recovering from a bipolar illness are excellent advocates and champions for psychiatric research."
>
> Martin Alda

Martin Alda believes that there have been gigantic advances in understanding psychiatric illness over the last 40 years. "Halifax had something like 20 times more psychiatric beds 40 years ago than it has now. Due to new treatments and medications, we don't have to hospitalize people as much." The fact that genes have been identified for certain psychiatric illness and that imaging can pinpoint brain changes has shown the public that psychiatric illnesses are no different from other illness, lessening the stigma that always attaches to the unknown.

All psychiatric disorders are complex diseases to which many genes are likely to contribute. Some of the contributing genes are probably rare but highly penetrant, meaning that a large proportion of individuals inheriting a particular alteration will develop the disorder. Some relevant genes are probably common but less penetrant. (Penetrance is the probability that a genetic trait will be behaviorally expressed). In other words, many people can carry an altered gene and yet not be ill.

For instance, in Alzheimer's disease (AD), mutations in three genes: a) presenilin 1, b) presenilin 2, and c) the amyloid precursor protein gene occur rarely but, when they do, they are highly likely to cause early-onset (prior to age 60) AD. In other words, AD develops by the age of 60 years in most people in whom one of these genes is mutated. But, because mutations in these genes are so rare, together, these genes are responsible for fewer than 1% of cases of AD. By contrast, the E4 form of the apolipoprotein gene is responsible for many more cases of Alzheimer's disease (usually in the mid-70s) than all the mutations combined. And yet only 8% of people with one E4 form of the gene (and 21% of people who carry both such forms) develop Alzheimer's disease. (By comparison, those who carry non-E4 forms of the apolipoprotein gene are at 3% risk for Alzheimer's). The relevance of carrying the E4 form of the apolipoprotein gene is that it is common. Approximately 26% of the North American population has one such gene and 2% of the population has two such genes. (Please see Chapter 1 for more on Alzheimer's disease). This is a model to keep in mind for understanding causation in psychiatric diseases such as bipolar disorder. It is thought that most psychiatric disorders result from multiple genes, many rare and some common, all with varying degrees of penetrance. To make matters more complicated, that probability may be enhanced or inhibited by as yet unknown environmental factors.

The human genome is thought to contain from 30,000 to 35,000 genes or coding regions (together making up less than 2% of the total DNA). Over 50% of the DNA is composed of repeat sequences that influence the genes in ways that are not well understood. We know the function of only 50% of human genes. While, in theory, all human genes are capable of causing disease if their DNA sequence is altered, mutations currently known to cause disease have only been identified in approximately 1,000 genes. Genes are transcribed into proteins and, through a mechanism known as "alternative splicing," the 30,000 to 35,000 genes of the human genome can code for more than 100,000 proteins. A number of known phenomena can change the coding effect of a gene. These constitute "epigenetics" and influence the expression and silencing of genes in specific tissues and at specific times of life.

While most genes are located in the DNA of the cell nucleus, several dozen genes involved with energy metabolism sit on the mitochondrial chromosome located in the cytoplasm of cells. Since ova are rich in mitochondria and sperm are not, mitochondrial DNA is usually only inherited from the mother (and not, like nuclear DNA, from combinations and recombinations of paternal and maternal chromosomes). Mitochondrial inheritance has been raised as a possible mechanism of inheritance in some bipolar disorder families.

When asked to compare U.S. psychiatric research with Canadian research, Alda thinks research in Canada has a number of advantages.

> Because of our public healthcare system, I think clinical research has done quite well here. In the States you have a situation that is more technology driven and, because of that, a number of research groups have done really, really well. On the other hand, Canadian research tends to be patient-driven. The clinical and basic research link is stronger here.

The complexity of brain research means that it advances more slowly than other types of medical research. This is a problem for private funders because, "of course, donors want to see results. They want to see where their investment is going and they expect dividends within a year or two. Psychiatry is a longer term investment." But the relatively slow pace is not a problem for Martin. As he speaks about his research, Alda's excitement shows. For him it is an intellectual challenge. "If I were a donor and wanted to fund something fascinating and cutting edge, psychiatry would be it."

> Many of us are attracted to psychiatry because the brain is the most complex of our organs and because you can study it at multiple levels – biological, or genetic, or physiological, or clinical, or behavioral.

Because psychiatric genetics is so complex, new discoveries in this field fuel the study of other diseases of complex etiology in other areas of health. Psychiatrists are leading the way in understanding the influence of disease-causing gene mutations. The most common way for a mutation to cause disease is through decreasing the quantity or activity of a protein. Less often, mutations lead to disease through a *gain* of function, increasing the level of a protein to the point of toxicity. There are several kinds of mutations. A point mutation is a change in a single DNA base. It is called a missense mutation if the substitution results in the formation of a new amino acid. It is called a silent mutation if there is no change in the protein product. A nonsense mutation is where the three-base sequence that codes for an amino acid is changed to a stop codon, stopping the protein in midstream. A frame-shift mutation shifts the start of the sequence, leading to a cascade of altered amino acids. There is a phenomenon called expanding trinucleotide repeats where three base pairs repeat over and over. Expanding trinucleotide repeats are responsible for several neuropsychiatric disorders such as Huntington's disease and fragile X syndrome. (Please see Chapter 3 for more on fragile X syndrome).

What motivates Martin Alda? A strong sense of personal responsibility. Even the communist regime in his native Czechoslovakia could not suppress that. "You make decisions and you have to live with the consequences. Life is fairly short. We have a certain amount of time here so we should use it well." Among the people who have used their time well, Martin cites Mogens Schou.

> Mogens Schou was born in Copenhagen 1918 and died in the Fall of 2005. In 1954, Dr. Schou and his associates published the outcome of a partly open, partly randomized and placebo-controlled trial of lithium, the first of its kind in psychiatric pharmacotherapy. It confirmed the anti-manic effect of lithium, first observed in 1949 by John Cade. Schou later showed that long-term lithium treatment was associated with an 87% long-lasting decrease in manic and depressive recurrences.

Alda hasn't quite unlocked the secrets of the perturbed mind. He hasn't yet discovered the susceptibility genes for bipolar disorder. His goals are more modest now. He hopes that his research will have a positive impact on patients' lives. "I hope this research will generate something significant for clinical areas." He feels there have been promising leads – several gene regions have been identified that contribute to the risk of developing both schizophrenia and mood disorders. He feels that these disorders may prove to be heterogeneous, i.e., in different families the responsible genes may differ. He collaborates with Dr. Anne Duffy, a former research fellow, who conducts longitudinal investigations of children of parents with mood disorders. Such studies are important for identifying both risk and protective factors. He is interested in neuroplasticity (the ability of the brain to shape or mold itself in response to environmental events). He does not think that "bad" genes will ever be engineered away but he trusts that processes such as the interplay of genes and stressors will, in time, be better understood.

> [Research] will open doors for better treatments and, one day, we'll be able to design better therapeutic molecules that will target specific areas and cause fewer side effects.

Further Reading

Alda M. Genetic factors and treatment of mood disorders. Bipolar Dis. 2001;3:318–324.

Alda M. Pharmacogenetic aspects of bipolar disorder. Pharmacogenomics. 2003; 4:35–40.

Alda M, Grof P, Rouleau GA, Turecki G, Young LT: Investigating responders to lithium prophylaxis as a strategy for mapping susceptibility genes for bipolar disorder. Prog Neuropsychopharmacol Biol Psychiatry. 2005; 29:1038–1045.

Grof P, Alda M, Grof E, Zvolsky P, Walsh M. Lithium response and genetics of affective disorders. J Affective Dis. 1994;32:85–95.

Kato T, Kato N. Mitochondrial dysfunction in bipolar disorder, Bipolar Disord. 2000;2:145–147.

Konradi C, Eaton M, MacDonald ML, Walsh J, Benes FM, Heckers S. Molecular evidence for mitochondrial dysfunction in bipolar disorder. Arch Gen Psychiatry. 2004;61:300–308.

Lindpaintner K. Pharmacogenetics and the future of medical practice. J Mol Med. 2003;81:141–153.

Schou M, Baastrup PC. Lithium treatment of manic-depressive disorder: dosage and control. JAMA. 1967;201:696–698.

Schou M, Juel-Nielsen N, Stromgen E, Voldby H. The treatment of manic psychoses by the administration of lithium salts. J Neurochem. 1954;17:250–260.

Chapter 5

Child Psychiatry:
The Legacy of Dr. Dan Offord

"Kids in Canada feel they are in a race. It is our job as adults to make sure that the race is fair to them, to level the playing field."

Dan Offord

Major advances in children's mental health have been made in recent years. Dan Offord from McMaster was not only an advocate for children but also a rigorous epidemiologist who focused on prevention.

Fifteen to twenty percent of Canadian children require help for mental illness or addiction. Hamilton child psychiatrist Dan Offord (1934–2004) knew this, and *much* more, about children. "I really enjoy kids," he once told a reporter.

Kids need to be enjoyed and I don't have to try. I really get a kick out of them. I remember vividly my own childhood and the people who did great things for me. I remember thinking that when I grow up, I will know exactly what kids need.

Central to that need, as far as Offord was concerned, was not clinical help but rather, the induction of values – the kinds of values one can learn at summer camp. He firmly believed that physical activity was an important source of healthy development. One of his tasks as Camp Director at Christie Lake, a camp for disadvantaged children, was to make sure that his campers received the same camping opportunities as all other children. He knew that recreation and sport activities not only improve skills like swimming, running and jumping; they also develop strength and endurance. He wanted his campers to feel good about their bodies. Feeling physically confident, they would grow socially and psychologically as well. He believed that mastery of age-appropriate skills nurtured children's self-esteem and buffered the vicissitudes that lay ahead. Offord was convinced that organized physical activities enhanced a child's ability to respond to the problems of life and offered an opportunity to enjoy relationships with caring adults. Sports spurred moral development because kids learned to give up instant gratification and appreciate fair play and the pleasure of seeing others succeed.

Throughout his life, much of Offord's time revolved around the camp. The challenge of determining which campers would be good in which sports led to an academic interest in epidemiology and prediction. In this he followed in the footsteps of Alexander H. Leighton, Canada's pioneer psychiatric epidemiologist.

Alex Leighton, an American, was named Canadian National Health Scientist in the Department of Psychiatry at Dalhousie University in 1948 and launched an epidemiological study of the prevalence of mental illness in Atlantic Canada. Known as the Stirling County Study, it found that approximately one in five adults suffers from mental illness. It showed that the most common forms of mental illness were depression, anxiety, and alcohol abuse. In 1975, Dr. Leighton became a resident of Canada and now holds dual citizenship in Canada and the United States. Currently directed by his wife, Dr. Jane Murphy Leighton, the Stirling County studies continue. Professor Emeritus, Harvard University, and Professor in the Departments of Psychiatry and of Community Health and Epidemiology, Dalhousie University, Alex Leighton remains an active participant in research. Epidemiologists working in psychiatric research have all been influenced by the methods he pioneered.

While it is said that scientists under the age of 35 are the ones most likely to make revolutionary discoveries (see Introduction), the older men of science, like Alex Leighton, are, in fact, the most influential. Leighton has inspired many Canadian psychiatric epidemiologists such as Julio Arboleda-Florez, Morley Beiser, Roger Bland, Stan Freeman, Paula Goering, Eliot Goldner, Nick Kates, Vivianne Kovess, Alain Lesage, Elizabeth Lin, Heather Stuart, Don Wasylenki, Carolyn Woogh, and many others.

He also inspired Dan Offord who, in 1983, initiated The Ontario Child Health Study (OCHS), one of the most important epidemiological studies of children's mental health ever conducted. It generated information not only about rates of different disorders in children but also about risk factors (poverty being key) that contribute to maladaptive behaviour. The results of this landmark study have led to improved mental health services for children in Ontario, throughout Canada, and in the United States.

Dan Offord and his team interviewed 1,869 Ontario families (3,294 children), randomly selected from Canada's 1981 census. They wanted to know the prevalence and distribution of mental health problems in children and adolescents and found that almost 20% of Ontario children had symptoms: the poorer the child, the more frequent the problems. Many children had more than one difficulty and only one out of six children had received treatment.

In adolescence, the rate rose in females and fell for males. The highest rates of problems were found in 12 to 16 year old girls and the lowest rates in girls 4 to 11 years old.

The Offord study showed that family difficulty heightened the risk for childhood problems, whereas being a good student, getting along with others, and taking part in activities reduced that risk. Psychiatric disorders went hand in hand with poor school

Mental Disorder among Canadian Children/Adolescents

Mental Disorder	% Prevalence Rate
Anxiety Disorder	6.5
Conduct Disorder	3.3
ADHD	3.3
Depressive Disorder	2.1
Substance Abuse	0.8
Pervasive Developmental Disorder	0.3
Obsessive-Compulsive Disorder	0.2
Schizophrenia	0.1
Tourette's Disorder	0.1
Eating Disorder	0.1
Bipolar Disorder	<0.1
ANY DISORDER	15.0

Source: Prevalence of Mental Disorders in Children and Youth, Mental Health Evaluation and Community Unit, Department of Psychiatry, University of British Columbia October, 2002

performance, chronic health problems, substance use and suicidal behavior. Interestingly, immigrant children were not at increased risk either for psychiatric disorder or for poor school performance. In fact, they needed mental health and social services significantly less often than did their non-immigrant peers.

An important finding was that both the prevalence and the pattern of disorder differed in significant ways depending on who was answering the study questions (e.g., parents versus teachers). Prevalence rates ranged from less than 1% to over 18% depending on who the informant was.

Adopted boys, but not girls, had more trouble with emotions and with school performance than biological children. In adolescence, however, more of the adopted girls than boys had substance abuse problems.

The siblings of the ill children from the Ontario Child Health Study were subsequently studied. They showed a two-fold increased risk for emotional disorders, including depression, anxiety, and obsessive-compulsive disorder, and a 1.6-fold increase in risk of poor peer relationships. However, they took part in the usual childhood recreational activities and did not have a particularly high rate of school problems. This suggested to Offord that, although economic disadvantage and family problems are important hazards, for many children, it is the individual risk factors that count the most.

The major aim of the initial cross-sectional OHCS study of 1983 was to obtain precise data about the prevalence of emotional, behavioral, physical, and substance use health problems among Ontario children. A follow-up study (1987) looked at outcome, prognosis, and risk. Results showed that conduct disorder, once present, did not disappear. Anxiety and depression were not always still there four years later but did tend to persist if family dysfunction and interpersonal problems were initially present. Low family income was perhaps the most important predictor of persistence of illness.

As a result of the widely acknowledged importance of this research, Offord received $600,000 in government funds to establish the Canadian Centre for Studies of Children at Risk, now called the Offord Centre. The Offord Centre addresses major childhood problems such as abuse, depression, autism, and offers help to children from poor families as well as to single mothers. It recommends a four–pronged strategy to improve children's health:

a) A civic community
b) Universal interventions
c) Targeted interventions
d) Clinical interventions

The Offord definition of a civic community is one in which "all children deserve the right of full participation in community life. In a civic community, adults take responsibility for more than their own children. In a civic community, there are family-friendly working places, so businesses make it easier to minister to children."

The Offord philosophy was that universal therapeutic programs for children have priority. That means that all children in a school or a neighborhood receive the therapeutic intervention.

> The advantages to these programs are that nobody is labeled or stigmatized. Further, when the middle class is involved, the programs tend to be well-run because parents insist on this. The third advantage of universal programs is that they till the soil for a particular targeted program. For instance, if a universal program in a school focuses on social skills, it can help to uncover which students might benefit from a more intensive program. The test of universality includes not just equal access but equal participation and, in the end, equal outcomes. Universality must include all the outside-the-home programs that we value for our kids but that tend not to be available to the kids who need them most.

Two disadvantages of universal programs are that they do not appeal to the public and politicians see them as squandering resources. Moreover, the children who seem to benefit the most are those who need them least.

For those not helped by universal programs, Offord recognized the necessity of targeted programs, geared to the specific needs of specific children. "If we can target kids accurately, we can give them a more intensive dose of whatever program it is that all the kids are getting."

Fifty nine years ago, in one of the very first peer-review funded projects ever awarded to a Canadian psychiatrist, Dr. Jack Griffin and his colleagues studied 8,000 school children and discovered that about 6.5% of them were shy, reclusive, and persistently timid. The researchers developed a manual to improve teachers' ability to understand these children and to spot early signs of trouble. Seventy percent of the children subsequently gained poise and self-confidence through specifically targeted education.

Targeted programs offer the opportunity of addressing problems early on, and are potentially efficient as long as targeting can be done accurately. Disadvantages include difficulties around screening and the possibility of labeling and stigmatization, a problem with many of the early programs. For those not able to access targeted school and community programs, Offord recommended clinical programs – evidence-based, well delivered, well-funded, and accurately targeted.

Offord realized that it was theoretically and practically important to determine cut-off points between normal child behavior and the kind of behavior that is labeled a disorder. He and his colleagues set out to do this empirically in 1996, using conduct disorder and hyperactivity disorder as test cases.

The use of different rationales to set thresholds for conduct disorder and hyperactivity will affect who is seen as ill, who is treated, and how they will be treated. For instance, a teacher's count of how many times a child gets up from his seat (a standard way of measuring hyperactivity) will define a group of children who require small classrooms in order to learn. A mother's count of the number of times a child is excluded from a friendship group will define a group of children who can benefit from learning social skills.

Offord took time from his work with children to enlist a team of scientists from McMaster University and the Clarke Institute of Psychiatry to design and carry out the Ontario Mental Health Supplement to the Ontario Health Survey. His motivation for leading this project, which primarily sampled adults, was the opportunity to understand what was happening to those aged 16–24, a group not previously studied. The survey included the then-controversial questions about the experience of sexual and physical abuse.

Of 1,000 adolescents, physical abuse was reported more often by males (31.2%) than females (21.1%), while sexual abuse during childhood was more often reported by females (12.8%) than males (4.3%). Severe physical abuse was the same in both sexes (9–11%).

The Offord team became known for its precision and rigor. Dr. Offord felt that risk research was much too important to tolerate less-than-rigoros gathering and reporting of results. He wanted empirical documentation to shape scientific knowledge, not hypotheses, speculations, or long cherished beliefs.

In the late 1990s, in an attempt to increase their rigor still further, the Offord group returned to the thorny issue of prediction. Two factors might correlate with each other but does one (early antisocial behavior for instance) actually predict the other (later conduct disorder for instance)?

Offord found that high levels of somatic symptoms first identified in community adolescents aged 13 to 16 represent a significant risk factor for major depression four years later.

Early and frequent marijuana use predicted substance abuse after four years. First use of alcohol at ages 11–14 greatly increased the risk of progression to serious alcohol disorders.

Dr. Offord and his group knew that reading problems in children were a well-established correlate of conduct disorder. Their findings showed that an eight-point increase in reading scores resulted in a 23% decrease in the risk of conduct problems 30 months later.

In 1999, Dan Offord's group spearheaded a tri-ministry project entitled Helping Children Adjust. This was a six-year prevention study to determine whether a combination of parent training, class-wide social skills training, and academic support (a partner reading program) could prevent adjustment problems in young children. The interventions were randomly offered in 60 schools. They were universal, i.e., offered to all children in the primary division, not only to those in need or to those who sought help. Information was collected from children and their families, teachers, and principals before and after the programs were implemented. In addition to the use of questionnaires, observers visited the schools to record child behavior in the classroom and playground.

The results were somewhat paradoxical. Most schools, whether or not they had a program in place, showed a general improvement in most measures over the first 18 to 24 months. Effects attributable specifically to the intervention were small. There were increases in observed social behavior in the playground and a reduction in behavior problems, as rated by both teachers and parents, but these improvements were modest. In fact, nine other school-based universal prevention programs have reported similarly mixed results. In other words, the process of observation and evaluation seems to make things better, regardless of whether specific interventions are offered. This shows that, no matter how promising a program seems, its effectiveness needs to be tested before major funds are assigned.

April 20, 1999 was the date of the Columbine High School tragedy in the United States. This dramatic event pointed to a critical need for understanding the roots of violence in children and adolescents. Even prior to this event, in 1994, Dan Offord had raised an alarm. Before the 1960s, he cautioned, kids had been violent with each other too but they used their fists, not weapons. Families and society have changed since then. While two-thirds of Canadian families in the 1960s consisted of a male wage earner and a stay-at-home spouse, this was only true for 12% of families in the 1990s when more than 70% of children required care outside the home. One-third of Canadian marriages were ending in divorce. There were increasing numbers of single parents or reconstituted families. Such services as existed for kids with violent tendencies had been designed for traditional families. Not many parents in the 1990s were able to take time off work to accompany their child to these programs. Offord insisted that Canada needed more recreation programs for children because the sense of community had weakened and belonging to gangs was filling the gap. He also advocated peer counseling.

To get children off to a good start in life, Dr. Offord emphasized the importance of the preschool time frame, i.e., early intervention. With Magdalena Janus, he developed the EDI (Early Development Instrument). Administered by teachers in the spring of senior kindergarten, it provides information about children's readiness to learn. The growing interest in the readiness to learn of Canadian children was reflected in the 1997 federal Speech from the Throne, which contained the commitment to "measure and report on the readiness to learn of Canadian children so that we can assess our progress in providing our children with the best possible start."

Excerpts from a speech delivered by Dr. Offord in May 2001, three years before his death reflect these objectives:

> Schools are a very difficult environment for many kids. If you are poor in Ontario, you are 10 times more likely to be identified by teachers as having problems....
> It takes only one good relationship to make a difference for a child at risk. This might be one teacher who believes in a child's abilities. Another factor is that a kid needs one area of competence...
>
> Kids with behavioral problems need a lot of contact with pro-social kids. Marginalizing them pushes them farther out....

If you ask kids what it is like growing up in Canada, the number one answer is that it is a race. This race has to be fair; and we must cut the penalties for losing.

Dan Offord illustrates the difference one person can make in a community. The lasting echoes of his words, "the burden of suffering, a level playing field for all kids, a civic community," will continue to inspire those who work with children everywhere in the world. His work also serves as an example of how science can inform program implementation so that governments are assured they are spending public money on interventions of proven effectiveness.

Further Reading

Bland RC. Demographic aspects of functional psychoses in Canada. Acta Psychiatr Scand. 1977;55:369–380.

Bland RC. Long term mental illness in Canada: an epidemiological perspective on schizophrenia and affective disorders. Can J Psychiatry. 1984;29:242–246.

Kates N, Munroe-Blum H. Psychiatric epidemiology in Canada. Can J Psychiatry 1990; 35:383–384.

Leighton AH. Contributions of epidemiology to psychiatric thought. Can J Psychiatry 1990;35:385–389.

Lipman EL, Offord DR, Boyle MH. What if we could eliminate child poverty; the theoretical effect on child psychosocial morbidity. Soc Psychiatr Epidemiol 1996;31:303–307.

Murphy JM, Horton NJ, Laird NM, Monson RR, Sobol AM, Leighton AH. Anxiety and depression: a 40-year perspective on relationships regarding prevalence, distribution, and comorbidity. Acta Psychiatr Scand. 2004;109:355–375.

Murphy JM, Laird NM, Monson RR, Sobol AM, Leighton AH.A 40-year perspective on the prevalence of depression: the Stirling County Study. Arch Gen Psychiatry. 2000;57:209–215.

Simonton DK, Creativity in Science: Chance, Logic, Genius, and Zeitgeist, Cambridge: Cambridge University Press, 2004.

Offord D. Ontario child health study: summary of initial findings. Ontario, Queen's Printer for Ontario, 1986.

Chapter 6

Forensic Psychiatry:
Bruno Cormier –
Rebel and Humanist

"Fidèle et indulgent aux yeux largement ouverts sur le monde et la science, poète lyrique d'un temps passé, Bruno le bon conseil, psychiatre imprudent mais efficace… Loyal and non-judgmental, eyes open onto the world of science, lyrical poet of bygone days, Bruno the good counsel, the reckless but effective psychiatrist."
Paul-Emile Borduas 1905–1960

Bruno Cormier (1919–1991) established forensic psychiatry in Canada in 1954. His credo was that incarceration impacts not only those who are confined but also those who do the confining. It demeans both the watcher and the watched.

Canada's pioneer researcher in forensic psychiatry, Bruno Cormier, was an idealist and a poet more than a physician. Avid art collector, especially of the work of the Automatistes, avant-garde Québecois painters, Cormier identified with their vision – freedom from restraints, whether artistic, religious, intellectual, or traditional. The Automatiste esthetic dictated that artists be childlike when they paint, that they paint automatically. The goal of automatic painting was not to create beauty, but to be natural, to give vent to unconscious emotions and impulses, to the free association of thoughts and feelings much like analysands on a Freudian couch. In 1948, the group wrote a liberation manifesto, the Refus Global (http://www.callisto.si.usherb.ca:8080/dhsp3/lois/Manifeste_Refus_global.html), which profoundly unsettled Québec society. It was penned by artist Paul-Emile Borduas with many signatories (see list below), of whom Cormier was the only non-artist. The manifesto questions traditional values and calls for ideological and cultural transformation. Its publication caused a furor in Québec, leading to Borduas' dismissal from his teaching position at the École de Meuble in Montréal. The Refus Global grew to the status of beacon for subsequent generations and is today credited with spurring fundamental changes in Québec's relationship with church and government, changes that ultimately led to the Quiet Revolution of the 1960s.

The manifesto called for individuality and freedom from shackles – themes that were to dominate Bruno Cormier's life. Bruno contributed an article that appeared (with other texts and reproductions of paintings) in the Refus Global pamphlet. His article was entitled, *"A Pictorial Work is an Experiment and an Experience."* Cormier was advocating multiple simultaneous viewpoints, urging his readers to consider the perspectives of those who paint and also of those who view and interpret. Later on, as a forensic specialist, he would reflect on the treatment of the offender from the standpoint of the criminal and the prison guard, the patient and the therapist – knowledge gained from experience as against knowledge gained from observation (see also Chapter 21 on a similar theme).

> The Refus Global (1948) called on French Canada to reject authority, embrace impulsivity, and live spontaneously through emotion, sensuality, and magic.

Bruno Cormier came from a family of seven children. His older brothers were union activists. His father ran a shoe store. His uncle owned a general store where Bruno earned the money that put himself through school. He studied Classics at Collège Sainte-Marie in Montréal, a Jesuit institution, and it was during the Collège years that he developed his eclectic interests in art, music, dance and literature. The library of the Catholic Collège allowed no books listed on the Index but Bruno was resourceful enough to read them anyway. Among his favorites was the work of Claudel, whose mysticism and sensuality seduced a generation of readers young and old. Influenced by Claudel, Bruno tried to write for the theatre; one of his plays was actually produced at the Gésu Theatre in Montréal. It was during this time that he forged his ties with the group of artists who were to become the Automatistes. It was also at the Collège that he first came into contact with psychoanalysis.

> Signatories of Refus Global: Paul-Émile Borduas, Jean-Paul Riopelle, Françoise Riopelle, Bruno Cormier, Françoise Sullivan, Fernand Leduc, Thérèse Leduc, Pierre Gauvreau, Claude Gauvreau , Jean-Paul Mousseau, Marcelle Ferron-Hamelin, Louise Renaud, Madeleine Arbour, Marcel Barbeau, Maurice Perron, Muriel Guilbault

After graduation, Bruno studied medicine at the Université de Montréal and obtained his degree in 1948, the year of Refus Global. By that time, his heart was already set on becoming a psychoanalyst. He trained first at the Allan Memorial in Montréal, then briefly in France, and then at the Maudsley clinic in London. On returning to Québec, he found that the authorities had not forgotten the part he had played in the Refus Global. A staff position at the Université de Montréal was out of the question. Not to be deterred, he applied to the Department of Psychiatry at McGill and, in 1954, opened the very first Canadian psychiatric service to operate inside a penitentiary. He also established an outpatient facility, the McGill Clinic in Forensic Psychiatry, to serve the mental health needs of those involved with the courts and those on parole or probation.

Under the leadership of Kenneth George Gray (1905–1970), a Forensic Service was also started in Toronto two years later. The research focus in Toronto was principally on sex offenders. In Montréal, it was on causes and outcomes of delinquency and criminality.

Cormier's predilection for looking at a problem from multiple viewpoints convinced him that punishment and confinement of offenders did more harm than good and, paradoxically, contributed to criminality. His first academic paper was on the psychopathology of deprivation of liberty – how incarceration affects not only those who are confined but also those who do the confining. It demeans both the watcher and the watched. This topic had haunted him ever since he learned what had taken place in Nazi concentration camps during the Second World War and it was to preoccupy him all his life.

Cormier grew to appreciate that crime, like other psychiatric symptoms, needed to be viewed longitudinally. He listened to and analyzed the narratives of those who had committed criminal acts and noted that, for some, criminal activity peaked at a young age and stopped while, for others, it continued indefinitely. If he could only understand why some offenders stopped offending, he felt he could put that knowledge to important therapeutic use. After much listening and analyzing, he came to the conclusion that a person stops committing offences when he/she experiences depression. The inability to do so is associated with persistent criminality. Cormier and his team also discovered that crime either continued or ceased depending on when in the life cycle it had first started. This was a first attempt at a scientific approach to prediction in the field of forensic psychiatry.

More recently, another Canadian, psychologist Robert Hare from the University of British Columbia, developed a checklist aimed at anticipating violence. Offshoots of Hare's original Psychopathy Checklist are now used throughout the world to predict dangerous behavior.

Hare's Psychopathology Checklist

The subject is given a score for each characteristic: 0 for "no," 1 for "somewhat," and 2 for "definitely"

1. Glibness/superficial charm
2. Grandiose sense of self-worth
3. Need for stimulation/proneness to boredom
4. Pathological lying
5. Conning/manipulative
6. Lack of remorse or guilt
7. Shallow affect
8. Callous/lack of empathy
9. Parasitic lifestyle
10. Poor behavioral controls
11. Promiscuous sexual behavior
12. Early behavior problems
13. Lack of realistic, long-term plans
14. Impulsivity
15. Irresponsibility
16. Failure to accept responsibility for own actions
17. Many short-term relationships
18. Juvenile delinquency
19. Revocation of conditional release
20. Criminal versatility

A major contribution of Cormier's team was investigating family patterns of incest. Reported cases usually involve sexual relations between two generations, the most common being father-daughter incest. The Cormier team found that incest could, in fact, involve three generations, i.e., be "transmitted" from one generation to the next. They found that the mother in a family of father-daughter incest had frequently herself been a victim of incest, rendering her psychologically incapable of preventing sexual entanglements between her husband and her daughters. The Cormier team also described another family pattern where the father in a father-daughter incest relationship had, in his youth, been the victim of father-son incest.

Cormier analyzed adolescent murderers and found that they characteristically denied the murder even in the face of incontrovertible legal proof. The denial often lasted for life. This was in contrast to the adult murderer who usually showed remorse or, at least, regret. Despite the denial, Cormier found that adolescent murder led to a very low rate of recidivism. He recommended that these cases be tried in juvenile court so that the adolescents would be spared a painful judicial process and years in prison, deprived of the opportunity to mature in a normal environment. At all times, Cormier's approach to offenders was humanistic, thoughtful, and therapeutic.

Bruno Cormier had to go to New York State to conduct his major experiment in turning a closed penal institution into a therapeutic community. This study, a collaboration between Dannemora State Hospital and the New York State Department of Corrections, exposed violent offenders between the ages of 25 and 35 to a consistent therapeutic milieu. Dr. Cormier's belief was that, by this age, psychopathic tendencies were on the wane and that these young adult prisoners could change their behavior if dealt with openly, realistically, and fairly. He believed that frank confrontation was needed to transform old interpersonal habits. His idea was for the prisoners to see themselves as others saw them and he used every means he could toward that end. He wanted to create emotional situations where prisoners could talk candidly without being punished. In order to do so, he first taught basic therapeutic principles not only to the inmates but also to his research staff and to the prison guards. The study was conducted between 1966 and 1972, with a final follow up visit by the Cormier team in 1975. Reading Cormier's book about the experiment, *The Watcher and the Watched*, one understands the intensity of the relationships that developed among inmates and between inmates and staff. Bruno Cormier believed in his technique and believed it would be effective in preventing criminal recidivism. He continued to believe until the end of his life but was never able to persuade Canadian penitentiary authorities to try his method.

Cormier did not approve of chains or restraints and in this he was true to the cherished principles of the Automatistes.

> "Ideally, I'd live without a passport. What I enjoy is moving freely."
>
>   Jean-Paul Riopelle (1923–2002)

Forensic psychiatry in Canada has moved in new directions but always acknowledges the debt it owes to the free spirit of Bruno Cormier.

Further Reading

Angliker CC, Cormier BM, Boulanger P, Malamud B. A therapeutic community for persistent offenders. An evaluation and follow-up study on the first fifty cases. Can Psychiatr Assoc J. 1973;18:289–295.

Barriga C, Boulanger P, Boyer R, Cormier BM, van der Vaart JM. Young adult offenders ages twenty to twenty-four. Can Psychiatr Assoc J. 1971;16:33–40.

Bloom H, Webster C, Hucker S, de Freitas. The Canadian contribution to violence risk assessment: History and implications for current psychiatric practice. Can J Psychiatry. 2005;50:3–11.

Breaking the chains: Bruno M. Cormier and the McGill University Clinic in Forensic Psychiatry, Two Volumes. Westmount, Québec: Robert Davies Multimedia Publishing Inc.; 1998.

Cooper I, Cormier BM. Inter-generational transmission of incest. Can J Psychiatry. 1982; 27:231–235.

Cormier BM. L'oeuvre d'art est une expérience. Montréal: Mithra-Mythe; 1948.

Cormier BM. On the history of men and genocide. Can Med Assoc J. 1966;94:176–291.

Cormier BM. Depression and persistent criminality. Can Psychiatr Assoc J. 1966;11: Suppl:208–220.

Cormier BM, Williams PJ. The watcher and the watched. A study on deprivation of liberty. Can Psychiatr Assoc J. 1971;16:15–19.

Cormier BM, Boyer R, Morf G, Kennedy M, Boulanger P, Barriga C, Cvejic J. Behaviour and ageing: offenders aged 40 and over. Laval Med. 1971;42:15–21.

Gauvreau, Claude. Écrits sur l'art. Montréal: L'Hexagone; 1996.

Gray KG. The sex offender. 1. Psychiatric services for the courts. Criminal Law Quart. 1960–61;3:443–447.

Hare RD. Without conscience: the disturbing world of the psychopaths among us. New York: Guilford Press; 1999.

Refus Global, Montréal, Les Éditions Anatole Brochu, 1972, pp.9–24 tiré dans Daniel Latouche et Diane Poliquin-Bourassa, Le manuel de la parole, manifestes québécois, Tome 2 1900 à 1959, Montréal, Éditions du Boréal Express, 1978, pp. 27–281.

Chapter 7

Memory: Cheryl Grady Images the Aging Brain

"The advantage of a bad memory is that one enjoys several times the same good things for the first time."
Friedrich Nietzsche

Memory processes have always intrigued human beings. Cheryl Grady from the University of Toronto uses functional magnetic resonance imaging to understand how the aging brain compensates for neuron loss.

With age, all body functions slow, weaken, and become less certain; memory is no exception. Episodic memory (memory of events) and working memory (the ability to hold and manipulate information over short periods of time) worsen with age. But, for most of us, semantic memory (vocabulary and memory for facts) does not change. New skills, however, become harder to learn – although many people over 65 do go back to university or start new careers. The older the person, however, the longer it takes to retrieve stored information at the time it is needed – exam time, for instance. One explanation is that the old have accumulated so many memories that the sheer bulk of the data makes searching onerous. Inattentiveness, distraction, or fatigue do not help, nor do diminished hearing, poor eyesight, alcohol and medications, or chronic pain – all frequent accompaniments of aging. Many medical conditions, such as an underactive thyroid, diabetes, infections, or heart or lung disease (that deprives the brain of oxygen) can exert extra negative effects on memory.

Dr. Cheryl Grady is trying to find out how the older brain differs in function from the younger brain. She uses neuroimaging, mainly functional Magnetic Resonance Imaging (fMRI), to help answer her questions. She has found evidence that older people whose memory is beginning to falter can improve their scores on cognitive tests by recruiting new areas of the brain to the task at hand – taking advantage of brain pathways that younger people do not normally use. Dr. Grady's work, carried out at the Rotman Research Institute at the Baycrest Centre for Geriatric Care in Toronto, has shown that functional adaptation – using novel brain circuits to accomplish a task rather than relying on the usual brain circuitry – improves performance in older people. The distinctive areas of the brain activated in the elderly when they are thinking through a problem are the frontal lobes. Even though brain activity is reduced in other parts of the brain, older individuals who activate their frontal lobes are able to perform well; their frontal lobes help them compensate for age.

Originally from Memphis, Tennessee, an American of southern stock, Cheryl Grady's description of herself as a youngster is: "I was a nosey kid, always asking questions." This naturally led to an interest in science and a decision to specialize in experimental psychology. Looking back on what influenced this decision, Dr. Grady singles out her High School Latin teacher. "She was open minded and our classes ended up being free ranging discussions. Studying Latin was a big help in general because it was a discipline that helped me think." After high school, Grady went to a small liberal arts college in Florida called Rollins College. She remembers that her professors at Rollins derived great joy from science and taught her not only the skill set she would need but also "the *art* of doing science."

She went to graduate school in Boston but, before she could complete her PhD, her thesis advisor accepted a position at the National Institutes of Mental Health (NIMH). At that juncture, Cheryl had almost finished writing her thesis. Her plan was to accompany her supervisor to Bethesda, quickly defend her thesis and be on her way. However, once there, she was recruited for a post at the Aging Institute. Those were the very early days of Positron Emission Technology (PET) scanning. Functional brain imaging was a very new methodology, just getting off the ground and Cheryl wanted to learn the new techniques. "It was the first real way we had of looking inside people's heads while they were doing a task." She had not been especially interested in aging until then but "somewhere along the way, I guess I discovered that aging actually was interesting. I fell into it and then decided I liked it and stayed with it."

In 1996, Dr. Grady accepted a position at the Rotman Research Institute in Toronto. The Rotman is unique as an Aging Institute in that so many people who work there are, like Grady, psychologists interested primarily in cognition and imaging. The group is dedicated to research. Teaching responsibilities are minimal so that the majority of one's time can be dedicated to research. The fit was right – Dr. Grady has worked there since.

As soon as Dr. Grady arrived in Toronto, she applied for three external research grants and was awarded all three.

> That hasn't happened since! Some good things about how Canada functions is that once you get a grant through the Canadian Institutes of Health Research (CIHR), they are pretty good about wanting to continue funding. Obviously the renewals are competitive, but they do try to renew as many grants as they can. I currently have the money to pretty much do what I want to do in my research, despite the fact that grants in Canada are smaller than in the U.S.

To determine how brain activity in older adults differs from that of young adults engaged in cognitive tasks, Dr. Grady has focused her work not only on the frontal lobes, but also on the connections among brain regions. This focus on "functional connectivity," or how activity in one part of the brain sparks activity in another part, has led to the finding that the brain networks used for retaining and retrieving memories alter with age. Older adults make use of their frontal lobes more often than do young adults, but this is not the only difference. Even when young adults do use their frontal cortex for a memory task, the specific frontal areas they activate are different from those used in older individuals. This was most clearly demonstrated in a recent study carried out by Dr. Grady and her colleagues at the Rotman, Gus Craik and Randy McIntosh, who measured brain activity while participants memorized lists of words and pictures of objects. In this experiment, activity in a brain region known to be critical for forming new memories, the hippocampus, increased during learning and this spike was highest in those who, when their memory was tested, showed the most accurate recognition. This was true regardless of age, but what differentiated the young from the old was how activity in the hippocampus was related to that of other brain regions. In young people, the hippocampus was functionally connected (simultaneously activated) to regions in the lower or inferior parts of the frontal lobes and parts of the visual cortex. In older people, the hippocampus interacted with areas of the frontal lobes that are involved in executive functions, so called because they are responsible for high-level organizational thinking and judgment. This age difference in the brain networks used during learning led Grady and her colleagues to a new hypothesis: aging results in a shift from relatively automatic learning strategies based on visual cues to specific organizational tactics that rely on deliberate effort. The serendipitous finding that greater activity in these executive function networks is associated with improved memory performance supports the idea that the engagement of novel brain networks in older adults helps them to retain their memory skills.

Using a similar approach, Dr. Grady has found that the ability to enlist frontal regions in the tasks of learning is also advantageous in older adults with dementing illnesses such as Alzheimer's disease. Previous neuroimaging studies had shown that individuals in the early stages of Alzheimer's disease, when performing cognitive tests, showed more activity in the prefrontal regions of the brain than did healthy age-matched controls. Dr. Grady and her team of investigators (including Dr. Sandra Black, Head of Neurology and senior scientist at Sunnybrook and Women's College Health Sciences Centre) found that Alzheimer's patients who were able preferentially to recruit the prefrontal cortex performed that much more accurately on memory tests. Dr. Grady feels that this is an area that needs more investigation. .

> The goal, until more definitive preventive treatment is found, is to develop more effective treatments that extend this compensatory effect and delay the degenerative effects of Alzheimer's for longer periods.

In the study, 12 healthy older adults and 11 older patients with probable early-stage Alzheimer's disease took part in a series of semantic and episodic memory tasks flashed on a computer screen. All of the Alzheimer's patients were taking medication for their cognitive impairment. Brain activity was inferred by measuring blood flow to various regions of the brain, using PET.

In the semantic exercise, a word or object appeared on either the right or left side of the screen, and a visual noise pattern appeared on the other side. Participants were instructed to make a decision whether the objects or words that appeared on the screen were living or non-living and to communicate the decision by pressing a button. During the episodic recognition task, objects or words were presented on either side of the screen – one was a new stimulus and one had been seen previously during the semantic task. Participants were asked to press the button whenever they recognized the stimulus.

Overall, Alzheimer's patients performed less accurately on the semantic and episodic tasks compared to the controls. However, the range of scores was quite large, with some patients performing within the normal range. The brain networks used by the patients and controls were determined by selecting a region in the left frontal cortex that was active in both groups during the semantic and episodic tasks, and seeing how activity in this region was related to activity elsewhere in the brain. The patients showed a much more extensive network of activity than the healthy elderly individuals; in particular, they recruited more frontal regions on the right side of the brain. The wider the network used, the better the patients performed on the tests.

In previous research, other scientists have identified similar compensatory activity occurring in the frontal regions of people who had suffered strokes or other forms of brain injury. The conclusion is that, as brains age (or become injured) they find ways to compensate for cognitive decline. The frontal cortex acts as an alternative network to aid cognition. The perceptual and cognitive demands of the task at hand are what decide the selection of brain areas that are recruited. All of this has implications for rehabilitation and cognitive remediation.

Discovering why particular types of memory are more vulnerable than others and how to maximize memory functioning throughout the aging process is what most excites Dr. Grady, who holds a Tier 1 Canada Research Chair in Neurocognitive Aging.

> I think it is my major joy, and I've had lots of joys, but if I were to pick one it would be doing science. I take a lot of pleasure in setting up an experiment and running it, and then seeing the data. Seeing the answer, having waited so long (people don't understand how long these experiments take – especially imaging experiments) to gather the data and then to take months analyzing it. But when you see the answer, of course, there it is.

Since she recognizes that the general public knows less about science than it should, Dr. Grady would like more effort and funding directed toward public education.

> The media seem particularly interested in some aspects of what we scientists do and I do get asked frequently to do interviews or appear on a TV show, and I usually try to do that. Not because I enjoy it, but I think we need to let people know what we do and explain its relevance. Why would anyone care, for example, about what I do? It's about trying to give them context so that they can understand that what I do may someday enable us to rehabilitate an older person who has a memory problem, that we might be able to figure out a way to change something in the brain to preserve memory. We actually have studies looking at that.

A challenge that Dr. Grady is beginning to face is that it is getting harder and harder to publish.

> It is not just me, because others have made this observation, and it is not just with neuroimaging because I've talked to people in other fields and it seems to be the same in other areas as well. It seems to be harder to get things published. If there is even the slightest question over how you have done something, the journal will reject the experiment without even giving you the opportunity to respond. Scientists live and die by publishing. If we don't publish, how do we show people that we are accomplishing anything?

When asked, she denies that this had anything to do with being a woman. "I've never felt discriminated against or that I've had to fight harder for what I wanted. Science is just competitive in general, for funds, for getting papers done." The biggest impact on her career has come from working at the National Institutes of Health (NIH).

And this was both for good and for bad. NIH is a huge place; it looks like a large university campus, at least it used to before they installed massive security systems and turned it into a government fortress. Before 9/11 it came across as a large college campus with about 50,000 people. It operates like a feudal system. Each laboratory is its own little fiefdom and the lab chief is the lord of the manor or chieftain. Because of these fiefdoms, there was no encouragement to collaborate.

Some labs are run progressively and people are treated equally, others operate very much from the top down and individual creativity and productivity is not valued. Unfortunately, that's the kind of lab I was in. What it did for me, besides making me tough and forcing me to develop a thick skin, was that it showed me what I didn't want from science. That whole model of hierarchy with everybody doing what the head of the lab wants them to do. That is not my idea of science. It is one model but that isn't the model that I think is the most effective.

In general, Dr. Grady believes that science works better when it is not part of a monolithic system like the National Institutes of Health. The system encourages territorial fights and that means that the best science is not being done. From her perspective, things run better when the scale is smaller.

I have never been interested in having a large lab or being in charge of a large group of people. I don't want to run things or set policies, I am more interested in asking the questions I want to ask and doing the work, and that is what I've wanted to do all along. It is just such an interesting thing to me: to ask questions and find answers. And I'm sure that this is the ultimate joy for all scientists, regardless of field.

Besides Cheryl Grady, there are not many researchers in Canada focused on aging and neuroimaging. One reason may be that neuroimaging is expensive and grants in Canada, with luck, amount to $100,000 to $200,000 in contrast to the several million dollars offered by large American grants. However, in the U.S. a grant would include the researcher's salary whereas that is not the case in Canada. The percentage of applications that end up being funded is about the same in the U.S. and Canada, says Dr. Grady, but there are more researchers in the U.S. and the atmosphere is more competitive. Dr. Grady advocates collaborations that form naturally (rather than being forced); she recommends providing researchers with relief from teaching and frequent sabbaticals. Researchers are in constant need of more time and more money.

While the mechanics of science funding may not seem crucial to the general public, it has inestimable bearing, as we shall see in other comments throughout this book, on the motivations of researchers, and, ultimately, on the calibre of discoveries made in Canada. Visually, science funding can be represented as an inverted U-curve on a graph. The dividends from grant applications should correlate with time spent applying. But past a certain point, when ever more time results in ever smaller gains, many researchers, even the most talented, lose heart. The challenge for funding agencies is to create the right mix of incentives such that grant writing does not retard the pursuit of science. Canadian granting agencies, alert to this concern, do re-evaluate their processes and guidelines frequently to ensure that they continue to fulfill their mission – encouraging good science.

Further Reading

Grady CL. Brain imaging and age-related changes in cognition. Exp Gerontol. 1998; 33:661–673.

Grady CL, Craik FI. Changes in memory processing with age. Curr Opin Neurobiol. 2000; 10:224–231.

Grady CL, Furey ML, Pietrini P, Horwitz B, Rapoport SI. Altered brain functional connectivity and impaired short-term memory in Alzheimer's disease. Brain. 2001; 124:739–756.

Grady CL, Bernstein LJ, Beig S, Siegenthaler AL. The effects of encoding task on age-related differences in the functional neuroanatomy of face memory. Psychol Aging. 2002; 17:7–23.

Levine B, Cabeza R, McIntosh AR, Black SE, Grady CL, Stuss DT. Functional reorganisation of memory after traumatic brain injury: a study with H(2)(15)0 positron emission tomography. J Neurol Neurosurg Psychiatry. 2002; 73:173–181.

Fernandes MA, Moscovitch M, Ziegler M, Grady C. Brain regions associated with successful and unsuccessful retrieval of verbal episodic memory as revealed by divided attention. Neuropsychologia. 2005;43:1115–1127.

Springer MV, McIntosh AR, Winocur G, Grady CL. The relation between brain activity during memory tasks and years of education in young and older adults. Neuropsychology. 2005;19:181–192.

Chapter 8

Mood Disorders:
Raymond Lam and SAD

"Keep your face to the sunshine and you cannot see the shadow."
Helen Keller

Depression is ubiquitous. Prevention will come from better delineating the processes that determine specific kinds of depression. Dr. Raymond Lam from Vancouver studies seasonal affective disorder and cannot understand why physicians are reluctant to use a proven and natural treatment: bright light.

"Restless Nights, Listless Days" is the title of a recent article in the prestigious science journal *Nature* describing winter depression or seasonal affective disorder (SAD), a condition that Raymond Lam has been investigating for the last 15 years. The prevalence of seasonal depression is estimated at four to six percent in the general population. An additional 10% to 20% of individuals may show features of this disorder, but too few to merit a diagnosis. The higher the latitude, the more common the seasonal changes in mood, making SAD a significant health problem for Canadians. Rates of SAD are highest in patients with a history of recurrent mood complaints. Of such patients, fully one third may be suffering from a seasonal disorder.

SAD is an oddly appropriate acronym, describing a pattern of wintertime misery and happy summers. This is a paradoxical depressive disorder. For instance, while most people with depression find it impossible to sleep, those with SAD tend to sleep too much. Most people with depression find it difficult to eat and dramatically lose weight as a result. In contrast, SAD sufferers crave carbohydrates, eat and gain weight, but only in winter. Throughout the winter months, they also feel tired and lack energy, as if in hibernation. There may, indeed, be an analogy between SAD and hibernation; much about this disorder remains unknown. Because exposure to bright, artificial light helps, the major theories about what causes SAD are currently linked to how light changes mood.

It seems like the punch line to a regional tale that a Canadian psychiatrist born and raised in rainy Vancouver should end up studying light and winter depression. But that is Dr. Raymond Lam's story. He is the fourth generation of his family to live and work in British Columbia, but by conventional reckoning a second-generation Canadian whose parents emigrated from China after the Second World War.

Raymond Lam's grandfather and great-grandfather worked in British Columbia throughout their lives but because of the times they lived in, their wives and children stayed in China. The first generations of workers from China were treated shamefully in Canada. They came to Canada around 1850, attracted to B.C. by the gold rush in the Fraser Valley. In the 1880s, about 15,000 Chinese workers were hired for very low pay to work under dangerous conditions building the Canadian Pacific Railway. As many as one third lost their lives. When the railway was completed, the Chinese laborers were laid off. Despite a climate of hostility and racial discrimination, some settled in B.C., becoming itinerant vegetable vendors and hired hands.

Family immigration from China was next to impossible in 1885 because the government imposed a head tax of $50 on every new Chinese immigrant. This was increased to $500 in 1903. At that time, $500 was the equivalent of two years' wages, so great-grandfather Lam could not afford to have his family join him. In 1923, the Canadian Parliament passed the Chinese Exclusion Act, barring Chinese immigration altogether. This Act remained in effect for 24 years until the Second World War when, even though not permitted to vote, hundreds of young Chinese men and women joined the Canadian armed forces. Chinese communities across the country raised $5 million for the war effort. In 1947, two years after the end of the war, the Chinese Exclusion Act was finally repealed and families were re-united. That is when Raymond Lam's parents came to settle in B.C. When he was a boy, Raymond assumed that his grandfather had worked on the railroad but he discovered as an adult that the man he knew as a chicken farmer started life as a houseboy to a doctor's family. Raymond's father was named after the young son of that Shaughnessy family.

Raymond is a first-born son and from a young age his parents expected him to be a doctor, in their view the most respected of all professions. Fortunately, Raymond excelled in academics, especially science, and happily shared their dream of his future. He was accepted into the University of B.C. medical school after only three years of undergraduate science.

After completing his medical degree in 1981 (a year after the discovery that bright light suppresses melatonin secretion in humans), Raymond Lam completed a rotating internship at the Jewish General Hospital in Montreal. At first, he thought he might be a general practitioner like his own family doctor, a distant cousin of his mother. When he realized that being a specialist was more in keeping with his interests, his fascination with brain and behavior led him to a choice between neurology and psychiatry. "I applied to and was accepted by both programs, and actually held both acceptance letters in my hand as I was trying to decide. In the end, I picked psychiatry because the patients and their conditions were more interesting and challenging to me…and I've never been sorry about my choice. Within psychiatry you can easily explore the brain, but in neurology it is much more difficult to explore behavior."

Raymond completed a four-year psychiatric residency at UBC. He acquired his first taste of research as a second-year resident working with Dr. Ron Remick, a Mood Disorders specialist and much sought-after teacher in the program. During this period, the dexamethasone suppression test was being hailed as the first laboratory test for depression and many psychiatrists were routinely using it to help diagnose depression. But Raymond saw many patients for whom the test was negative, even though they were clearly depressed. He became particularly interested in this group of patients. He read the research studies for the validity of the test and quickly realized that it had too many limitations to be clinically useful. As a young resident, he wondered why experienced clinicians hadn't critically read and integrated the research literature on the test.

Two of the interests that were to govern his career had been born: an interest in atypical depression and an interest in translating research findings into clinical practice.

During the course of the rotation with Dr. Remick, one of their patients experienced a manic episode while participating in a clinical trial of a new medication for depression. The unusual reaction led Raymond to review the literature and present the case study of medication-induced mania at a meeting of the North Pacific Society for Neurology and Psychiatry. Twenty-eight years old, Raymond Lam received a prize for best paper presentation and decided then that research would be a prime focus of his career.

Influenced by a scientific report on the newly discovered syndrome of SAD (and indulging his affinity for ocean-front campuses where he could play tennis all year round) Raymond decided to study melatonin and mood disorders at the University of California at San Diego (UCSD). Funded by a fellowship award from the Canadian Psychiatric Research Foundation (CPRF), he worked with Dr. Chris Gillin (see Chapter 14) and Dr. Dan Kripke at the UCSD Clinical Research Center, sponsored by the U.S. National Institute of Mental Health. UCSD is a place where medical research is valued; Dr. Francis Crick, who co-discovered the structure of DNA, was one of fifteen Nobel Prize winners on faculty at UCSD. Gillin and Kripke, renowned psychiatrists and investigators in sleep and circadian rhythms, became Raymond's mentors in academic research. Coming home to Vancouver as a new Assistant Professor in the Department of Psychiatry, he started his own SAD clinic at UBC, treating depressed people with light.

"It is remarkable," says Raymond, "that something as simple as bright light can profoundly alter mood states. People almost change right before your eyes…one week a patient comes in feeling terribly depressed and by the next week they are feeling much better." Many studies have shown that light therapy, usually using a fluorescent light box, is an effective treatment, with about two-thirds of people with SAD showing a good response.

Light is a natural treatment with minimal side effects and safe for developing fetuses, so it can be used during pregnancy and breast-feeding (especially important because of the high female to male ratio in depression – see Chapter 15). About 20% of patients may experience mild side effects, including headache, eye strain, and "feeling wired." The therapeutic effects occur via light entering the eyes, but there is no evidence that exposure to bright light as prescribed for SAD can harm the retina; a five-year prospective study of patients receiving regular light therapy did not find any significant damage to the eye.

Although light therapy is effective for SAD, Dr. Lam advises against self-diagnosis because there are many medical causes for depressive symptoms. If light therapy is prescribed, he recommends that physicians follow clinical guidelines for treatment of SAD that he developed with a team of Canadian experts.

When Raymond Lam first started investigating SAD, he hoped that the apparent link between animal models of seasonal rhythms influenced by light and treatment with bright light exposure in depressed people would soon lead to a full understanding of the underlying cause of winter depression. The past two decades of research, however, have shown SAD to be more complicated than first thought. The underlying cause of SAD or exactly how light works for this condition is still not known.

Raymond Lam has focused his SAD research in four major directions – eyes, brain chemistry, genes, and immune function. First, he investigated the possibility that the eyes rather than the brain are the problem, that the retinas of people vulnerable to SAD may not absorb enough light. He used a technique called electro-retinography (measuring electrical impulses produced by exposure to flashes of light) to test the eyes of those who suffer from SAD and he found reduced sensitivity to light among this group.

Second, he examined the serotonin neurotransmitter system in SAD patients. He showed that depressed SAD patients secrete less growth hormone in response to serotonin than other people. But, after treatment with light, their growth hormone response normalizes. His team also showed that when serotonin is decreased by rapidly depleting blood tryptophan (a dietary amino acid that is converted to serotonin in the brain), the antidepressant effect of light therapy stops – indicating that bright light acts by affecting serotonin. This important result has now been replicated by three independent laboratories. Lam and his colleagues subsequently conducted a brain-imaging study using Positron Emission Tomography (PET) to examine the effects of tryptophan depletion on brain serotonin receptors. They found that not only serotonin but also other brain neurotransmitters, such as dopamine and noradrenalin, are implicated in the expression of SAD.

Third, working with geneticists, Lam has found that seasonality (mood changes linked to the seasons) has a strong genetic link that varies with personality type. In collaboration with other scientists, he is now investigating serotonin and dopamine genes that may be involved in SAD. Fourth, based on many animal studies showing large seasonal fluctuations in immune response, his team is exploring brain immune function in SAD. They are testing a theory that the decrease in light during winter leads to an increase in melatonin secretion, which in turn activates immune cells such as macrophages and T-helper lymphocytes. This results in a shift in inflammatory brain chemicals called cytokines. Cytokines – the signaling molecules of the immune system – have the same effects on the brain as psychological and physical stresses; increasing levels of cytokines could therefore result in the characteristic symptoms of SAD. This theory would help to explain why patients with SAD are depressed even though the levels of stress hormones, high in most depressions, are unchanged or even decreased – because melatonin secretion, high in SAD, suppresses the release of stress hormones, but not of inflammatory cytokines.

Studying SAD can be a way of exploring and better understanding other forms of depression. Because it has a predictable start and end, the same person can be studied when depressed and when not depressed to see what biological markers are associated with the depressed state and what environmental factors (other than season and light) trigger or buffer depression. Lam and his group have also conducted clinical trials of treatment for SAD, showing that ultraviolet wavelengths are not necessary for the therapeutic effect of light therapy. The important result is that commercial light boxes now have UV filters.

Raymond Lam and several other Canadian colleagues conducted the first well-controlled study to compare antidepressants and light in the treatment of SAD. Both treatments worked well, but bright light therapy offers an advantage over antidepressants in that the effect is quicker. Most patients experience an effect within the first week of light therapy while, typically, an oral antidepressant takes several weeks to work. What remains a question is whether a combination of medications and light therapy is more effective than either alone.

Raymond has not limited his research to SAD. He has demonstrated that other psychiatric disorders (the eating disorder, bulimia nervosa, and premenstrual depression for instance) also show seasonality and that light therapy might benefit these conditions. He also studies new antidepressant medications and combined medication/psychotherapy treatments.

Raymond Lam has another mission in life: to overcome physicians' reluctance to change their practice even in the face of scientific evidence that a new treatment works better than an older one. He feels this is especially true with non-medication treatment that physicians are not used to dispensing. His assessment is that the decades of work showing the effectiveness of light therapy on SAD has ended up not having much of a clinical impact. "Even though the evidence that light therapy works is solid, it's a shame that more patients do not have access to it because their physicians aren't aware of it."

As a result, he became interested in the question of how physicians can be persuaded to change their behavior – the translation of research evidence to the clinic. It is difficult to obtain funding for studies that help physicians incorporate scientific evidence into their practice and Dr. Lam feels strongly about this: "In our present scientific grant system, it is often easier to get funding for an esoteric biological study than one that compares how well different treatments work so that you can influence clinical practice."

In the end, Lam decided he could best influence physicians by educating the general public. "If you encourage people to actively participate in managing their illnesses and increase public awareness about new treatments, their doctors will have to learn about them too." Raymond believes that some of his most influential work has not been published in medical journals, but in Cosmopolitan magazine! He also engages in many public education events and has been honored for this work by the Canadian Mental Health Association. He feels it is particularly important for people to hear that "depression and other types of mental illness are very treatable."

The healthcare system in general, Raymond says, is even harder to change than individual doctors. He believes strongly in the ideal of Canadian healthcare, which is why he returned to Canada instead of remaining in the U.S. after his fellowship, but he no longer believes that a system that is entirely publicly funded can provide the highest quality care for patients. "Unfortunately, a healthcare system that wants to be equal for all is geared to mediocrity…in our system, there is no incentive or encouragement for innovation or excellence." Many Canadians do not have access, for example, to the newest medications because Pharmacare is singly concerned with the costs of drugs. New medications do seem more expensive than the old ones, but no one is measuring the potential cost-savings in other areas, such as lower hospitalization rates, earlier return to work, or faster integration back into normal family life.

The healthcare burden of depression is exceedingly large but it is often a hidden burden. The focus in healthcare is frequently on dramatic illness presentations like schizophrenia in the homeless or psychosis in the emergency room, so funding finds its way to hospitals and emergency departments. Raymond Lam insists that there needs to be a shift:

I see a lot of promising things happening. Society is recognizing the high cost of mental illness in general and finally some attention is being paid to the hidden burden of depression and anxiety. I'm glad that our health ministries are starting to develop and fund, for example, chronic disease management programs for depression in primary care (care by family doctors).

However, I see great potential in partnering with business on initiatives for depressed workers. It is easier for the business sector to recognize how big a problem depression is because it relates directly to their bottom line. And, if you demonstrate benefit of innovative programs that, for example, get depressed people back to work earlier, companies will put money towards them.

Similarly, Raymond thinks Canada should develop research centers that concentrate on specific areas of excellence. That means setting priorities in funding. "We can't be fair to all people in research." Unlike the U.S., in Canada, "we are more balanced in our priorities, we have a smaller population and we have to realize we can't be all things to all people."

Raymond believes that, whether in Canada or the United States, being a researcher is tough work.

It is certainly difficult to do clinical research anywhere – it is not well-funded or encouraged. At least in the U.S. you can ask for salary support in research grants. Here in Canada we expect the universities and hospitals to cover research salaries but there is insufficient funding to do so. On top of that, very little funding is dedicated to supporting clinician scientists.

He acknowledges that many clinicians are drawn away from research by the lure of clinical earnings. "I certainly don't make as much money as a full-time clinician, but I have the flexibility to see patients, teach students, and study the questions that interest me." It is a fact that, especially with new doctors carrying increasing debt from medical school, it is a personal sacrifice to go into academics.

This is not a new problem and many funding agencies are trying to address it. My first research grant to study SAD came from the CPRF. It was extremely important to me, as a junior researcher, to have access to funding to begin clinical studies. That initial grant allowed me to start the research program that later would receive federal funding from the Medical Research Council of Canada (which later became the Canadian Institutes of Health Research).

Another way the system hasn't worked well in the past is that collaborations among health disciplines were not encouraged.

Treating mental illness needs to be particularly collaborative. There is still a tension among psychiatrists, psychologists, and other mental health workers. This is improving through integrative programs. Unlike the past, we no longer argue about whether psychotherapy or biological treatments work better. What we try to do now is understand who does better with which therapy and what combination of therapies could work even better. I'm optimistic on this level.

One motivation for Raymond Lam to become a clinical scientist came from a family source. During his internship in Montreal, his sister in B.C. developed a potentially fatal medical condition. The doctors gave her four years to live. At one point she was placed on a heart-lung transplant wait list but the doctors were reluctant to operate because she was so ill. And then she was given an experimental drug that led to an "unexpected and miraculous response – she hasn't looked back since." Twenty years later, she is doing well. That reinforced for Raymond the value of pushing the envelope of science to discover new and improved treatments. "I'm an academic psychiatrist because I am not satisfied with what we are currently doing for our patients." His patients deserve more and he is determined to give them more.

In part, he feels he owes it to them because his own life has been a healthy and fortunate one. Although he regularly works long hours (especially at grant deadlines!), Raymond always takes ample time off to be with his family: his wife, Tracy, and their two sons. He is close to his extended family in Vancouver – the main reason why he has so far stayed, despite the cloudy skies and the many job offers to go elsewhere. And golf has become a recent passion for him that removes him from work concerns.

This pioneering Canadian scientist thinks that Canada has been particularly successful at integrating psychological and biological approaches – he himself sees no gulf between the two since the effect of both is mediated through the brain. And he is proud of Canadians for, at long last, beginning to overcome the stigma surrounding mental illness – he feels that people are not as reluctant as they once were to talk about their experiences with depression. He believes that the Canadian public will lead the way and steer the profession in the correct direction – making effective use of interventions scientifically proven to work.

Further Reading

Abbott A. Restless nights, listless days. Nature. 2003;425:896–898.

Jang KL, Lam RW, Harris JA, Vernon PA, Livesley WJ. Seasonal mood change and personality: an investigation of genetic co-morbidity. Psychiatry Res. 1998;78:1–7.

Hébert M, Beattie CW, Tam EM, Yatham LN, Lam RW. Electroretinography in patients with winter seasonal affective disorder. Psychiatry Res. 2004;127:29–34.

Lam RW. Seasonal affective disorder. Diagnosis and management. Primary Care Psychiatry. 1998;4:63–74.

Lam RW, Levitt AJ, editors. Canadian consensus guidelines for the treatment of seasonal affective disorder. Vancouver BC: Clinical & Academic Publishing; 1999.

Lam RW, Levitt AJ, Levitan RD, Enns MW, Morehouse RL, Michalak EE, Tam EM. The CAN-SAD study: randomized controlled trial of the effectiveness of light therapy and fluoxetine in patients with winter seasonal affective disorder. Am J Psychiatry. In press 2006.

Lam RW, Song C, Yatham LN. Does neuroimmune dysfunction mediate seasonal mood changes in winter depression? Med Hypotheses. 2004;63:567–573.

Lam RW, Zis AP, Grewal AK, Delgado PG, Charney DS, Krystal JH. Effects of tryptophan depletion in patients with seasonal affective disorder in remission with light therapy. Arch Gen Psychiatry. 1996;53:41–44.

Lewy AJ, Wehr TA, Goodwin FK, Newsome DA, Markey SP. Light suppresses melatonin secretion in humans. Science. 1980;210:1267–1269.

Rosenthal NE, Sack DA, Gillin JC, Lewy AJ, Goodwin FK, Davenport Y, Mueller PS, Newsome DA, Wehr TA. Seasonal affective disorder: a description of the syndrome and preliminary findings with light therapy. Arch Gen Psychiatry. 1984;41:72–80.

Sohn CH, Lam RW: Update on the biology of seasonal affective disorder. CNS Spectrums. 2005;10:635–646.

Chapter 9

Personality Disorders: Herta Guttman works with the Family

"Africans believe in something that is difficult to render in English. We call it ununtu botho. It means the essence of being human. You know when it is there and when it is absent. It speaks about humanness, gentleness, hospitality, putting yourself out on behalf of others, being vulnerable. It recognizes that my humanity is bound in yours, for we can only be human together."

Desmond Tutu.

Personality disorders are, by definition, ingrained in character structure and not easy to modify. Herta Guttman from Montreal has found a treatment that works through its effect on the family.

Personality disorders are enduring patterns of behavior that cause distress to the person and to those around him. About six to nine percent of the general population fit current criteria for a personality disorder. A specific personality disorder characterized by unstable interpersonal relationships, fluctuations in self-image and emotion, and impulsivity in such areas as spending, sexual conduct, driving, eating, and substance abuse has been called borderline personality disorder (BPD). Self-mutilation, suicide threats, gestures, and attempts often occur in this condition. For people suffering from BPD, relatively minor everyday events and interactions can trigger feelings of depression, anxiety, and anger. People diagnosed with this condition may also experience dissociative symptoms, symptoms of depersonalization, and paranoid symptoms. Individuals with BPD complain of a feeling of emptiness; they both expect and fear abandonment, and they often act without reflecting. One of the interpersonal hallmarks of this form of personality disorder is an oscillation between idealizing and devaluing others. The disorder occurs in approximately two percent of the population; 75% of those fulfilling the current diagnostic criteria are women.

BPD has always been associated with early life difficulties but, more recently, it has been hypothesized that the specific antecedents are emotional, physical, and sexual abuse. Over 50% of people diagnosed with BPD also fulfill the criteria for posttraumatic stress disorder (PTSD). The two conditions may be variants of the same disorder or, alternatively, the prior presence of BPD may predispose to PTSD when a person is exposed to trauma. Because of the intense neediness of BPD patients and their high risk of self-injury and suicide, they have been notoriously difficult for psychiatrists to treat. Specific forms of cognitive behavioral therapy individually and in groups have shown great promise. Dr. Herta Guttman in Montreal is a pioneer in the family treatment of persons with borderline personality disorder.

Born in Montreal, Herta is the child of immigrants from Vienna. Herta's father was a chemical engineer who had served in the First World War. He came to Canada because there was no work in Austria postwar. He had a reverence for science and a belief in scientific progress that Herta would inherit. From her mother, she absorbed a love of the arts and a passionate interest in women's issues. The family was always achievement-oriented. Both parents believed women should have careers; the conflict was whether or not they should also get married. At the time, it was considered very difficult to do both.

Having suffered two polio attacks as a child, Herta became interested in how the body worked and how one goes about trying to fix it. By the age of thirteen, she had discovered Freud. She was fascinated to learn through her readings that the mind followed laws and that the unconscious determined behavior. This led to an undergraduate degree in psychology at McGill University where Donald Hebb (1904–1985) was one of her professors.

Originally a Nova Scotian, Hebb was Chair of the Department of Psychology at McGill. His 1949 book, *The Organization of Behavior: A Neuropsychological Theory*, established the Hebbian rule that neurons that "fire together, wire together," an influential concept in the brain sciences. Herta consulted him about her future – should she continue in psychology or go into medicine? She remembers his response: "If you want to treat people; go to medical school. Psychology is for research."

Herta married Frank Guttman right after undergraduate school and, together, they attended medical school in Geneva. She received her medical degree in 1958 (her first baby was born in 1956) and the Guttmans returned to Montreal. A second daughter was born in 1960 and Herta took time away from Medicine to rear her children. One day, her husband, who was interning at the Jewish General Hospital, came home and excitedly said, "You have to see this guy and how he interviews families!" He was referring to the new chief of psychiatry at the Jewish General, Dr. Nathan Epstein, a pioneer in family therapy. Nathan Epstein had trained with Nathan Ackerman in New York and is credited with having introduced family therapy to Canada.

Herta began attending the family interviews at the Jewish General and was hired as a part-time research assistant on Dr. Epstein's team. While there, she devised a coding system for family interaction. By 1965, with the children in school, she went back to school herself – to do a residency in psychiatry. She has worked since then as a clinician, educator, researcher, and administrator at the Jewish General and the Allan Memorial in Montreal and the Clarke Institute in Toronto. As a tribute to her accomplishments, Herta Guttman has recently been awarded a lifetime achievement award from the American Family Therapy Academy.

Guttman and her colleagues have discovered a pattern wherein the parent with BPD uses the child as a target of projections and reality distortions, a harm that the other parent sometimes fails to buffer. They found that young women with anorexia often experience lack of family cohesion and undue family conflict, maternal control, intrusiveness, and overprotection. Women with BPD, they discovered, suffered *more* intrafamilial verbal and physical abuse than those with anorexia nervosa. And the abuse tended to start early, recur frequently, and take place in multiple forms, as corroborated by parents.

The Guttman group showed that family members of women with BPD scored high on levels of alexithymia – an inability to experience feelings or, at least, to put a name to them. Moreover, BPD daughters rated their parents as unempathic. Herta Guttman concludes that early impairment of attachment to the caregiver in those destined to develop BPD is at least partly attributable to a lack of empathic parenting. She feels that effective communication in these families is marred by inability to experience or express feelings and that this, in turn, makes it difficult for the family to engage in problem solving together. Mutuality does not occur and intimacy does not develop. The multiple abuse is often specifically directed at daughters. The symptoms of the daughter can be understood as representing both predispositional characteristics and reactions to the family system.

Working with laboratory animals, Michael J. Meaney and his group at the Douglas Hospital Research Centre in Montreal have lent support to these clinical findings by delineating the mechanisms by which adversity in early life can alter brain development and expose individuals to psychopathology. This research group has proposed that the individual differences that matter are those that regulate behavioral and endocrine response to stress, notably central corticotropin-releasing factor (CRF) systems. Individual differences in maternal care, they have shown, can modify an offspring's cognitive development, as well as its ability to cope with stress later in life.

Like many interviewees in this book, Herta Guttman believes that there are considerable obstacles to research in Canada.

It seems to be a question of money. Many good projects don't get funded. It is easier for better-known researchers but very hard for the young ones. That is why the Canadian Psychiatric Research Foundation's policy of funding new researchers is so important.

Another obstacle to a research career for Herta, as for other psychiatrists, has been the powerful need that doctors have to heal. That can lure young people away from the bench and toward the clinic. Lack of a strong mentor is another problem. In Herta's case, the solution has been to work collaboratively with others.

Despite the obstacles, Dr. Guttman is of the opinion that Canadians have contributed greatly to expanding knowledge in psychiatry. In her field, the main contributions have been: a) the realization that mental illness has reciprocal impact within the family, b) the elaboration of cognitive family therapy, c) the recognition that psychoeducation to families has to be delivered repeatedly before it can do any good, d) the recognition that abuse is part of the constellation of BPD, and e) the demonstration of the long-term consequences of having a parent who suffers from serious psychiatric disorder.

The actual experience of mental illness can be a strong driving force in research according to Dr. Guttman, so that clinicians who deal with patients daily seem to do more relevant research than non-clinicians, even though their time is more limited. With respect to personal experience with mental illness, Herta's family, like all families, knows what it is at close hand. An uncle shot himself after the First World War – the result, she thinks, of a hitherto unsuspected mental illness.

Herta started practice when there were still few women in Medicine. She founded a group of women psychiatrists who met regularly and called themselves "the seven sisters."

Whereas the playing field has leveled, there are still glass ceilings in Psychiatry. The importance to most women of doing many things well is a detriment in research, where you have to be single-minded.

She worries that, despite so many women now entering Medicine, all the professors will continue to be men and women will remain foot soldiers.

Today Herta has reached retirement age and asks herself the question: Is there life after psychiatry?

> One inevitably pays a price by concentrating on a profession – retirement can lead to many rewarding activities for which one has never had time.

Herta's husband, Frank, has been involved since 1967 with the group called Canadian Friends of Peace Now (CFPN). The association is dedicated to the establishment of peace in the Middle East. Herta, too, is concerned about peace. Living in Quebec has shown her that two different cultures can co-exist and work together in harmony. World peace is her major hope. She is a true ideological descendant of famed Canadian psychiatrist, Brock Chisholm (1896–1971), first Director General of the World Health Organization. She is involved in helping refugees through Amnesty International and is also active in Polio Québec.

> Psychiatry is at the core of humanitarian thinking. The tradition of the care of the patient and the understanding of patient needs was pioneered by psychiatry.

Herta Guttman believes, as her father did before her, in science and in the concept of progress. She has overcome hardship in her life, notably her experiences with polio and the post-polio syndrome, as well as career difficulties resulting from being a woman in a man's field. But she does not easily get overwhelmed. She loves when others turn to her for advice. She has had a long and happy marriage and her husband and family are number one on her priority list. She loves being a grandmother. No wonder she leaves a legacy in family therapy.

Further Reading

Brown RE, Milner PM. The legacy of Donald O. Hebb: more than the Hebb synapse. Nat Rev Neurosci. 2003;4:1013–1019.

Chisholm GB. Social responsibility. Science. 1949;109:27–31.

Epstein NB, Bishop DS. Family therapy. State of the art – 1973. Can Psychiatr Assoc J. 1973;18:175–183.

Feldman RB, Guttman HA. Families of borderline patients: literal-minded parents, borderline parents, and parental protectiveness. Am J Psychiatry. 1984;141:1392–1396.

Guttman HA, Spector RM, Sigal JJ, Rakoff V, Epstein NB. Reliability of coding affective communication in family therapy sessions. Problems of measurement and interpretation. J Consult Clin Psychol. 1971;37:397–402.

Guttman HA, Spector RM, Sigal JJ, Epstein NB, Rakoff V. Coding of affective expression in conjoint family therapy. Am J Psychother. 1972;26:185–194.

Guttman HA, Laporte L. Empathy in families of women with borderline personality disorder, anorexia nervosa, and a control group. Family Process. 2000;39:345–358.

Guttman H, Laporte L. Alexithymia, empathy, and psychological symptoms in a family context. Compr Psychiatry. 2002;43:448–455.

Guttman HA. The epigenesis of the family system as a context for individual development. Fam Process. 2002;41:533–545.

Hebb DO. The organization of behavior: a neuropsychological theory. New York: Wiley, 1949.

Hebb DO. Heredity and environment in mammalian behavior. Br J Animal Behavior 1953;1:43–47.

Irving A. Brock Chisholm: doctor to the world. Markham, Ontario: Fitzhenry & Whiteside; 1998.

Laporte L, Marcoux V, Guttman HA. [Characteristics of families of women with restricting anorexia nervosa compared with families of normal probands] Encephale. 2001;27:109–119.

Laporte L, Guttman H. Abusive relationships in families of women with borderline personality disorder, anorexia nervosa and a control group. J Nerv Ment Dis. 2001;189:522–531.

Meaney MJ. Maternal care, gene expression, and the transmission of individual differences in stress reactivity across generations. Ann Rev Neurosci. 2001;24:1161–1192.

Milner PM. The mind and Donald O. Hebb. Scientific American. 1986;268,124–129.

Chapter 10

Psyche and Soma:
Mindfulness and Zindel Segal

"View all problems as challenges.
Look upon negativities that arise as opportunities to learn and to grow.
Don't run from them, condemn yourself, or bury your burden in
saintly silence.
You have a problem? Great.
More grist for the mill. Rejoice, dive in, and investigate."
Bhante Henepola Gunaratana, "Mindfulness in Plain English"

Mindfulness-based cognitive therapy (MBCT) combines cognitive therapy with the traditional Buddhist practice of meditation. Zindel Segal of Toronto has shown that MBCT protects against recurrences of depression.

Psychotherapy helps patients in many ways. Through an empathic relationship with a skilled therapist, patients learn about their emotional problems and about the circumstances that tend to induce symptoms. They learn to identify and avoid situations that have led to previous episodes of illness and to view themselves and their life situations more realistically. They learn to become less reactive to stress and to improve their interpersonal skills. Psychotherapy is a powerful tool for change and the responsibility for studying its specificity and efficacy at the University of Toronto falls on the shoulders of Zindel Segal, the Morgan Firestone Chair in Psychotherapy. As Chair, part of his responsibility is researching the mechanisms underlying effective psychotherapy. Mr. Morgan Firestone, a well-known business leader and supporter of health care causes, endowed this Chair (and also the Chair of Psychiatry at McMaster University held by Dr. Richard Swinson – please see Chapter 2) because of his conviction that psychotherapy powerfully contributes to quality of life.

Zindel Segal's *particular* research interest is preventing relapse in individuals who have previously suffered depression. Depressions tend to recur. Patients with at least three past depressive episodes have a 70–80% chance of a new setback within three years. The good news is that the risk of recurrence diminishes the longer a person stays well, and a growing body of evidence suggests that psychological interventions administered *after* recovery from a depressive episode substantially improve the outlook. The challenge that Dr. Zindel Segal set for himself was to develop a form of psychotherapy that would protect patients from depressive relapse. Dr. Segal (with Dr. Mark Williams at Oxford and Dr. John Teasdale at Cambridge) developed a therapy called mindfulness-based cognitive therapy (MBCT) designed specifically to prevent relapse in those who have recovered from depression. This approach combines cognitive therapy with the practice of an Eastern form of meditation called mindfulness.

What patients first learn is to recognize how their belief system (their inner thoughts) reinforces the tendency to depression. Then, in small steps, they are taught how to be mindful or aware of their thoughts. They need to train themselves to keep mild states of sadness from escalating. MBCT involves developing a capacity to allow distressing feelings, thoughts and sensations to occupy awareness, but, at the same time, to moderate one's response to them. Training in mindfulness fosters a "decentered" view of the thoughts passing through one's mind. Patients learn to view these thoughts from the comfort of a seat in the theatre rather than from centre stage. They learn to attend to them in an emotionally detached way, as if standing on a bridge and watching the river flow by. Thoughts are seen as passing events in the mind, transitory and fleeting, no longer fraught with consequence.

Dr. Segal comes from a family caught in the Holocaust in Europe. His father's whole family lost their lives. Ancestral trauma of this magnitude can infect younger generations through the phenomenon of transgenerational inheritance. Deep-seated convictions such as "the world is not safe," "the future is uncertain," "evil exists around us" can be and are passed down to children and grandchildren of trauma survivors. Drawing on basic research in cognition and emotion, Dr. Segal set out to develop a model of treatment that could eradicate deep-seated convictions without basis in present reality. Once a person has been repeatedly depressed, the mere feeling of sadness, even if transient, rekindles a number of previously held beliefs that have been well-rehearsed and reinforced during previous periods of depression. In this way, sadness can evoke believing that one is unloved, in danger, worthless, or hopeless because these are the very beliefs that were held during previous depressive episodes. Working with depressed patients, Dr. Segal came to the conclusion that stopping chain associations such as these could prevent relapse into depression. Not that feelings of sadness can ever be eliminated. Nostalgia and melancholy, disappointment and longing, grief and sorrow are a part of the human condition. The core element of MBCT is not to avoid such feelings but to become aware, instead, of the automatic linking of feeling and conviction (from sadness to unwarranted beliefs about oneself), to be mindful of the association and to recognize that the beliefs result not from objective evidence but from fleeting states of mind. Such beliefs are transient mood-dependent thoughts not reflective of a permanent reality. Awareness of automatic patterns of thinking triggered by transient events or emotions allows the chain to be recognized early, stopping the spiraling that leads to relapse. Classical cognitive behavioral therapy tries to alter negative thinking but MBCT focuses on the awareness of thoughts, regardless of their content. After awareness comes an emotional disengagement and the adoption of a more panoramic view of one's own cognitions, a form of meditative practice that lets such thoughts come and go, much as the waters of a river flow by. Buddhists have pursued similar practices for centuries in order to still the mind and achieve equanimity in the face of psychological stress.

The practices are designed to help develop an observational stance toward experience by starting with easy cues such as bodily sensations and the act of breathing in and out. The Body Scan is a traditional method that requires paying attention to body sensations (Can you feel your left middle toe without wiggling it?). In this practice, attention is focused in a narrow horizontal band that is slowly brought down through the entire body as if giving oneself a mental CAT scan. Similarly, concentrating on breathing in and breathing out means not dwelling on other thoughts. The saying "you can only take a breath in the present" is an illustration of how a person can keep his or her mind from wandering into the future or worrying about the past. This ability to give pause to the onrush of concerns and apprehensions gives patients the space they need to prevent an automatic response to familiar triggers and stress points. With time, the old cues are experienced as passing events in the mind, transitory and fleeting, no longer fraught with consequence, no longer capable of evoking the old distress.

Starting with an undergraduate degree in psychology from McGill University and continuing with a doctorate from Queen's University, Dr. Segal came to Toronto to do a Fellowship with Dr. Brian Shaw. At this time, Dr. Shaw was developing cognitive therapy for the treatment of depression. After his Fellowship, Zindel was offered a faculty position at the Centre for Addiction and Mental Health. His more recent mentor has been Dr. John Teasdale from Cambridge University with whom he began to investigate the psychological vulnerabilities to depressive relapse.

Dr. Teasdale had done some of the best basic science on cognition, memory, and emotion and I was fortunate enough to work very closely with him. I learned a lot about how to embed the insights from cognitive models of the mind into a clinical approach capable of calming a reactive mind.

In a multi-centered randomized controlled trial conducted by Dr. Segal and his UK associates, 145 volunteers were allocated to either treatment-as-usual or treatment-as-usual plus eight classes of MBCT. All the participants had had at least two episodes of depression in the past but were free of depression at the time of the trial. They were then followed for twelve months to see how many relapsed. The results showed MBCT was helpful for those who had suffered the most number of previous episodes of depression. It reduced the risk of relapse from 66% to 37% in those who had had three or more previous episodes. But it had no demonstrable effect in those with only two previous bouts of illness. Psychologists Ma and Teasdale in Cambridge have replicated these findings in a subsequent trial.

Dr. Segal and his colleagues are now examining how well their treatment compares with maintenance pharmacotherapy.

Maintenance pharmacotherapy is currently the gold standard for helping patients stay relapse-free but there are problems with keeping people on medication for a very long time. Often they don't want to or they discontinue the medication as soon as they feel well again even thought there is a substantial amount of research literature suggesting that patients who are recovering still require some sort of protection against relapse. We'd like to find out whether this treatment we've developed can work synergistically with antidepressant medication so that, in the end, people may get well because of pharmacotherapy but stay well because of the skills in emotion regulation that we can teach them. That would be a very important outcome of the research and would help a lot of people.

For this chapter, Dr. Segal was asked to describe a high point in his career:

It was when I received an MRC fellowship that allowed me to formulate a research program investigating psychological predictors of relapse. The initial studies were funded by the Laidlaw Foundation and I used some of that money to conduct a study that showed that there were some significant psychological predictors (of relapse) that have to do with the kind of ways that thinking styles change when recovering depressed patients begin to feel sad or experience a temporary shift in mood. This was a significant predictor of relapse. It was the risk marker we used to develop our new treatment. Our first funding came from the Laidlaw Foundation and then from the Ontario Mental Health Foundation.

We had the typical difficulties in making our case and having initial grant applications rejected. But we collected some pilot data from our clinics and that bolstered our applications. Then we were able to make the case for larger scale funding. Then, after we did that, we published in top-tier peer reviewed journals and, after that, funding was easier to come by. I've been funded from sources outside of Canada, the NIMH in Washington and even from some agencies in the United Kingdom. But overall, the interest in funding research on psychotherapy has dwindled. I believe that this is shortsighted because, when research into psychotherapy is tied to a specific model of psychopathology, the opportunities for discovery are immense. Once you have an effective treatment, you can go on to discover the mechanism of its action and that will give you clues to the origins of the disorder. Things become very interesting if you have a theory that says condition X can be managed by achieving changes in the serotonin system and effective pharmacological treatment lets you do that. If you are able to achieve comparable change for the better with a nonsomatic intervention such as psychotherapy, it adds to the complexity of the model you are testing. Maybe it's the repetitive thoughts that depressed people have that lead to the changes in the serotonin system that antidepressants alleviate.

Because a false dichotomy (biology vs. psychology) continues to exist even among scientists, much time, effort, and energy go into convincing the relevant granting agencies that psychological interventions are relevant for biological illnesses such as depression. But working hard comes naturally to Zindel.

As a child of immigrants, one grows up watching one's parents work very hard in order to establish a foothold in a new country. One of the lessons learned from that is that hard work pays off but another is that one shouldn't take things for granted. Achievements such as establishing a career in a respected profession are very important in my family and that definitely had an effect on me. Because I'm a child of Holocaust survivors, I have always felt the need to try to make sense out of the incomprehensible. History has sensitized me to the fact that there is a lot of suffering in the world and that people have to learn to deal with difficulty in their everyday lives. Perhaps that type of awareness steered me into a profession that helps people cope with their difficulties and to use research to try to understand mechanisms and develop better ways of coping.

My parents' generation suffered enormous emotional difficulties. Some managed to stay healthy and some didn't. I want to find out why that is. Cognitive processes have a lot to do with the structure of belief systems and how information is represented in the mind. That is intimately related to mental health and mental illness.

Further Reading

Beck AT, Rush AJ, Shaw BF, Emery G. Cognitive therapy of depression. New York: Guilford Press; 1979.

Brave Heart MY, DeBruyn LM. The American Indian Holocaust: healing historical unresolved grief. Am Indian Alask Native Ment Health Res. 1998;8:56–78.

Chaitin J. "Living with" the past: coping and patterns in families of Holocaust survivors. Fam Process. 2003;42:305–322.

Dickson-Gomez J. The sound of barking dogs: violence and terror among Salvadoran families in the postwar. Med Anthropol Q. 2002;16:415–438.

Goldapple K, Segal Z, Garson C, Lau M, Bieling P, Kennedy S, Mayberg H. Modulation of cortical-limbic pathways in major depression: treatment-specific effects of cognitive behavior therapy. Arch Gen Psychiatry. 2004;61:34–41.

Kellermann NP. Transmission of Holocaust trauma – an integrative view. Psychiatry. 2001;64:256–267.

Ma SH, Teasdale JD. Mindfulness-based cognitive therapy for depression: replication and exploration of differential relapse prevention effects. J Consult Clin Psychol. 2004;72:31–40.

Scott KM. A perennial mourning: identity conflict and the transgenerational transmission of trauma within the African American Community. Mind & Human Interaction. 2001;11:11–26.

Segal ZV, Williams JMG, Teasdale JD. Mindfulness-based cognitive therapy for depression. New York: Guilford Pub; 2002.

Teasdale JD, Segal ZV, Williams JMG, Ridgeway VA, Soulsby JM, Lau MA. Prevention of relapse/recurrence in major depression by mindfulness-based cognitive therapy. J Consult Clin Psychol. 2000;68:615–623.

Teasdale JD, Moore RG, Hayhurst H, Pope M, Williams MS, Z. Segal Z. Metacognitive awareness and prevention of relapse in depression: empirical evidence. J Consult Clin Psychol. 2002;70:275–287.

Van Ijzendoorn MH, Bakermans-Kranenburg MJ, Sagi-Schwartz A. Are children of Holocaust survivors less well-adapted? A meta-analytic investigation of secondary traumatization. J Trauma Stress. 2003;16:459–469.

Williams JMG, Teasdale JD, Segal ZV. Soulsby J. Mindfulness-based cognitive therapy reduces overgeneral autobiographical memory in formerly depressed patients. J Abnorm Psychol. 2000;109:150–155.

Chapter 11

Psyche and Soma: Harvey Max Chochinov and the Needs of the Dying

"Learn as if you were going to live forever. Live as if you were going to die tomorrow."
Mahatma Gandhi

Soma and Psyche, body and soul are involved in the research of Harvey Chochinov of Winnipeg who tries to discover and attend to the unmet needs of those who are dying.

Many cultures speak of "good" deaths and "dying with dignity," but few scientists have directly asked what these terms mean to those who are dying. Winnipeg psychiatrist Harvey Chochinov has. He has also studied the many factors associated with end-of-life dignity, such as physical comfort, autonomy, meaningfulness, preparedness, and interpersonal connection. Emerging from these conversations and this research is a brief psychotherapeutic intervention called dignity therapy that Dr. Chochinov designed for patients who are nearing death. The therapy, described in a recent editorial in the Journal of Clinical Oncology as "a major contribution to advancing care for the terminally ill," improves mood, fosters hope, and decreases suffering.

Dr Chochinov's model of dignity therapy in the terminally ill addresses three areas: a) "illness-related concerns" that involve symptom management, b) the "dignity conserving repertoire" that concentrates on the patient's psychological and spiritual needs, and c) the "social dignity inventory" that focuses on social and environmental factors affecting a person's sense of dignity. This includes features such as staff showing consideration for the person, respecting physical privacy, and making sure to ask permission before performing routine care.

Dr. Balfour Mount, Professor of Palliative Medicine at McGill University and Canada's pioneer palliative care expert has said:

> The "death with dignity" research by Dr. Chochinov and colleagues is clarifying the individual-specific contributors to the dying person's sense of well-being, and suggesting relevant types of support care. It should open the door for improved care and lessened suffering at the end of life.

The main intervention consists of a 30-to-60 minute tape-recorded session between a patient and therapist. Patients are invited to talk about issues of importance to them, aspects of their lives that they would most want remembered. An edited transcript of the session is then given to the patients who are invited to share it with their family. In a clinical trial of dignity therapy involving 100 terminally ill cancer patients from Canada and Australia, the researchers found that 91% of participants reported satisfaction with dignity therapy and 81% of participants said the therapy had either already helped, or would in the future help their families. Over two thirds of those asked said that the therapy increased their sense of dignity, sense of purpose, and sense of meaning. When pre-and post-intervention surveys were compared, the authors found that the therapy had significantly reduced both suffering and depression. Almost half of the participants reported an increased will to live. Those who are initially the most distressed appear to benefit the most.

"There are few drug-based therapies available that can lessen someone's distress about death or reinforce their sense of worth as they near death," says Dr. Chochinov. "Our study has shown that this relatively simple and straightforward psychotherapy can help patients attain the sense of peace they need to die with dignity."

From the start of his training, Harvey Chochinov knew that psychiatry was where he belonged. He decided early on to work at the interface between psychiatry and medicine. Although psychotherapy was most used in the young and relatively healthy, he felt that psychological intervention was in fact most needed among those with chronic illnesses, and especially among cancer patients. In 1985, one of the few psychiatrists working in this area (she had first coined the term psycho-oncology) was Dr. Jimmie Holland at the Memorial Sloan-Kettering Cancer Center in New York City. Young Dr. Chochinov, in the fourth year of his psychiatric residency, went to do a one-week observership with Dr. Holland. At the end of the week, Dr. Holland called him to her office to say he had passed the interview for the fellowship. He said: "What interview? What fellowship?" and she said: "A one year fellowship is something you should consider. We'll hold a position open for you till July 1st."

Harvey talked it over with his wife, Michelle, (she was pregnant with their first child, Lauren) who convinced him he could not possibly turn down such an opportunity. He went to New York on July 1, with Michelle and Lauren joining him a few weeks later, and spent a year in New York working with Jimmie Holland, Kathleen Foley, and William Breitbart, three individuals who indelibly influenced his life.

New York was a clinical (rather than a research) experience. "If anything, I looked at all these world class people who were trying to do everything; research, clinical work, administration, and to me, they were setting an agenda for themselves that I thought was incompatible with a life outside of work." Harvey came back to Winnipeg determined to be a full time clinician, and became the psychiatric consultant for Cancer Care Manitoba. "At the time," he recalls, "our department had a psychologist by the name of Keith Wilson; my sense is that his job was really to cajole psychiatrists into considering research as part of their work. So Keith would come to me and say, "you should really do some research." I'd nod my head, largely ignore him and move on to my next clinical task."

Then Chochinov read an article published by fellow Winnipeg psychiatrist Jim Brown and colleagues in 1986 on the question of whether it was ever "normal" for a patient to desire death.

Brown JH, Henteleff P, Barakat S, Rowe CJ. Is it normal for terminally ill patients to desire death? Am J Psychiatry. 1986;143:208–211.

Among 44 terminally ill patients, the majority (N = 34) had never wished death to come early. Of the remainder, three were or had been suicidal and seven more had desired early death. All 10 patients who had desired death were found to be suffering from clinical depressive illness. The methodologic difficulties encountered by the authors were the lack of a brief, efficient interview schedule suitable for debilitated patients, and criteria for depressive disorder that do not depend on suicidal thoughts or on symptoms that can also be caused by physical disease.

It was clear that this was a groundbreaking article, in that nobody had previously explored this issue. But the conclusions they reached left me feeling that something more needed to be done, and that these questions needed to be revisited. For example, they concluded that all patients who desired death had a co-morbid clinical depression. That was interesting, but perhaps too simple an answer for such a complicated question?

I recall going straight to Keith Wilson's office and saying: "I think I have an idea." We started working on a protocol to expand Jim Brown's work. Within a month a proposal was submitted to a granting agency, and shortly thereafter we had funding to look at depression and desire for death in the terminally ill. That's how my research career began. Each study has led to another study, and each question to another research question; I have continued to follow that thread of end-of-life care inquiry, and continue to find it intriguing.

Harvey Chochinov comes from a Russian Jewish family that immigrated to Winnipeg around the time of the Russian Revolution. His paternal grandfather, Max Chochinov, was a very wise man who transmitted important values to successive generations of Chochinovs. Harvey is proud of all his own characteristics that come from his Zaida Max, and, to show his pride, he took on the middle name Max following his grandfather's death. The family on both paternal and maternal sides is a close one. Mutual respect and support for one another were and are family norms. Harvey's father, Dave Chochinov, was born in Winnipeg – a remarkable man with boundless, practical know-how. He worked in the restaurant business, the insurance business, the upholstery business, and, prior to retirement, owned a sunflower seed company. Harvey's mother looked after the three children – his eldest sister Ellen (born with cerebral palsy), Harvey, the middle child, and a younger daughter, Brenda, who subsequently became a schoolteacher. At first, Harvey wasn't sure what he wanted to do in life. He was an avid musician, interested in the liberal arts and also in the sciences. He did a year of medicine, then took a year off to re-evaluate, and then returned. After being exposed to psychiatry in his second year of Medical School, he knew he was in the right place. He credits much of this to his psychotherapy mentor, Dr. Michael Eleff.

His current work combines his interests in medicine and psychiatry, his expertise in psychotherapy, and the values he learned at home.

Some people think of palliative care as being futile, and yet there are so many opportunities to improve the quality of life for people nearing death. I want to understand the emotional landscape of people who are dying, and the interface between that landscape and other aspects – physical, psychological, and spiritual – of their experience. It is a largely unexplored area, and an honor to work on issues that might have positive effects on how a person dies. So long as the mortality rate remains at one per person, this area will affect all of us. Being able to impact the quality of end-of-life care feels both a responsibility and a genuine privilege.

Currently, there are some new projects near and dear to Dr. Chochinov's heart. He is embarking on an international randomized controlled trial – funded by the National Institutes of Health in the U.S. – to generate further evidence to support his new psychological intervention for patients nearing death. He hopes that the intervention will help both patients and family members, since the last period of a loved one's life remains a permanent memory for those left behind. "I hope to help the field understand the notion of dignity in dying, and the tools to begin targeting dignity as an important outcome for people at the end of life." Chochinov is writing a book about his new therapeutic intervention and another book on psychiatry as it relates to palliative care.

Several problems in end-of-life care have been described in the literature: inadequate or unskilled communication of information to patients and their families, psychological withdrawal by the physician, labeling of patients as no longer medically interesting, and lack of attention to physical and mental pain and spiritual needs. Dr. Chochinov:

> Our work has helped uncover evidence around various emotional and psychiatric issues as they pertain to end-of-life care. Our studies point out the importance of recognizing clinical depression at the end of life. The desire to no longer be alive is often, although not exclusively, related to depression, pain, and lack of support. This can fluctuate in the face of various types of stress, and can be buffered by various sources of support.

Enrolling patients in clinical studies is always difficult because it means putting them to the extra trouble of answering standardized questions when they are preoccupied with their suffering. How much more difficult to enlist *dying* patients into research studies! How does one reconcile optimal end-of-life care with the conduct of clinical research? The goals of good clinical research never compromise taking the best care possible of a terminally ill patient. This is achievable, as long as all patients are treated with equal skill and compassion, whether or not they participate in research, and as long as the needs of families and caregivers are taken into account.

> The wonderful thing about palliative care is having an opportunity to make a difference in the lives of patients and families. Knowing we can improve how people live in their last months, weeks, days, or hours of life – and the ripple effect this will have on their families – is very gratifying.

Being able to do research comes down to being funded in a continuous way, so that research ideas can develop, ever more specific hypotheses can be explored, and new directions can be established. Dr. Chochinov:

> Can you prove to a granting agency that what you are doing has merit? In Canada, funding for operating grants is separate from salary support. If you receive

an operating grant and spend your time doing research, you have to somehow make sure that your salary continues, even though you are not bringing in clinical earnings. You have to carve out time from your clinical responsibilities to do the research, always with the challenge of both supporting yourself and the needs of your research program. In my area, there have been interesting opportunities. Who would have thought that one could make a career of doing research at the interface between psychiatry and end-of-life care? And yet, that's where I live. This has meant being able to access some unique sources of funding, such as the National Cancer Institute of Canada.

I also received funding through an American organization called the Project on Death in America (PDIA) via the Soros Faculty Scholarship Program, funded by the philanthropist George Soros. The PDIA decided it wanted to do something to transform the culture of death and dying in North America. They created a grants program, but also funded individuals who were charged with becoming agents of change in their institution. Four Canadians received funding. I was the only psychiatrist. One specific task of this program was to create a professional development plan – part of the application was to convince them that I would come out of their program a better researcher. So, in 1996, I re-entered the classroom and got more training in qualitative and quantitative methods, and earned my PhD in Community Health in 1998.

But all of these funding opportunities have an expiration date. Funding is always very competitive and the work has to have a creative edge. Most recently, the funding has been wonderful. Being named to a Tier I Canada Research Chair in Palliative Care offers long-term stability.

Working in palliative care increases dramatically the number of people one is touched by and subsequently loses. Dr. Chochinov is acutely aware of this:

Research ideas are often based on clinical experiences. I have recollections of many patients, most of whom are no longer with us. If you really listen to people and try to understand their experience, that will inform your research. Working in palliative care doesn't immunize anyone from the struggle of coping with personal loss. However, I take comfort in knowing that people we've known and loved help shape us. When I think of those who are no longer here, I hope that I take forward something of what they were; that my worldview has been enriched by having been touched by them.

Further Reading

Agrawal M, Danis M. End-of-life care for terminally ill participants in clinical research. J Palliat Med. 2002;5:729–737.

Chochinov HM. Dignity-conserving care – a new model for palliative care: helping the patient feel valued. JAMA. 2002;287:2253–2260.

Chochinov HM, Hack T, McClement S, Kristjanson L, Harlos M. Dignity in the terminally ill: a developing empirical model. Soc Sci Med. 2002;54:433–443.

Chochinov HM, Hack T, Hassard T, Kristjanson LJ, McClement S, Harlos M. Dignity in the terminally ill: a cross-sectional, cohort study. Lancet. 2002;360: 2026–2030.

Chochinov HM, Hack T, Hassard T, Kristjanson LJ, McClement S, Harlos M. Dignity and psychotherapeutic considerations in end-of-life care. J Palliat Care. 2004;20:134–142.

Chochinov HM, Hack T, Hassard T, Kristjanson LJ, McClement S, Harlos M. Understanding the will to live in patients nearing death. Psychosomatics. 2005;46:7–10.

Chochinov HM, Hack T, Hassard T, J. Kristjanson LJ, McClement S, Harlos M. Dignity therapy: A novel psychotherapeutic intervention for patients near the end of life. J Clin Oncol. 2005;23:5520–5525.

Hack TF, Chochinov HM, Hassard T, Kristjanson LJ, McClement S, Harlos M. Defining dignity in terminally ill cancer patients: a factor-analytic approach. Psychooncology. 2004;13:700–708.

McClement SE, Chochinov HM, Hack TF, Kristjanson LJ, Harlos M. Dignity-conserving care: application of research findings to practice. Int J Palliat Nurs. 2004;10:173–179.

Chapter 12

Research Policy: Rémi Quirion, the Eagle-Eyed

Mental health research attracts less than 5% of Canadian health research dollars, yet mental illnesses directly affect 20% of Canadians.

Rémi Quirion

As head of the Institute of Neurosciences, Mental Health and Addiction at the Canadian Institutes of Health Research, Rémi Quirion, like the eagle of legend, looks wider, views farther, swoops swifter.

Rémi Quirion is one of Canada's most cited scientists. *"Nul doute qu'un cerveau exceptionnellement brillant se cache derrière le regard taquin du docteur Rémi Quirion."* – There is no doubt but that a brilliant mind lurks beneath the playful gaze of Dr. Rémi Quirion – (Part of a tribute on the occasion of winning the Wilder Penfield prize 2004, prix de Québec). In recognition of his contribution to neuroscience, Quirion, the first scientific director of the Institute of Neurosciences, Mental Health and Addiction (IN-MHA), one of thirteen Canadian Institutes of Health Research (CIHR), in 2004 also became a National Mental Health Champion. This designation is conferred by the Canadian Alliance on Mental Illness and Mental Health, an organization that represents relevant non-governmental agencies across Canada.

In Aboriginal legends, eagles are portrayed as flying high, far, and wide on wings said to be silent. Eagle eyes, though not as large as human eyes, are four times sharper. An eagle soaring at 500 feet can spot a fish from a mile away and pounce on it at a speed of 100 miles per hour. In a similar way, Rémi Quirion can spot a good research idea from afar and incorporate it instantly into the mission of INMHA. This is how Rémi Quirion grew to be an eagle: He was born in 1955 into a large Québecois family, eight brothers and sisters, in Lac-Drolet, a very small village between Beauce and Estrie in the Eastern Townships, close to the border with Maine. His parents owned the only restaurant in town and their credo was hard work. It has been said that a man who gives his children habits of industry provides for them better than a man who gives them fortune – and this has proven true for Rémi. By the age of twelve, he was expert at preparing food at the restaurant but, because school learning came so easily to him, his teachers encouraged him to leave behind the family business and go first to CÉGEP (College) and then to University. He applied to the University of Montréal for geology and to the University of Sherbrooke for biology and was accepted by both schools. Rémi preferred geology but his father offered him a car if he went to Sherbrooke with one of his brothers – so he chose Sherbrooke, the car, and biology.

At first, he wanted to major in botany but transferred to biochemistry because he found botany boring. By the end of his BSc, he had developed an interest in cell division and was accepted into a laboratory that studied cancer-related proteins. But fate intervened. Just when he was to start, his supervisor-to-be lost his funding. Rémi wasn't certain what to do next because, by that time, it was late to be applying anywhere. He decided to take it a step at a time, which is his motto. That literally meant going to the top floor of the Faculty of Medicine at the University of Sherbrooke and walking down the stairs floor by floor until he found someone who would accept him. The top floor was floor 10 – cell biology. The Chair of the department said; "you're too late, there's no space in the department." So he went to the 9th floor and the 8th floor and the 7th floor and the 6th floor and received the same answer each time. Pharmacology was on the 5th floor. The head of the department, Domenico Regoli, asked him: "Do you come from a large family? How many brothers and sisters do you have?" "Eight." "Okay, when do you want to start?" (This proved to be an important lesson in both perseverance and the benefit of large families). So Rémi did his PhD in cardiovascular pharmacology (1980) but decided to do postdoctoral work in neuroscience. Somewhere along the line, he had become interested in the brain. The fact that one of his brothers had developed a major depression must have influenced his choice – he realized that mental illness was pervasive and could be disabling.

He applied for a postdoctoral fellowship at the National Institute of Mental Health in Maryland (NIMH) because it was reputed to be the world's best; they offered him a position. What clinched the deal for him was that NIMH also offered a position to Pierrette, Rémi's wife. On first arrival, the Quirions found the laboratories run down and dirty and the competitiveness vicious. But they stayed on until 1983 when Rémi, with his eagle eye, spotted a new opportunity in Montreal that suited him well. He came home to Canada to launch and head the Neuroscience Laboratory at the newly established Douglas Hospital Research Centre (http://www.douglasrecherche.qc.ca/index.asp?l=e).

Over the years, Quirion has had wide-ranging research interests, including Alzheimer's disease, brain peptides, growth factors, pain, drug dependence, and schizophrenia. Dr. Quirion is undoubtedly a brilliant researcher and educator. But it is in his role as the scientific director of INMHA (Institute of Neurosciences, Mental Health and Addiction) that he was interviewed for this chapter. The goal of INMHA is to subsidize innovative research that holds promise to provide new knowledge about neurological, mental, and addictive disorders. INMHA's mission is to foster excellence in Canadian research and also to encourage knowledge translation (application of research findings to clinical diagnosis and treatment). Its broader aim is to improve the quality of life for Canadians through health promotion, excellence in health care provision and recovery from psychiatric illnesses.

Although Canada has too few clinical scientists, Quirion feels optimistic about the future of Canadian mental health research. In the past, the Canadian government trimmed its research budget while the budget of the National Institute of Mental Health (NIMH) in the U.S. was doubled. Inevitably, Canada lost neuroscientists at that time. But since the Medical Research Council evolved into CIHR (Canadian Institutes of Health Research) five years ago, things have markedly improved. The federal government has invested in research infrastructure (Canadian Foundation for Innovation – CFI), and into two levels of Chair programs, so that now, while still not easy, recruitment has definitely improved.

In addition to investigator-initiated research, CIHR supports targeted multidisciplinary research across institutes. CIHR grants are now about one third as large as those of the U.S. National Institutes of Health. Tier 1 CIHR Chairs are tenable for seven years and renewable. They are intended for outstanding researchers acknowledged by their peers as world leaders in their fields. For each Tier 1 Chair, the chair holder's university receives $200,000 annually for seven years. Tier 2 Chairs are tenable for five years and are renewable once. They are for exceptional emerging researchers. For each Tier 2 Chair, the university receives $100,000 annually for five years. Chair holders are also eligible for infrastructure support from CFI to help acquire state-of-the-art equipment essential to their work.

Tier 1	2005 Chair Holders in Research Related to Psychiatry
Martin Alda	McGill University (see Chapter 4)
Glen B. Baker	University of Alberta (see Chapter 15)
Anne Bassett	University of Toronto
Pierre Blier	University of Ottawa
Neil Cashman	University of British Columbia
Harvey Chochinov	University of Manitoba (see Chapter 10)
Katherine Cianflone	Université Laval
Anne Marie Craig	University of British Columbia
Adele Diamond	University of British Columbia
Eric Frombonne	McGill University
Susan R. George	University of Toronto
Cheryl Grady	University of Toronto (see Chapter 6)
Brian MacVicar	University of British Columbia
Ashok K. Malla	McGill University
Michel Maziade	Université Laval
Jacques Y. Montplaisir	Université de Montréal (see Chapter 14)
John Roder	University of Toronto
Guy Rouleau	Université de Montréal
Michael Salter	University of Toronto
Elise Stanley	University of Toronto
Hubert H.M. Van Tol	University of Toronto

The support for research on the part of the federal government has increased five-fold over the last five years. CIHR now spends about $53 million yearly on mental illnesses, mental health, and addiction research and about $97 million yearly on neuroscience research. With his eagle vision, Dr. Quirion can see the science vista and states publicly that these amounts need to be increased. "We have to go farther. We need to invest much more in neuroscience, mental health, and addiction research."

The Canadian Foundation for Innovation and Genome Canada are important funding bodies that supplement CIHR and bring additional funding through matching funds from the provinces. Co-ordination among funding agencies is essential. A major difference between Canada and the U.S. is the relatively small role that Canadian business plays in the support of research (see Chapter 19). Nonetheless, in the field of neuroscience, Canadian research compares very favorably with that of the U.S. if one looks at numbers and quality of research publications and rates of citations. One Canadian advantage, Quirion believes, is the single-payer health care system that does not squander scarce dollars on superfluous administration. Another is a national tradition of excellence in neuroscience. Canadian neuroscience is ranked third in the world (after the U.S. and Great Britain).

But mental health research, and especially addictions, is unfortunately not as strong. Mental health researchers face difficult challenges because the origins of most mental health problems remain unknown and few animal models exist for psychiatric problems. The other difficulty is the stigma of mental illness, "something than can happen to others but not to me." Research funding flows to cancer and cardiovascular disease because more is known about these illnesses, because there are good research animal models, and because people are open about their brushes with these diseases. Openness means that everyone understands that research dollars are needed for cancer and cardiovascular disease. When it comes to mental illness, secrecy and stigma cloud understanding. With time, stigma *is* diminishing. Most people nowadays know that mental illnesses are health problems, not fatal flaws or curses or punishments for sins, but considerable public misinformation still exists. Like the eagle who spots the glint of a fish he wants underneath the ocean current, Quirion and INMHA have targeted stigma as an emergent area of research focus for Canada.

The tradition of research funding for psychiatric conditions in the U.S. contrasts with that of Canada. The National Institute of Mental Health (NIMH) has a long history of public support and receives massive media attention. Mental health is constantly in the news in the U.S. NIMH research is discussed in Congress and in the U.S. Senate. Findings from NIMH research appear on the front page of the New York Times. Canadians, on the other hand, traditionally hate to sing their own praises and CIHR-INMHA is very Canadian, characteristically humble. Quirion, taking the eagle's view, thinks more publicity is needed, more front page stories about Canadian breakthroughs such as the discovery of genes associated with suicide, epilepsy, mood disorders, schizophrenia, and Alzheimer's. Once the public is aware of the potential of neuroscience research, public opinion will propel the government to act. For example, as of today, says Dr. Quirion, the Canadian Institute of Public Health has nothing on its agenda for mental health. Their mandate is prevention and they have programs for severe acute respiratory syndrome (SARS) and obesity prevention – yet nothing directed specifically at mental health, even though preventive general health measures like fitness and diet and hygiene depend on a person's level of motivation and motivation is primarily a mental health issue. It is important to pressure members of Parliament, Quirion advises, about matters such as these – politicians respond best to voices that are well organized, as is the case for cancer and stroke.

> We need to organize coalitions among our groups and present a united front to the politicians. AIDS groups are a good example of collaborations that worked together to reduce stigma and ensure that the right messages hit the front pages of newspapers. In the same way, mental health should be on all politicians' minds.

Perusing the territory from an eagle's perspective, Quirion believes that improved funding is not the only solution. There is much that researchers themselves can do to further collaboration and, thus, effectiveness. Communicating, networking, and linking study records are examples of what can be done by the scientists themselves. Although there is little documentation that proves that active collaboration leads to better research, it seems clear that, in today's fast-paced research world, single investigator studies are unlikely to produce the major breakthroughs. Quirion also feels that an anti-celebrity ethos exists among Canadian scientists while, in his view, success deserves to be celebrated. He also thinks funding agencies need to provide support for databases and longitudinal studies because some answers only come after a prolonged follow-up period. In general, clinical research (as compared to basic laboratory research) merits better support. Industry needs to be more involved in mental health research and the public needs to be better informed about the relevance and contribution of mental health research to important social problems such as delinquency, homelessness, alienation, unemployment, disability, suicide, and violence.

Quirion is especially proud of an INMHA program called BrainStar. Every two weeks an award of $1,000 goes to a trainee who has published relevant research as a first author in a peer-reviewed journal. Another novelty is the annual meeting of IN-MHA that includes not only scientists but also lay participants and trainees. A patient, a trainee and two world-class experts address each topic. Each perspective adds to understanding.

For this chapter, Dr. Quirion was asked what the important areas are likely to be for the future of Canadian mental health research. The next forefront for psychiatry will be molecular genetics, thinks Dr. Quirion. Very strong epidemiologic data point to genetic transmission of many, if not most, psychiatric illnesses. Thus far, however, linkage studies (trying to link specific chromosomal regions to specific illnesses) have been largely disappointing. Part of the problem is delineating genetic entities. Although the DSM-IV classification system has made major strides in definition and delineation, psychiatry needs to further refine its categories. Clearer demarcations have to be made among disorders and between what is and what is not disorder. Collaboration is key since researchers with complementary skill sets are needed for the process to succeed. For instance, better ways are needed to deal with complex and voluminous data sets, requiring expertise in bioinformatics. Epidemiologists have to study populations prospectively and longitudinally to better understand interactions between genes and the environment. Brain imagers, predicts Dr. Quirion, will continue to revolutionize psychiatry. Linking genetic studies with brain imaging with bioinformatics with epidemiology with cell biology and with large scale clinical trials is the way of the future. This will individualize and optimize treatment.

Because of unique populations and large families in Québec and the Eastern provinces and because these families have tended to remain in their original localities, Canada has led the way in genetic population studies. In the not-too-distant future, proteomics (the unraveling of individual proteins coded by genes) holds great potential,

Some of Canada's Luminaries in Brain Sciences	
Wilder Penfield	1891–1976
Donald Hebb	1904–1985 (see Chapter 9)
Herbert Jasper	1906–1999 (see Chapter 14)
Hans Selye	1907–1982 (see Chapter 2 and Chapter 15)
Heinz Lehmann	1911–1999 (see Chapter 13)
Brenda Milner	1918–
David H. Hubel	1926–
Endel Tulving	1927–
Ronald Melzack	1929–
Fergus Craik	1935–
Doreen Kimura	1940–

but this, predicts Quirion, will be a more difficult research task than genomics. Each human being has approximately 25,000 protein-coding genes but at least five times as many proteins. Research into proteins will require a whole new research infrastructure and even wider collaborations.

Rémi Quirion is like the legendary eagle who scans the landscape far and wide and, with piercing eyes, is able to zero in on immediate needs. What mental health research in Canada needs, according to his panoramic view, is accelerated training of future generations of scientists. To get there requires not only higher levels of funding for groups like INMHA but also the celebration of home-grown world-class achievements.

> Canada needs to do more to foster the careers of its young researchers in the field of mental health. Higher targets for research funding must be set to reflect the burden of mental illness and improve the acquisition and translation of new knowledge.

Further Reading

The Brain from Top to Botttom. Available at: http://www.thebrain.mcgill.ca/flash/index_d.html
    Canadian Institutes of Health Research. Available at: http://www.cihr-irsc.gc.ca/
Le Cerveau à Tous les Niveaux. Available at: http://www.lecerveau.mcgill.ca/flash/index_d.html
Institute of Neuroscience, Mental Health and Addiction (INMHA). Available at: http://www.cihr-irsc.gc.ca/e/17913.html
Les Prix du Québec. Available at: http://www.prixduquebec.gouv.qc.ca/recherche/desclaureat.asp?noLaureat=310
Quirion R. A Canadian experiment: the Institute of Neurosciences, Mental Health and Addiction. How to link up the brain via a virtual institute. Trends Neurosci. 2002;25:268–270.

Quirion R. The Douglas Hospital Research Centre celebrating 25 years of innovation in mental health research. J Psychiatry & Neurosi. 2005;30:312–314.

Rémi Quirion's Lab. Available at: http://www.douglashospital.qc.ca/quirionlab/remiq.htm?l=e

Rémi Quirion's Lab – recent publications. Available at: http://www.douglashospital.qc.ca/quirionlab/Publications.htm

Regoli, Domenico. Available at: http://www.amlfc.com/Articles/1999_05_03.html

Vercauteren FG, Bergeron JJ, Vandesande F, Arckens L, Quirion R. Proteomic approaches in brain research and neuropharmacology. Eur J Pharmacol. 2004;500:385–398.

Whately, Richard (1787–1863): Oxford philosopher, educator, theologian, social reformer and economist, Anglican Archbishop of Dublin.

Chapter 13

Schizophrenia:
Philip Seeman – Driven to
Discovery

*"All truths are easy to understand once they are discovered; the point is
to discover them."*

Galileo Galilei

Schizophrenia is the most serious of psychiatric illnesses. It usually strikes in early
adulthood and subsequently interferes with all aspects of life. For almost 50 years,
Philip Seeman of Toronto has been pursuing clues that will ultimately lead to a
more complete understanding of this intractable disease.

Philip Seeman does not remember this but when he was three, his mother lost him. She looked all over the house, listened for sounds… nothing. Hours passed. She frantically called the neighbors and the police. He was found sitting quietly on the balcony trying to join egg cartons together to make a passenger train. This trait was to characterize him all his life: a dogged, some would say obsessed, pursuit of a challenge. He firmly believes that Einstein was right, that God does not play dice with the universe, that nothing is attributable to chance. He always felt, and continues to feel that order exists even in apparent chaos and, if he tries hard enough, the rule that explains away all paradox will somehow emerge.

The balcony where his single-mindedness first came to notice was in Winnipeg. His parents had immigrated to Canada in the 1920s from a small town near Turka in Galicia, now Ukraine.

Most would describe Philip Seeman as practical. If a job needs doing, he will do it. What makes him an extraordinary doer is that he tackles the seemingly impossible because he believes that, with enough hard work, any mystery can be solved. He is not one to wait and see what happens and then make a decision. He makes the decision first and events had better fall into line, or else!

One might have thought that a man who believed in order would choose physics as a career, not psychiatry. He did, in fact, consider physics, but he then came under the influence of Arnold Burgen, McGill University's youngest ever full Professor, now Sir Arnold. Seeman did a Masters degree in physiology and then got hooked on medicine – not medicine to practice, because he never felt the need to save the world, but medicine to disentangle the supposed order of how things worked in the body. The body proving not enough of a challenge, he then decided to figure out how things were ordered in the mind, and not any mind at that, but the minds of those who suffered from schizophrenia, perhaps the hardest minds in which to look for order. He had the vague idea that by understanding processes of thinking during a psychotic crisis, one could learn about thinking in general. (Please also see Chapter 4 in which Martin Alda starts his career with a similar notion).

When asked whether personal motives led him to research antipsychotic drugs, whether family members suffered from mental illness, Philip Seeman notes that his wife's grandfather was treated for bipolar illness in Vienna by no lesser an eminence grise than Julius Wagner-Juarregg who won the Nobel Prize in 1927 for healing general paresis (tertiary syphilis) by malaria inoculation. "Mental illness affects one in every five people," Seeman reminds us. "Every family copes with one mental illness or another. Those who say there is no mental illness in the family haven't inquired too deeply into the well-being of their relatives."

Because his wife was a psychiatry resident working, at the time, at Manhattan State Hospital in New York City, Philip had ready access to people diagnosed with schizophrenia when he began his doctoral work. And he had a PhD supervisor, nobel laureate Dr. George Palade, who let him pursue his interest. His dilemma was that he did not really know what to ask of these very ill people that would allow him to understand why their thinking was unusual. Then he got an idea. People with schizophrenia were being treated with drugs, relatively new at the time, reputed to straighten out distorted thoughts. If he could determine how the drugs worked (which was unknown), perhaps he could figure out precisely what the trouble was that the drugs ostensibly "fixed."

He worked with red blood cells, his own. (His wife took a sample of his blood every morning before the children were awake). He bathed these cells in chlorpromazine, the prototype antipsychotic drug, put them under the electron microscope and noticed that the outer membrane of the cells grew fat. He concluded that when the membrane expands in neuronal cells, the patient with schizophrenia thinks more clearly. *The surface activity of tranquilizers* was published with Harvey Bialy in Biochemical Pharmacology in October, 1963. The theory was that the expansion caused stabilization of the cell, hence tranquilization and more logical thought.

Forty years later, Philip is still trying to figure out how antipsychotic drugs work. Once he has that question solved, he plans to go on to the next step – what is wrong in schizophrenia that the drugs are able to control. He started by looking at the cell membrane and the calcium and sodium and potassium transport across the membrane, thinking this might account for membrane expansion. He and his team found that all anaesthetics expand the cell membrane, a mechanism useful for the understanding of anesthesia, but how did it explain schizophrenia or, for that matter, the side effects of antipsychotic drugs (the tremor, restlessness, and muscle stiffness that patients complained of)?

In the sixties, scientists had found that several antipsychotics enhanced the secretion of three substances (noradrenaline, serotonin and dopamine) within the brain, but the main antipsychotic target was still not clear. A Dutch scientist, Jacques Van Rossum, speculated that antipsychotic drugs blocked dopamine receptors, but there was no evidence for this hypothesis. In order to test the Van Rossum idea, Seeman decided to search for targets in the brain that were sensitive to extremely low concentrations of antipsychotic drugs because he wanted to recreate the conditions that existed in the brain of persons actually treated with these drugs. He asked Paul Janssen, the pharmaceutical giant who synthesized the antipsychotic drug, haloperidol, to have a Belgian industrial company prepare radioactive haloperidol for his target receptor test. He also asked Dr. Leslie Humber at the Ayerst drug company in Montreal to help him. Humber developed a pair of antipsychotic drugs that were mirror images of each other. One, called [+]butaclamol, showed activity in animal tests while its mirror twin, [−]butaclamol, did not. So Seeman set out to see if there were targets in brain tissue that could be occupied by radioactive haloperidol in the presence of [−]butaclamol, the inactive form, but not in the presence of [+]butaclamol (which, being active, would itself occupy the receptor, keeping haloperidol out). This proved to be a breakthrough. The antipsychotic receptor was discovered. This target receptor was later called the dopamine type 2 receptor (one of a family of receptor proteins) and, quite amazingly, the proclivity with which different drugs blocked that receptor turned out to correspond to the actual clinical doses patients were prescribed. Philip and his colleagues published their discovery in the Proceedings of the National Academy of Science in 1975, and extended their work later, as reported in 1976 in Nature.

As Paul Janssen once said, every new discovery is met with disbelief and arguments are mustered to prove that it just can't be. When the arguments are defeated (and this takes years), the refrain becomes "Okay, but it's a trivial discovery, it doesn't help anyone." When you can show (and Philip did show that the receptor test can screen for new and better antipsychotic drugs) that it really is important, then the chorus changes to "Well, it's true, and it's important, but you're not the one who discovered it. It had been known for ages." This is pretty much what happened with the D2 receptor and the subsequent work on what percentage of receptors needed to be occupied before a drug would actually work in schizophrenia, and what percentage had to be occupied before side effects emerged.

Newer drugs for schizophrenia came along at the end of the century; they were said to be different, to not act through the D2 receptor, but Philip knew that order had to exist in the world of antipsychotic drugs. In collaboration with Dr. Shitij Kapur and the brain imaging group at the Centre for Addiction and Mental Health in Toronto, Seeman looked at the clinical evidence. Clinical evidence is important to any good theory. Talking to clinicians, this is what he heard: patients treated with the newer drugs were less lethargic than those treated with the older drugs; they appeared to have more energy, to be more "with it" in terms of interest, motivation, and ambition; they seemed brighter intellectually, laughed more readily; they seemed more sociable, more likely to enter into intimate relationships; their mood was better, they were more active physically, and sexually as well; they were less likely to smoke or use alcohol and street drugs, and they were hungrier, actively seeking food. Another clinical observation: women on these drugs were menstruating regularly (interruption of the menstrual cycle had been a common side effect of the older drugs). Women were not only menstruating; they were getting pregnant, a relatively rare occurrence before. One definite down side of the new drugs, however, was that it didn't take long, once patients stopped taking their daily dose, before relapse occurred. A patient taking one of the older antipsychotic medications could sometimes stop for a whole summer and be none the worse for it. This was not true of the newer medications. For some patients, one or two days of a drug-free holiday could lead to the return of the original symptoms.

The research group wondered what these clinical observations could mean. (The advantage of working collaboratively is that ideas can be challenged and tested). After many experiments, the group finally came to the conclusion that the new drugs were allowing some of the dopamine to get through the antipsychotic blockade. With dopamine getting through in the striatal region of the brain, stiffness, tremor, and muscle spasms were eliminated. With dopamine getting through in the hypothalamus, the level of the hormone, prolactin, would be held in check by dopamine. There would, therefore, be no missed periods in women and no infertility. Sex drive would make a come back for the same reason. If dopamine were getting through in the limbic system of the brain, mood would improve, interest in life would return, and patients would feel more alert.

Seeman and Kapur found that the new drugs still worked through the dopamine D2 receptor but they slid off the receptor faster, letting dopamine through.

Over the years, the research strategy in the Seeman lab has not changed – finding out how the drugs do their work will ultimately lead to the pathophysiology of schizophrenia. Seeman measured D2 receptors in the brains of schizophrenia patients after death and found receptor levels to be higher than expected. He took a particular interest in the high affinity state of these receptors. Receptor shapes are in constant flux but one kind of three-dimensional structure of the D2 receptor binds dopamine tightly and is therefore called "high affinity." Seeman found that, when the high affinity state predominated, laboratory animals became behaviorally supersensitive to dopamine. In other words, they startled readily and, when given a dopamine-like drug, became hyperactive. By searching the literature, he was able to locate many animals that were made supersensitive to dopamine in a variety of ways, for instance by having specific genes knocked out or inactivated. He collected all these animals and found that they all showed elevations of high affinity dopamine receptors in their brains. He and his many colleagues published the results recently in the Proceedings of the National Academy of Science. The implications are important. The work suggests that supersensitivity to dopamine, a potential final common pathway to schizophrenia, can result from a multitude of prior events including many varieties of brain compromise and many different faulty genes.

Researching the effects of antipsychotic drugs originated in Canada with Dr. Heinz Lehmann (1911–1999). Lehmann was born in Berlin of a mixed marriage; his mother was Protestant, his father, a physician, was a Jew. Lehmann received his MD from the University of Berlin in 1935. Had he stayed in Germany, he would have suffered the fate of millions of European Jews but, in 1937, he asked and was granted permission to go to Canada for a skiing vacation. It is not known whether he did any skiing. It *is* known that, once in Canada, he applied for and received refugee status and a temporary medical licence. He became a naturalized Canadian citizen in 1948, but it was not until 1963 that Lehmann received a permanent Quebec license to practice medicine and not until age 60, in 1971, did the Royal College of Physicians and Surgeons of Canada finally certify him as a specialist in Psychiatry.

Few psychiatric drugs were available to patients when Lehmann first arrived in this country in 1937. There were vitamins and sedatives such as barbiturates, chloral hydrate, and paraldehyde. Injections of hyoscine and apomorphine were used to calm agitated patients. Somewhat later, amphetamines were used for stimulation. In the 1940s, Lehmann set up a psychophysiological laboratory (the precursor of Rémi Quirion's Neuroscience Laboratory – see Chapter 12) at the then Verdun Protestant Hospital (now Douglas Hospital) in order to test the nervous system under different conditions. He didn't do all his testing on humans. In the late 1950s, Lehmann picked dandelions from the grounds of the hospital and placed them in individual glasses of water to which he added a variety of drugs: a barbiturate, an amphetamine, chlorpromazine (the first antipsychotic), prochlorperazine (a somewhat newer antipsychotic), and imipramine (the first antidepressant). The dandelions were unaffected by water and prochlorperazine; the barbiturate made the flowers fold in on themselves, while the imipramine-and-chlorpromazine-treated dandelions were partly open, partly closed. The dandelions on amphetamine were open wide, wider than normal. In this way Lehmann showed that chlorpromazine was less sedating than barbiturates but more sedating than prochlorperazine. He was fond of doing this sort of research. He referred to it as "bootstrap research," low cost, unpretentious, but far-reaching.

In 1953, Lehmann noticed an article in the French journal, L'Encéphale, written by Jean Delay and Pierre Deniker, on the effects of chlorpromazine on psychosis. He ordered a supply from the pharmaceutical firm, Rhône-Poulenc, and tried it out on 230 patients with schizophrenia. In 1954, in the first North American paper on chlorpromazine, he reported the drug's unprecedented therapeutic benefits.

Most of Lehmann's research was done with no written protocol, no specific subject recruitment strategy, no placebo controls, no informed consent from the patients or their families (this was not required at the time), no research oversight, and no external funding. It is interesting to speculate what Lehmann might have accomplished in today's climate of relative research plenty. As it was, he published over 300 scholarly papers and mentored and inspired countless younger researchers.

Schizophrenia is a highly complex disorder that affects approximately 1% of the world's population. It has a high heritability rate of about 80%, meaning that 80% of the risk for illness lies in a person's genome. The risk of getting ill with this disorder is approximately 45% to 50% if an identical twin has the illness, but only 15% to 17% if the twin is fraternal. There is a 10% risk of illness for the child of someone with schizophrenia and this holds true even when the child grows up apart from biological parents. Symptoms include hallucinations (misperceptions), delusions (false beliefs, often frightening ones), disorganization (trouble focusing, thinking, speaking, or behaving rationally), lack of engagement with others, lack of interest in activity, and lack of pleasure in everyday living. Mood is often unstable and it is hard to think clearly. Psychological testing shows impaired ability to abstract, deficits in memory, and a decline in IQ. Early symptoms often go undiagnosed for up to 4–5 years; the diagnosis is made, on average, at around age 20, earlier in men than in women. (Please see Chapters 18 and 27 for personal descriptions and Chapters 19 and 28 for descriptions by family members).

There are many unsettled questions about schizophrenia. Because there is no objective diagnostic test (as there isn't for most psychiatric disorders), the fear is that unusual people who are different from others can be labeled "schizophrenic" and unfairly stigmatized. Another fear is that those with schizophrenia are more dangerous than others. A common fear is that patients with this diagnosis will be "drugged," oversedated with antipsychotics.

In this regard, it is interesting to read an excerpt from a talk by Dr. David Healy delivered at the Queen Street site of the Centre for Addiction and Mental Health in Toronto on November 30, 2000. (This was the now famous talk after which Dr. Healy's offer of a position at the Centre and at the University of Toronto was rescinded. He sued. A settlement was reached). At this talk, Dr. Healy showed a slide of Philip Seeman's work correlating the prescribed dose of various antipsychotic medications with their potency at the dopamine D2 receptor. Healy: "This was one of the triumphs of modern psychopharmacology. It remains as true and accurate today as when it was first published 25 years ago. But these binding data introduce something else as well, for which neither Seeman nor (Solomon) Snyder, nor others who developed radio labeled techniques can be held responsible… after 1974… far from this being a science that worked in the interests of patients, it led on to megadose regimes of neuroleptics. No longer answerable, it seems, to how the patients in front of us actually looked, following the science, we moved on to these megadose regimes that may have caused as many brains to be injured as were ever injured with psychosurgery." The reasoning by which Dr. Healy transforms an understanding of the receptor action of drugs into a rationale for overdosing patients is somewhat elliptical.

Schizophrenia can be studied in different ways. Patients are sometimes asked to do behavioral and cognitive tasks under standard conditions in an attempt to see what functions are interfered with and what circumstances make the interference worse. Blood is drawn for chromosomal and genetic testing. Brain imaging helps to detect morphological and functional changes. With prior permission from the patient, after death, the brain can be dissected for histological clues to illness. Treatment studies measure the effects of a variety of interventions on specific outcomes. Treatments known to be effective (antipsychotic drugs, for instance) are analyzed to try to understand how they work (the strategy used by Dr. Seeman and his colleagues).

The web site http://www.phac-aspc.gc.ca/publicat/miic-mmac/chap_3_e.html has a good summary of schizophrenia for those who would like to know more about this illness. Perhaps what is now called schizophrenia is a cluster of different diseases, each with its own cause. This is for future generations of young scientists to determine.

"Psychiatric research has not been easy to do in Canada, but sometimes, because it's hard, the challenge is greater and the inspiration stronger," says Philip Seeman. Considerably older than three, he is still doggedly pursuing challenges.

Further Reading

Hoenig J. The concept of schizophrenia. Kraepelin-Bleuler-Schneider. Br J Psychiatry. 1983; 142:547–556.

Kapur S, Seeman P. Does fast dissociation from the dopamine D2 receptor explain the action of novel antipsychotics?: new hypothesis. Am J Psychiat. 2001;158:360–369.

Kapur S, Seeman P. Atypical antipsychotics, cortical D2 receptors and sensitivity to endogenous dopamine. Brit J Psychiat. 2002;180:465–466.

Lehmann HE, Hanrahan GE. Chlorpromazine; new inhibiting agent for psychomotor excitement and manic states. AMA Arch Neurol Psychiatry. 1954;71:227–237.

Seeman PM, Bialy HS. The surface activity of tranquilizers. Biochem Pharmacol. 1963;12:1181–1191.

Seeman P, Lee T. Antipsychotic drugs: direct correlation between clinical potency and presynaptic action on dopamine neurons. Science. 1975;188:1217–1219.

Seeman P, Chau-Wong M, Tedesco J, Wong K. Brain receptors for antipsychotic drugs and dopamine: direct binding assays. Proc Natl Acad Sci USA. 1975;72:4376–4380.

Seeman P, Lee T, Chau-Wong M, Wong K. Antipsychotic drug doses and neuroleptic/dopamine receptors. Nature. 1976;261:717–719.

Seeman P. Atypical antipsychotics: mechanism of action. Can J Psychiat. 2002;47:27–38.

Seeman P, Weinshenker D, Quirion R, Srivastava LK, Bhardwaj SK, Grandy DK, Premont RT, Sotnikova TD, Boksa P, El-Ghundi M, O'Dowd BF, George SR, Perreault ML, Mannisto PT, Robinson S, Palmiter RD, Tallerico T. Dopamine supersensitivity correlates with D2High states, implying many paths to psychosis. Proc Natl Acad Sci USA. 2005;102:3513–3518.

Chapter 14

Sleep Disorders:
Rachel Morehouse and the Science of Sleep

> *"A ruffled mind makes a restless pillow."*
> Charlotte Brontë

Sleep: a third of our life is spent sleeping but sleep is a million times less well understood than wakefulness. Rachel Morehouse from Saint John, New Brunswick is working to uncover the secrets of sleep.

The mission of the Canadian Psychiatric Research Foundation (CPRF) is to jump start the careers of young researchers, and there is no better illustration of the success of this mission than the scientific trajectory of Dr. Rachel Morehouse. Rachel grew up in New Brunswick where she is currently Director of Research in the Department of Psychiatry of the Saint John Regional Hospital. Her first ambition was to be a neurologist. After medical school she needed to take one year of internal medicine to qualify for a residency in neurology. However, the program in neurology did not accept anyone the year she applied. Rachel decided on a year of psychiatry to fill in the time until she could re-apply. By the time the year was over, she was a convert.... and neurology lost a brilliant researcher, though not altogether. Sleep disorders are part neurology, part internal medicine, part psychiatry – an ideal mix for Rachel Morehouse.

After completing her psychiatric residency in 1987, Dr. Morehouse did a Fellowship year with Dr. Christian Gillin (1938–2003), a renowned sleep specialist and professor of psychiatry at the University of California in San Diego. Dr. Gillin had observed that sleep deprivation could quickly reverse depression (within hours, but the depression unfortunately returns once the patient catches up on his/her sleep). Gillin found that the greater the improvement in mood after sleep deprivation, the greater the reduction in metabolic activity in the brain's anterior cingulate lobe – the first identification of an anatomic area in the brain associated with a positive response to a psychiatric intervention. Because a good antidepressant drug response produced the same effect in the same part of the brain, Gillin believed that sleep and chronobiology could be used as windows through which psychiatric disorders such as depression could be studied. In collaboration with others, he investigated bright light treatment for depression (see Chapter 8), the relation of immunology to sleep, and the sleep abnormalities associated with depression, recovery, and abstinence in patients with alcoholism.

Dr. Morehouse came back to Canada in 1988 and joined the Department of Psychiatry at Dalhousie University in Halifax. When CPRF awarded the young researcher a grant in 1991, she used it to establish the first investigative centre for sleep disorders in Atlantic Canada. At that time, short Rapid Eye Movement Latency (REML) had been identified as a biological marker for depression. It was, in fact, one of the first ever biological markers for a psychiatric disorder. Dr. Morehouse decided to study this phenomenon in a group of patients with a puzzling illness known as chronic fatigue syndrome, one of whose symptoms is depression. Her first significant project was to recruit individuals with chronic fatigue syndrome, assess them for depression and study their REM latency. This trial marked the beginning of a long chain of further sleep research.

Without severing her connection to Dalhousie University, Dr. Morehouse came back to St. John in 1998. Her mother's family had moved there from England in the 1870s. Her father's family was from Nova Scotia where they had decided to settle, being United Empire Loyalists, during the American Revolution. On his way west to seek his fortune, Rachel's father met her mother in Saint John, and stayed. Rachel and her brother were born and raised there. Her father worked at an oil refinery and her mother was a medical secretary. The Morehouses had a motto: whatever you decide to do in life should be something you love.

> My parents were fine with whatever I wanted to do. They were a little surprised I went into medicine, and it totally baffled them that I went into psychiatry, though it shouldn't have. Close to where I grew up in Saint John was a tertiary, provincial psychiatric hospital; it was between my house and my school. So, as a child, I had a daily exposure to patients with chronic schizophrenia. As a little kid I would walk by, see adults on swings going back and forth. I saw it all through a child's eyes. It was all part of the neighborhood. For instance, the patients would work on a farm on the other side of the neighborhood and they would go by on their hay wagons and say "hi" and bum a cigarette from my father and sometimes I would even ride with them and pick blueberries with the ladies. It's only in retrospect that I realize that most of these people probably had a diagnosis of chronic schizophrenia and were probably heavily medicated, but it was just an ordinary part of my childhood. The patients would farm, pick blueberries and sell them to us. They were part of the community, part of our daily life. I thought it was great when I could hitch a ride with them to school.
>
> And then a children's hospital school was built close to where we lived, where kids with severe retardation and physical disabilities would go for care and education. It was a combination of a hospital and school and my mom worked there as a medical secretary. As a student, I would work there during the summer. So, in retrospect, psychiatry was a natural choice for me.

Most patients who suffer from psychiatric disorders have problems with sleep, but sleep problems are not restricted to psychiatric illness:

- About 40% of menopausal and post-menopausal women experience difficulties with sleep
- Ten percent of the Canadian population suffers from persistent insomnia
- 30% suffers from occasional insomnia
- Between 5% and 10% are believed to have obstructive sleep apnea
- A prevalence rate of 5–10% has been recorded for restless legs syndrome
- About 8% is the estimate for nightmares and recurring dreams
- Eight percent suffers from bruxism (grinding of teeth during sleep)
- Ten percent of children and 1% of adults walk in their sleep

Canadian readers will remember the story of Kenneth Parks, a 23-year-old Toronto man, who got up early in the morning of May 23, 1987 and drove 23 kilometers to his in-laws' home where he stabbed his mother-in-law to death. Parks also assaulted his father-in-law, who survived. He then drove to the police and said "I think I have killed some people."

Because he could not remember anything about the murder and assault, had no motive for the crime, and had a history of sleepwalking, defense experts concluded Ken Parks was "asleep" when he committed the crime, and therefore unaware of his actions.

Parks' sleepwalking defense proved successful and, on May 25, 1988, the jury rendered a verdict of not guilty. The government appealed the decision and in 1992 the Canadian Supreme Court upheld the acquittals, legitimizing sleepwalking as a *bone fide* disorder.

Sleep disorders lead to a lack of alertness and accidents, low productivity, a decline in quality of life and in cognitive performance. Yet in spite of the scope of the problem, governments have not invested sufficient funds into sleep research. Dr. Morehouse feels that the study of sleep is more visible in internal medicine (research into sleep apnoea for instance) but "is not a major player on the psychiatric landscape despite the fact that every major psychiatric disorder has an associated sleep disorder complaint."

> The joys [of doing this work] are that there is a very real possibility that I can help somebody: someone with a psychiatric disorder or a sleep disorder or both. What is rewarding for me is that I can sometimes find a sleep issue that is treatable in psychiatric patients who have appeared nonresponsive to other treatments. I guess that is the biggest joy.
>
> My main frustration is that there is never enough time and money. A successful clinical researcher is pulled in so many directions at once. We try so hard to maintain a balance but it is a losing battle. Also, many of us are overwhelmed by clinical demands, more patients than we can deal with. In addition, we teach and we manage departments. Most of us are juggling four different jobs and that is extremely tough. The people who are successful at the national level are able to limit their teaching and administration responsibilities. Maybe that is the answer, giving up everything else, but I am not willing to do that. So I guess I'll never be a high profile researcher.

Dr. Morehouse is currently investigating treatments for depression, seasonal affective disorder, restless legs syndrome, and insomnia. She is also interested in the links among obesity, sleep apnoea and sexual abuse in women. She is prolific. She has written and spoken about all aspects of sleep: wakefulness, shift work, the prescription of hypnotics, sleep apnoea, sexual abuse, the use of L-Tryptophan for sleep, sleep and depression, the effect of age on sleep, biological markers in psychiatry, seasonal changes in behavior, adolescent sleep and school, drowsy drivers, sleepwalking, why yawning is contagious, noise and sleep, snoring, dreaming, and the sleep problems of menopausal women.

> What I do is work in an area that is on the border between psychiatry and internal medicine and what this does is promote a very holistic view of individual

patients. You can't treat depression when the patient can't breathe at nighttime. You can't expect to improve the rapid cycling bipolar disorder with medication if the patient can't sleep.

In addition to Dr. Gillin, an important mentor for Rachel Morehouse has been Dr. Harvey Moldofsky, a Toronto psychiatrist who investigated the inter-relationship of brain and behavior in various medical and psychiatric illnesses such as chronic pain, fatigue, and depression. From 1993 to 2000, he served as the founding Director of the University of Toronto Centre for Sleep and Chronobiology. He studied eating disorders, Tourette's syndrome, and especially rheumatic disease. He is best known for discovering the connection between musculoskeletal pain and nonrestorative sleep. More recently, he has focused on neuroimmune and neuroendocrine mechanisms in sleep and wakefulness. In 1997 and 1998, Moldofsky and a group of colleagues collected data from an American astronaut and five Russian cosmonauts who spent several months aboard the Russian Mir space station. The men provided blood samples, kept sleep diaries, and wore equipment that monitored their brainwaves, eye movements, and muscle tone during sleep.

Moldofsky found increases in the levels of cytokines in the blood samples drawn in space – a normal response to increased stress – but cortisol levels, which normally rise with stress, unpredictably fell. The increased levels of cytokines persisted after return to earth but reverted to normal by two months. The astronauts did not sleep as much in space as they did on earth; they also had less deep sleep, the most physiologically restorative stage of sleep. Either sleep loss or microgravity or radiation are suspected to have caused the immune changes (see Chapter 8 for more about cytokines in seasonal affective disorder).

Another Canadian pioneer in sleep research is Dr. Jacques Montplaisir who received his medical degree at the University of Montréal in 1967, and his doctorate in neuroscience in 1972 under the supervision of Professor Herbert Jasper. Montplaisir did a three-year postdoctoral fellowship in sleep studies with James Olds at the California Institute of Technology and with William Dement at Stanford. He then returned to Canada and trained in psychiatry at McGill University. In 1977, Dr. Montplaisir established the Sleep Disorders Centre at the Hôpital du Sacré-Coeur, Université de Montréal. He is one of nine researchers credited with founding the discipline of sleep research. Dr. Montplaisir has investigated sleepwalking and narcolepsy and has been a pioneer in the study of restless legs syndrome (RLS). He has investigated over 2,000 patients with this condition. Since 2001, he holds a Canadian Institutes of Health Research Chair in Sleep Disorders and is hunting for the genes responsible for RLS and narcolepsy. Many sleep disorders appear to result from complex interactions between genes and the environment. Susceptibility genes for RLS have so far been discovered on chromosomes 9p, 12q, and 14q. (p is the short arm, q is the long arm of chromosomes).

Dr. Morehouse's most important research contribution to date has been the finding that adolescent girls with a strong family history of depression (but never having suffered depression themselves) show low temporal coherence of their electroencephalogram (EEG) rhythms during sleep, as compared to girls of similar age but without a family history. Temporal coherence is a measure of the rest-activity cycle of arousal and organization in the brain. Impairments in this measure have been found in depression. In the Morehouse study, half of the girls with a family history showed low temporal coherence even though they had never been depressed. More importantly, on clinical follow up two years later, almost half of the girls identified as having the most abnormal coherence values were already showing symptoms of depression. This is significant because it means that sleep markers can be used to identify individuals at risk for depression *before* they become depressed. Appropriate interventions directed toward such at-risk groups could prevent the occurrence of illness.

Yet prevention will only be possible if early psychiatric intervention is not seen as stigmatizing, if it is viewed in a non-discriminatory manner, much like immunizations or vaccinations that prevent infectious disease. Rachel Morehouse would like psychiatry to be considered a branch of medicine, co-existing on a level playing field with the other major medical specialties. "But more importantly, I'd like a level playing field for our patients... they suffer far more than we (mental health workers) do from stigma and discrimination." Dr. Morehouse's primary goal is to make a significant contribution toward correcting the imbalance.

Further Reading

Benca RM, Ancoli-Israel S, Moldofsky H. Special considerations in insomnia diagnosis and management: depressed, elderly, and chronic pain populations. J Clin Psychiatry. 2004;65 Suppl 8:26–35.

Broughton R, Billings R, Cartwright R, Doucette D, Edmeads J, Edwardh M, F. Ervin, Orchard B, Hill R, Turrell G. Homicidal somnambulism: a case report. Sleep. 1994;17:253–264.

Dickstein JB, Moldofsky H. Sleep, cytokines and immune function. Sleep Med Rev. 1999;3:219–228.

Gillin JC, Buchsbaum M, Wu J, Clark C, Bunney W Jr. Sleep deprivation as a model experimental antidepressant treatment: findings from functional brain imaging. Depress Anxiety. 2001;14:37–49.

Kato T, Rompre P, Montplaisir JY, Sessle BJ, Lavigne GJ. Sleep bruxism: an oromotor activity secondary to micro-arousal. J Dent Res. 2001;80:1940–1944.

Moldofsky H. Sleep and pain. Sleep Med Rev. 2001;5:385–396.

Moldofsky H. Management of sleep disorders in fibromyalgia. Rheum Dis Clin North Am. 2002;28:353–365.

Montplaisir J. Abnormal motor behavior during sleep. Sleep Med. 2004;5 Suppl 1:S31–34.

Morehouse RL. Sleep problem? Consider a psychiatric or medical link. Med North America. 1992;49330:4208–4311.

Morehouse RL. Dilemmas of the clinical researcher: a view from the inside. Health Law Canada, 1994,15:52–54.

Morehouse RL. Shiftwork: the special challenges for women. Am Assoc Occup Health Nurses J. 1995;43:532–535.

Morehouse RL, Flanigan M, MacDonald DD, Braha D, Shapiro C. Depression and short REM latency in subjects with chronic fatigue syndrome. Psychosom Med. 1998;60:347–351.

Morehouse RL, Kusumakar V, Kutcher SP, LeBlanc J, Armitage R. Temporal coherence in ultradian sleep EEG rhythms in a never-depressed, high-risk cohort of female adolescents. Biol Psychiatry. 2002;51:446–456.

Chapter 15

Stress Disorders: Kathy Hegadoren and Women's Mental Health

I feel there is something unexplored about women
That only a woman can explore.
Georgia O'Keefe

Kathy Hegadoren's research in Edmonton straddles biology and psychology, clarifying the relationship between hormones and life experience in women who are stressed. Her work sheds light on the 3/2 gender ratio in illnesses such as depression and anxiety.

Kathy Hegadoren is both a nurse and a basic neuroscientist who holds a Canada Research Chair in Stress-Related Disorders in Women. She is the first person to have established a basic science laboratory within a Faculty of Nursing in Canada. She works out of the University of Alberta, with multidisciplinary teams of researchers, and collaborates widely, both nationally and internationally. Dr. Hegadoren received her nursing diploma in 1971, her BScN in 1987, her MSc in psychiatry in 1990, her PhD in medical sciences in 1995. Still not satisfied with the amount of knowledge she had accumulated, Kathy did a further postdoctoral fellowship in molecular biology. In January of 1998, she became the first nurse in Canada to be awarded a grant from the Canada Foundation for Innovation. The infrastructure grant translated into significant funding and allowed her to build a basic science laboratory that integrates biological and psychosocial approaches to women's health.

Hegadoren straddles biology and psychology by investigating the relationship between hormone fluctuations and life events. She hopes, one day, to explain the high female/male ratio in such psychiatric disorders as depression, post-traumatic stress disorder (PTSD), and other anxiety disorders. "There is something about women that makes them more vulnerable [than men] to stress." What that something is, is precisely the mystery that Dr. Hegadoren is trying to solve. Hormones are part of the answer. Twenty to 40% of menstruating women experience premenstrual mood and behavior changes (they become more irritable and more down in the few days leading up to their menses). Premenopausal women between the ages of 18 to 45 account for the largest proportion of patients suffering from clinical depression. Ten to 15% of women experience a clinical depression during pregnancy or after the birth of a baby (please see Chapter 23). In women with a prior history of mood disorder, that percentage increases threefold. Once a woman has experienced a postpartum depression, her risk of having another is approximately 70%. As many as 80% of all women report a low mood or postpartum blues after giving birth. In any given year, seven percent of women experience depression and another eight percent experience anxiety. Ten percent per year suffer at least one panic attack and this figure rises to 16% in the youngest adult age group, ages 15 to 24. Women require mental health services more frequently than men, receive treatment more often, are prescribed more medication, and are hospitalized more often for psychiatric problems.

What makes women so vulnerable? To answer this question, basic laboratory research into gender differences is needed, as well as accurate psychiatric demographics, clinical studies into the gender-specific effectiveness of treatments (including pharmacologic, psychotherapeutic, non-medical, self-help, peer support, and complementary medicine), health services research into gender aspects of access to health services, sociocultural studies into the effects of poverty, violence, and relative lack of autonomy in women, and ethnographic studies on the impact of care-giving on female carers. Health policy needs to address the specific needs of women psychiatric patients by involving them, as partners, in the process of enquiry. Women need to shape and participate in research that pertains to them.

This is precisely what Dr. Hegadoren does. She involves women in research studies on the effect of stress on women's health.

> Many women have trauma histories, like childhood sexual abuse or adult interpersonal trauma. That led me to look at the impact of context on women's lives and that became my whole research program: to understand what psychological, sociological, and biological factors lead to the extra vulnerability in women. And that, inevitably, leads to neuroendocrinology as a window through which to understand the impact of traumatic stressful events on women's lives. It gives you a nice biological, but complex, window through which you can observe the interaction between reproductive hormones and stress hormones.

Hegadoren hopes that studying changes in the stress hormone system might provide a means to differentiate between subtypes of depression in women and to help predict their response to antidepressant treatment. But one of the positive outcomes of looking at stress adaptation in women is that it is not concerned only with pathology. It leads to therapeutic intervention and prevention, i.e., learning how to build resilience and enhance strategies needed for coping.

Not everyone (in the male world) saw it as a positive when Hegadoren first started applying for operating grants.

> People like the idea of biopsychosocial integration in theory, but not, apparently, if they are reading a grant. The first grant I ever submitted to CIHR, in 1998, the reviewer's comment was: "if this person thinks they are a researcher, they are delusional." For a while, I thought of abandoning it all and returning to clinical nursing but... getting a Canadian Research Chair now, I want to go to this person, and point out how quick he (presumably it was a he) was to make judgments about a new investigator rather than assessing the value of the proposed project. A small voice within me also wants to shout out, "SEE!"

For Kathy Hegadoren, among the most influential people in her life have been the women who have agreed to take part in her research, the women who have answered her advertisements and have shared the stories of their lives.

> These are courageous women with horrible histories, and yet they still have some reason to get up every morning. They have a reason not to give up and you can't help but feeling humbled. Sometimes [talking to me] is the first time they've shared these histories and it is pretty powerful that they are willing to do this, to help other women – it is in large part altruism and also something they feel they need to do as part of healing. To have that honor, [of being trusted with their stories], is what made me continue with my research even when I had those funding issues at the beginning.

Hegadoren believes that listening to research participants' stories can teach researchers about the kinds of research questions that are important to ask.

> In one of my studies, I recruited women from a trauma therapy group. When I'd completed my data collection and prepared it for publication, I returned to the group and presented my findings to see whether they made good sense to the participants. They did. The women had always been told that it was all in their heads but now they saw that it was the early trauma that was affecting their health, years down the road. We need to include participants more than we do in evaluating research results.

Besides her women subjects and her collaborators, Kathy owes much to her supportive family and to her scientific mentors. One of them is Dr. Glen Baker, Chair of the Department of Psychiatry at the University of Alberta and a Canada Research Chair in Neurochemistry and Drug Development. He is well known for his work in the neurochemistry of symptoms and treatment strategies in psychiatric disorders and has been a strong supporter.

Dr. Hegadoren might have devoted her life to studying adolescent rather than adult stress because she started her career working with teens. Although the work was very satisfying, not all her experiences were positive: A 15 year old adolescent was placed in an intensive treatment program that only operated Monday through Friday. He needed a home for weekends so Kathy and her husband agreed to have him join their family while he was attending the program. This young man suffered from severe behavior problems. He would spy on people in the neighborhood. He would go to the corner store and take things without paying. Before long, the neighbors became involved. Kathy would receive calls saying: "that boy is hiding behind our garbage can again." "He's taken a pop [from the corner store owner], do you want me to put it on your tab?"

The community remained loyal even when the boy was expelled from his treatment program and began living full time with the Hegadorens. One day, he came home very drunk and verbally threatened the family. Kathy and her husband, Dale, called the crisis unit. When he was picked up, he claimed that the Hegadorens had battered him. The staff who worked for Social Services believed him and created a Hegadoren file, which means that Kathy and Dale can never again look after foster children (this, despite letters of clarification from the attending psychiatrist). It is a disconcerting story. The boy went to a longer-term hospital, a chronic unit, and the Hegadorens lost all contact and still don't know what eventually happened to the boy.

Perhaps as a result of this personal experience, Kathy's interests were redirected to the examination of the psychological and biological factors that increase women's vulnerability to stress-related disorders following traumatic experiences. She is developing models that link trauma to illness and recovery. She conducts multidimensional studies using psychological measures, brain imaging, and the measurement of stress hormone levels collected from women who have experienced different sorts of early and more recent traumas. The outcomes will clarify the issue of the role of *type* of trauma on women's health as well as the *timing* of trauma. She has also developed tools to identify at-risk individuals. As well, she studies the longer-term impact of interpersonal trauma on women's health, particularly during reproductive periods – pregnancy, childbirth, and early mothering. In collaboration with other researchers, she is trying to determine the influence of a woman's reproductive cycle on both her hormonal stress responses and her reaction to antidepressant therapies.

Dr. Hegadoren hopes her work will lead to improvement in gender-specific psychoeducational programs and interventions. Many women using mental health services not only have a history of childhood trauma but are currently raising children singlehandedly on a low income, suffer from domestic violence, or are sole caregivers of an elderly parent. These are crucial issues that contribute to women's stress levels yet, unfortunately, the psychiatric services that address these needs do not always feel safe for women. To increase the feeling of safety, separate sleeping, washing and toilet facilities have been advocated for men and women in psychiatric treatment. There needs to be fail-safe protection from violence, sexual harassment and professional sexual abuse. In order to feel safe, many women who are psychiatrically ill need access to women staff. Importantly, psychiatric drug therapy may, for a variety of reasons not be safe for all women, either because of weight gain, the risk of abnormality to a fetus during pregnancy, or the induction of menstrual irregularity and lactation problems.

Dr. Hegadoren's research into stress builds on a foundation of Canadian stress research founded by Hans Selye (1907–1982). Born in Hungary, Selye did his pioneering work in Montreal where he stumbled upon the idea of the now generally accepted general adaptation syndrome (GAS) or stress reaction, "the nonspecific response to any demand placed on the body." It consists firstly of the alarm reaction, (the body preparing itself for "fight or flight."), secondly, of resistance (the actual fight or flight), and finally, of exhaustion. The fight or flight concept, which includes all the emotional, cognitive, behavioral and biological processes involved in stress, has more recently been critiqued through a gender perspective. Taylor and colleagues (see Further Reading below) have suggested that it does not hold for everyone and that, particularly in women, stress can elicit another behavioral pattern they have called "tend and befriend," a tendency to seek out friends in times of stress rather than preparing to flee or fight. The tend and befriend response, mediated by neurochemicals such as oxytocin and endogenous opioids, may be more relevant to women than the original fight-or-flight (adrenergic and steroid) responses to stress, studied largely in men.

Asked whether it is difficult to do mental illness research as a woman in Canada, Kathy Hegadoren replies:

> I'd have to say there are some system issues that make things difficult for everyone, man or woman. Neuroscience research and Mental Health research compete for the same pot of money, but neuroscience researchers have an advantage.

Working with test tubes or animals is cleaner, the experimental designs are much easier to sell, the goals much easier to accomplish. Recruitment of human subjects is much harder than ordering animals or using cell lines and, thus, publication of results is a much slower process in clinical studies. No matter into which category we place mental health, no matter with whom we're grouped: we always seem to come out the poorer cousin. Mental health research used to have its own peer-review funding pot in Alberta. When the Alberta Heritage Foundation for Medical Research took over the administration of those funds, that money was subsumed under a larger umbrella and we lost that dedicated research resource. A proposed new provincial mental health plan includes dedicated research funds, so maybe there is good news on the horizon."

She is quick, however, to acknowledge the benefits of the new structure of the main federal research funding agency, the Canadian Institutes of Health Research (CIHR).

The spirit of CIHR is to encourage independent researchers to become part of research teams that include basic and clinical researchers, a bench-to-bedside approach. The single independent researcher can no longer do things on his or her own. You don't just look at a specific receptor; you look at its behavioral implications. With such teams, we can decrease the amount of time it takes for research results to enter into clinical practice and change health policy. It is claimed that it takes 17 years for research to reach clinical practice. We need to accelerate that, and the only way to do it is through these interdisciplinary, multidimensional research collaboratives. So this is a huge advance in the way research is supported in Canada. But, as I said, it's hard for mental health to compete against neuroscience.

Another advantage of CIHR, according to Kathy Hegadoren, is its Institute of Gender and Health where gender-specific research is highlighted and women's health has broadened to include "more than uteruses." There is an attempt to look at gender as a health determinant, to see health through a wider lens. The Canadian Government has adopted a Women's Health Strategy, which aims to increase knowledge about women's health, promote the health of women, support the provision of effective health services to women and to ensure that Health Canada's policies and programs are responsive to the unique needs of women.

Researchers in other fields such as heart and stroke, cancer, or diabetes have many funding sources. Mental health researchers have few. It is socially acceptable to have a sick heart or a sick pancreas, so donors generously support research foundations such as the Heart and Stroke Foundation or the Canadian Diabetes Association. "But people don't want to think of sick minds." Dr. Hegadoren is also very much aware that progress in mental health research is slowed by the fact that psychiatric disorders are complex. This also slows funding donations because philanthropists want relatively quick results from their investments; they are discouraged when cures are long in coming. The pharmaceutical industry is also influenced by the stigma attached to mental illness. The suicides associated with SSRI antidepressants, for instance, could have encouraged pharmaceutical companies to research the problem and develop safer drugs, rather than simply to limit their use. Hegadoren points out the contrast between Viagra and the SSRIs in how the potential for life-threatening side effects was handled in the two cases. Clear directions about not combining Viagra with nitrates ended the media coverage in the first case but, with SSRIs, sensationalist headlines about suicides continue. Sensitive to the uproar, the pharmaceutical industry tends to stay with copy-cat drugs, rather than more fully exploring novel drug targets for depression.

Kathy Hegadoren reflects on the social status of depression today:

> When it became okay to talk about depression at a cocktail party and say openly that you were on antidepressants, in some ways that was good, but it was a double-edged sword – it gave the impression that depression was easy to treat. For some, it is not like that at all; it takes longer. People say: "you've been on treatment for four weeks and why the hell aren't you better?" and "get out of bed, get back to work." There is an intolerance for suffering; you are supposed to get identified, get treated, and then you are supposed to be fine.

Asked about the effectiveness of such psychotherapies as cognitive behavioral therapy (CBT) (please see Chapters 2 and 11), Dr. Hegadoren says:

> CBT is undervalued and under-utilized; this reflects a system problem. Therapists who use this form of therapy are not covered by health insurance so they have to charge the individual. Many people can't afford to take advantage of CBT for that reason. Our current health system seems only to be able to afford drug therapies; other therapies are called "adjunct." Using depression as an example, with antidepressants, there is less than full recovery for a third to a half of patients. We need to better identify those who require more than one type of treatment and start them on psychotherapy early, instead of waiting 4 to 6 weeks until the individual has shown a failure to respond to antidepressants."

The overall answer, Kathy Hegadoren believes, is in active collaboration among different kinds of health professionals. Perhaps this solution comes easily to her because she was born into a family of eight children; co-operation was essential. She believes that "in the end, collaboration is the only way we'll advance." Her hope is to take the research Chair that has been awarded to her and use it to work with future generations of students, to operate in closely knit partnerships, to integrate biology, psychology, and sociology in all three domains: research, education and practice.

What has been one of her greatest joys? "Being awarded a Canada Research Chair after someone called me delusional!"

Further Reading

Cahill L. His brain, her brain. Sci Am. 2005;292:40–47.

Canadian Community Health Survey. Mental health and well-being, 2002.

Carter-Snell C, Hegadoren K. Stress disorders and gender: implications for theory and research. Can J Nurs Res. 2003;35:34–55.

Coupland NJ, Hegadoren KM, Myrholm J. Beclomethasone-induced vasoconstriction in women with major depressive disorder. J Psychiatry Neurosi. 2003;28:364–369.

Gabriel G. Hans Selye: the discovery of stress. Available at http://www.brainconnection.com /topics/?main=fa/selye

Health Canada. Health Canada's women's health strategy. Ottawa: Health Canada; 1999.

King SL, Hegadoren KM. Stress hormones: how do they measure up? J Biol Nursing. 2002; 4:92–103.

Levitan RD, Parikh SV, Lesage AD, Hegadoren KM, Adams M, Kennedy SH, Goering PN. Major depression in individuals with a history of childhood physical or sexual abuse: relationship to neurovegetative features, mania, and gender. Am J Psychiatry. 1998; 155:1746–1752.

O'Donnell T, Hegadoren KM, Coupland NC. Noradrenergic mechanisms in the pathophysiology of post-traumatic stress disorder. Neuropsychobiology 2004;50:273–283.

Romans SE, Seeman MV. Women's Mental Health. A life cycle approach. Philadelphia: Lippincott, Williams & Wilkins; 2005.

Taylor SE, Klein LC, Lewis BP, Gruenewald TL, Gurung RA, Updegraff JA. Biobehavioral responses to stress in females: tend-and-befriend, not fight-or-flight. Psychol Rev. 2000;107:411–429.

Chapter 16

Substance Abuse:
Juan Carlos Negrete – Under the Influence

"Alcohol is the anesthesia by which we endure the operation of life."
George Bernard Shaw

It is not generally known that alcohol exerts different effects on brain and behavior depending on one's native culture. According to Juan Carlos Negrete, the problem of addictions will be solved when the tools and methods of two kinds of sciences – the physiological sciences and the social sciences– are fused.

As illustrated by the quotation from George Bernard Shaw, overusing alcohol has not, until relatively recently, been viewed as illness and, in may parts of the world, it is still seen as a lifestyle issue, a social problem perhaps, but not a disease. In Canada, many scientists believe that calling addiction a disease medicalizes it unduly, letting affected persons off the hook, not holding them responsible for their behavior. What justification is there, they ask, in embracing the disease concept of addiction and looking for genetic predispositions, enzymes gone awry, or changes in the brain that single some people out as vulnerable and therefore not accountable? Psychology has developed some very effective behavioral treatments for addictive behavior and psychologists worry that a disease concept of addiction carries with it the implication that only biological treatments can work.

Juan Carlos Negrete is a medical doctor, a psychiatrist, who believes that addictions *are* illnesses, but he also believes in the effectiveness of behavioral treatments. His special contribution to the field is the recognition that the expression of addictive illness is shaped by the culture in which one lives (i.e., by a lifetime of learning). Like other scientists in other chapters of this book, Dr. Negrete views the mind as one views a muscle, a biological entity, to be sure, but malleable when flexed, and expandable.

Juan Carlos Negrete was born in Tucuman, in northern Argentina. His eldest brother, older by 14 years, was a heavy smoker and died of lung cancer in his 40s. Perhaps, unconsciously, this influenced Juan Carlos' decision to study the biosocial components of addiction. As an adolescent, however, he was more interested in languages, literature, and history than in science. He first attended a military college – not that he was interested in the military but this happened to be a good school with very good teachers. Juan Carlos spent five years at this school. The decision to go on to study medicine at university was influenced by family tradition. One of his grandfathers and a grand uncle had been physicians. His initial idea was to go to medical school to appease the family and, after finishing the required six years, decide what he *really* wanted to do. It was during his final year of medical school that he met Henri Ellenberger and determined to stay in medicine and specialize in psychiatry, and it was also because of Ellenberger that he came to Canada.

Short history of Henri Ellenberger

Of Swiss-French Huguenot descent and born to missionary parents in South Africa, Henri F. Ellenberger (1905–1993) was brought up in France. He graduated from medicine in Paris in 1934. He trained in psychiatry in France and Switzerland and, in 1952, while on a scholarship in the U.S., was recruited to the Menninger Clinic in Topeka, Kansas. In 1959, he came to McGill to work in the field of ethnopsychiatry with Eric Wittkower and H.M.B. Murphy. In 1961, he visited Argentina and met Juan Carlos Negrete.

In 1962, he was appointed Professor of Criminology at the Université de Montréal where he stayed for the rest of his career. He wrote more than a hundred papers on psychiatry, psychology, criminology, and the history of medicine. A man of encyclopedic knowledge, Henri Ellenberger is best known for his masterful historical work, The Discovery of the Unconscious.

In Argentina in 1961, psychiatric training was all psychoanalytic. When Henri Ellenberger came there to visit his friend and colleague, Professor Juan Dalma, Juan Carlos was in his final year of medicine and a Teaching Assistant in the Department of Psychiatry. Ellenberger was a breath of fresh air, opening the window onto the larger world of psychiatry beyond psychoanalysis. He described the early psychopharmacology trials that Heinz Lehmann was conducting at the Verdun Protestant Hospital (now Douglas Hospital) in Montreal (see Chapter 13). He told Juan Carlos about the Allan Memorial Institute's day therapy program, the first of its kind in the Western world. He told him about the world famous family therapy centre at the Montreal Jewish Hospital (see Chapter 9), about Wilder Penfield at the Montreal Neurological Institute and Donald Hebb in the McGill Psychology Department (please see Chapter 9). And he told him about Eric Wittkower's outstanding group in transcultural psychiatry. It is to that program that Juan Carlos came to do his residency training in psychiatry, under the supervision of H.B.M. Murphy. He came to Montreal with his wife and child, planning to only stay four years.

Short history of Eric Wittkower

Eric Wittkower (1899–1983) was born and educated in Berlin but discharged from his post as Privat-Dozent at the University of Berlin in 1933 because he was Jewish. His interest in the impact of culture on human beings must certainly have been influenced by this experience. After practicing psychiatry in Great Britain, he joined the McGill Department of Psychiatry in 1951. In 1955, Drs. Eric Wittkower and Jack Fried set up the section of Transcultural Psychiatric Studies as a joint venture between the Departments of Psychiatry and Anthropology at McGill. Subsequent world-renowned psychiatrists in this program have been H.B.M. Murphy, Raymond Prince, and Laurence Kirmayer.

When Juan Carlos told his Argentinian colleagues that he was going to specialize in psychiatry, they asked (and this was the prevailing feeling among medical doctors of the time): "Why go into psychiatry when you are smart enough to be a real doctor?" Not only was psychiatry seen, among physicians, as an uninspiring specialty but, in addition, the field of addictions was seen as a lackluster subspecialty among psychiatrists. Negrete's early paper on the influence of alcohol on the specifics of criminal behavior in different parts of the world elicited the following comment from his professor: "That is all very nice, but couldn't you work on a subject of interest to psychiatrists?"

But Juan Carlos was not to be deterred. Even before graduating from medical school, he had decided that this would be his life's work. Since then, essentially all Juan Carlos' scholarly contributions (over 160) have been in the area of substance abuse. This is not, he hastens to make clear, because he has anything against drinking:

> I grew up in a society heavily influenced by Mediterranean culture; my family is of Italian and Spanish descent. These aren't exactly cultures of abstinence and, because of this, I do not have a moral stance against alcohol. I must tell you that I drink; I'm not a teetotaler and neither is anybody in my family. Nor, on the other hand, has anyone in my family suffered from alcoholism.

Both Italy and Spain boast high rates of alcohol consumption, Negrete explains (although, interestingly, a recent study of alcohol trends in 15 European countries showed that, among men, the abstinence rate was highest in Italy – see Further Reading). Rates of dependence on alcohol may be similar across European countries but the behavior of people under the influence varies. The often heavy chronic alcohol intake in Mediterranean countries can lead to long term physical complications such as liver and brain damage, heart disease, certain types of cancer, blackouts and loss of memory, sexual impotence, reproductive problems, stomach ulcers, and pancreatitis. In northern European countries, the complications are more likely to be behavioral – loud parties, arguments and exchanges of insults, family disputes, vandalism, drinking and driving, and violence. When Italians compare themselves to the British, for instance, they think they have relatively less of a problem with alcohol because intoxication does not equate to violence in Italy. This difference may depend on the incidence of binge drinking – one study that included ten countries concluded that Canadian men (and Swedish women) reported the highest incidence of bingeing (see Further Reading).

> Nobody in my university (in Argentina) or here in Montreal when I came to train in psychiatry was interested in the subject of alcohol. So I was not influenced by a particular role model at the time, although I developed a role model – Griffith Edwards from England, whom I met in the '70s when I was already well into my career. That is why this clinic where I work today is called Griffith Edwards House.

Griffith Edwards is a world expert in alcohol and drug addiction. The founder of the National Addiction Centre in the U.K. and editor of the journal, Addictions, the most prestigious scientific journal in this field, he is a medical scientist who has studied substance abuse for 40 years. A man who is always developing new ideas, he is the author, most recently, of a major new book, *Alcohol: the Ambiguous Molecule*.

> I've tried to follow his [Griffith Edwards'] path more than anybody else's. When I developed this clinic, we did not want to put a poster outside saying "Addiction Clinic." We thought that would be inappropriate, so we picked a proper name. I

consulted Griffith Edwards: "I want to name it after you, what do you think?" He answered: "Do it immediately before you change your mind!"

Because, until quite recently, addiction has been considered a minor and marginal field of endeavor for psychiatrists, only a very few leading academic psychiatrists in Canada have made their careers in this field. As of 2005, there are only four full professors of psychiatry in Canada who can be identified as *bona fide* addiction psychiatrists. But the field of addictions has nevertheless spawned the development of neurobiology within psychiatry as a whole.

Using a technique first developed by Avram Goldstein, in 1973 Candace Pert and Solomon Snyder located the brain opiate receptor (See Further Reading). This led to a new understanding of how morphine and heroin affect the brain but, more importantly, it transformed scientific appreciation of neurotransmission, the transfer of chemicals from one neuron to another, the principle that neurochemicals and their antagonists compete for the same receptor sites on nerve cells.

Despite the fact that addiction study has led to this basic neurobiological concept that has resulted in major psychopharmacological discoveries, addictions, to a large extent, have remained within the *social* sciences. As mentioned at the beginning of the chapter, they are often seen primarily as problems of behavior – not only individual behavior (drinking or abstaining) but also culturally determined behavior (that which one's tradition reinforces). That is where Juan Carlos Negrete comes in. "I think it [addiction] is the biopsychosocial problem par excellence, the archetype."

There is a "how" to people getting drunk in different parts of the world and a "what" to their behavior when they are drunk. That is not determined by alcohol's effect on the brain (which does not differ much among the world's peoples, although some differences do exist) but by interpersonal psychology and culture. Juan Carlos Negrete feels that the same holds true for the manifestations of other psychiatric illnesses (depression, anxiety) and that this cultural fact is not sufficiently appreciated. His contribution has been to describe the psychosocial determinants of the manifestation of the addictions and the varied subjective experience of addiction. Addiction is a disease of the brain, he believes, no less medical than any other disease of the brain. But its behavioral components, important to its impact on the person, are the direct consequence of values, social mores, and customs.

As an example, the traditional Russian approach to alcoholism was that it was amenable to treatment through social/political policies such as taxes, restrictions in production, and education. This approach has not worked and Russia is now moving toward a more medical model. American research looking at drinking patterns among ethnic minorities found that the lifetime alcohol use rate among Chinese, Japanese, Korean, and Filipino Americans is much lower than that of the general U.S. population. Japanese Americans had the highest (though still low) percentage among the Asian groups, and Chinese Americans had the lowest. There has been some suggestion that genetic factors can account for these patterns. For example, up to 50% of Asians carry a gene that causes an unpleasant flushing reaction in response to alcohol, but many Native Americans, whose alcohol rates are high, carry the same gene. Confucian and Taoist philosophies may influence Eastern drinking styles. The emphasis on conformity and harmony in those philosophies is believed to promote moderation. It has also been said that cultures where drinking takes place in prescribed social situations limit the likelihood of alcohol abuse.

There is nothing more biological than the liver that metabolizes the alcohol that affects the brain of individuals, yet even the liver can be seen and expressed through the prism of culture:

(A portion of Oda al Higado (Ode to the Liver) by Pablo Neruda, 1904–1973, Chilean poet, Nobel Laureate in Literature, 1971. Translation by Oriana Josseau Kalant and published in Alcohol Liver Pathology (J.M. Khanna, Y. Israel, and H. Kalant, editors) 1975:

> Modest,
> organized
> friend,
> underground
> worker,
> let me give you
> the wing of my song,
> the thrust
> of the air,
> the soaring
> of my ode:
> it is born
> of your invisible
> machinery,
> it flies
> from your tireless
> confined mill,
> delicate
> powerful
> entrail,
> ever alive and dark.
> ....there, inside,
> you filter
> and apportion,
> you separate
> and divide,
> you multiply
> and lubricate,

you raise
and gather
the threads and the grams
of life, the final
distillate,
the intimate essences.
Submerged
viscus,
measurer
of the blood,
you live
full of hands
and full of eyes,
measuring and transferring
in your hidden
alchemical
chamber.
Yellow
is the matrix
of your red hydraulic flow,
diver
of the most perilous
depths of man,
there forever hidden,
everlasting,
in the factory,
noiseless.

Juan Negrete is in a unique position to compare the science of addictions around the world.

> In Europe and Latin America, addiction has always been within the realm of psychiatry. But in North America, largely due to neglect on the part of psychiatry, but also due to a large movement of non-psychiatric physicians who had experienced the problem of addiction themselves and were therefore motivated to study it, addiction work fell largely outside the realm of mental health.

Dr. Negrete admits there are controversies in his field:

> Firstly, the taking over of the treatment of addictions by the philosophy of self-help and mutual help, which held professional intervention as somewhat incompetent to solve the problem. Initially that was quite right, but sadly this has kept clinical

Canadian Addiction Specialists

Drs. Harold and Oriana Kalant (University of Toronto) worked together starting in the 1950s and became international authorities on the study of drug dependency and toxicity.

Roy Wise taught for 28 years at Concordia University until 1997 when he became Deputy Director and Chief of the Behavioral Neuroscience Branch of the National Institute on Drug Abuse in the U.S.

"Neurochemical events involved in relapse to cocaine or heroin use induced by cues, drugs and stressors can be dissociated, suggesting that no single treatment approach to treatment prevention will be adequate." *Jane Stewart, Concordia University*

"It is widely accepted that addiction is a brain disorder due primarily to disregulation of neurotransmitter systems, including the monoamine, glutaminergic and opioid peptide pathways." *Anthony Phillips, University of British Columbia*

"Genes and their putative functions, differential sensitivity of particular brain regions and particular psychosocial factors have all been implicated in high-risk populations." R.O. *Pihl, McGill University*

"*The dead drug leaves a ghost behind. At certain hours it haunts the house.*" Jean Cocteau. "The "ghost" is summoned by the memory of the drug, typically elicited by places, times, or circumstances that have been associated with the drug in the past." *Shepard Siegel, McMaster University*

"Gamblers attempt to control and predict events that are objectively uncontrollable." *Robert Ladouceur, Laval University*

"[Gamblers display] dysfunctional beliefs about luck, emotional reasoning, [their own] exaggerated skills… superstitious behaviors, attributional biases, interpretive biases and memory impairments." *Tony Toneatto, University of Toronto*

scientists away from the field. This philosophy has influenced the type of treatments that have been developed in North America: it was around the twelve-step movements that most of the initial treatment centers were organized. There have been problems between laboratory and academic scientists and proponents of these approaches (which incidentally are a lot more scientific than scientists think).

Today, the self-help movement manages about 80% of addiction treatment. (Please see Chapters 20 and 29)

I do not believe in such distinctions. Look at this clinic. There are 20 professionals. Only four are psychiatrists. Most of the rest are not medical professionals. We work in harmony; we approach patients in a very comprehensive way.

Dr. Negrete has worked in this field for 43 years.

> I was very lucky to have started working in a field that had relatively few takers. I have never felt the need to push my way into anybody else's place. I have been given ample support, always.

Because addictions was historically an area in need of development, there was little competition at the time so Negrete had no problem getting started. His first research study in Canada was a cross-cultural comparison of French Catholic and Anglo Protestant men with alcohol problems – a group in their forties who had lived through the Second World War. On the basis of their cultural identity, Negrete was able to predict what their behavior would be like under the influence of alcohol.

Subsequently, he became interested in clinical aspects of addiction and has also done experimental work trying to identify psychobiological mechanisms of drug use. He is especially interested in the interaction of psychoactive substance use with psychiatric disease. Negrete was one of the first to study cannabis use in psychosis and its effects on the symptoms of schizophrenia. He is an expert in the dual diagnoses – alcohol or drug addiction co-existing with depression, schizophrenia, or other psychiatric illness. Such concurrent disorders are notoriously difficult to treat (See Chapters 20 and 29).

Dr. Negrete feels that Canada is a major contributor in the area of addictions.

> But we live next door to the U.S. and, as with everything else, they have more resources and a chance to do things on a larger scale. The basic problem with resources within research in addictions in Canada has been that medical research money is usually not given to addictions, and social research money is usually not given to medical researchers in addictions. The result is that medical researchers in addiction in Canada are poorly resourced.
>
> We need to establish a higher profile among those who influence the setting of priorities by the Canadian Institutes for Health Research. We are making good progress, for sure, but we are not completely there. We should, more and more, demonstrate that our science is as good as any other science within health. We have the problem of behavior that is so easy to define but so difficult to research. Interventions that are not chemical ones are very difficult to test and scientists look upon them with suspicion. Psychosocial interventions are seen as less serious scientifically and less certain as to response. Even within psychiatric research organizations, we tend to look with less respect on psychological intervention research as opposed to biological intervention. There is also a problem with biological research. It has been taken over by the pharmaceutical industry to a large extent, and funding agencies assume that the pharmaceutical industry will fund it, so they stay away. That is a mistake.

Dr. Negrete has a life outside addictions. He is the father of five children. His wife, Carolyn, is an oncologist, the Chair of the Department of Radiation Oncology at McGill. Second to his family, Juan Carlos Negrete mentions as his major joys a) seeing the scientific development of the area of addictions and b) the recruitment of young people into research and service in addictions. He has no desire to stop working – McGill University has no compulsory retirement age so he plans to go on doing what he is doing for many years to come. "I am working full time and perhaps even more than before." He finds that his aspirations and ambitions have not really changed over the years. He estimates he is learning more these days per unit of time than ever before because so much new knowledge is being produced every day. He never finds he knows enough; there is always more to know. "I could stay doing this for many years."

In Canada, 29% of men and 11% of women drink over 5 drinks at one sitting more than 12 times a year. Ten percent of men and 5% of women have used cannabis in the last year. One and a half percent of men and 0.7% of women have used LSD, heroin, or amphetamine. Cocaine has been used in the last year by 0.8% of men and 0.5% of women in Canada.

According to Negrete, the problem of addictions will be solved when the tools of two kinds of sciences – the physiological sciences and the social sciences – are fused. Empiricism rather than conjecture, he is certain, will eventually lead to the prevention, treatment, and cure of addictions.

Further Reading

Babor TF, Edwards G, Stockwell T. Science and the drinks industry: cause for concern. Addiction. 1996;91:5–9.

Bloomfield K, Stockwell T, Gmel G, Rehn N. International comparison of alcohol consumption. Alcohol Res & Health. 2003;27:95–109.

Cleghorn RA, Dongier M. Memory and appreciation: Eric D. Wittkower 1899–1983. Can J Psychiatry. 1983;28:314–315.

Corin E, Bibeau G. HBM Murphy (1915–1987): a key figure in transcultural psychiatry. Cult Med Psychiatry. 1988;12:397–415.

Dongier M. Festschrift for Eric Wittkower, M.D. Introduction. Can J Psychiatry. 1979;24:381–382.

Edwards G, Anderson P, Babor TF, Casswell C, Ferrence R, Giesbrecht N, et al. Alcohol policy and the public good. Oxford: Oxford University Press; 1994.

Edwards G. Alcohol: the ambiguous molecule. London: Penguin Books; 2000.

Edwards G. Oriana Josseau Kalant, 1920–2001: a remarkable scientist, a remarkable woman. Addiction. 2002;97:1356–1357.

Galvan FH, Caetano R. Alcohol use and related problems among ethnic minorities in the United States. Alcohol Res & Health. 2003;27:87–94.

Humphreys K. Alcoholics Anonymous and 12-step alcoholism treatment programs. Recent Dev Alcohol. 2003;16:149–164.

Murphy HBM, Negrete JC, Tousignant M. Exploring a new type of alcoholism survey. Int J Epidemiol. 1979;8:119–126.

Negrete JC, Murphy HBM. Psychological deficit in chewers of coca leaf. Bull. on Narcotics. 1967;19:11–18.

Negrete JC. Cultural influences on social performance of chronic alcoholics: a comparative study. Quart Studies Alcohol. 1973;34:905–916.

Negrete JC, Knapp WP, Douglas DE, Smith WB. Cannabis affects the severity of schizophrenic symptoms: results of a clinical survey. Psychol Med. 1986;16:515–520.

Negrete JC. Do role-model societies exist? Addiction. 1995;90:1443–1445.

Negrete JC. Harm reduction: quo vadis? Addiction. 2001;96:543–545.

Pert CB, Snyder SH. Opiate receptor: demonstration in nervous tissue. Science. 1973;179:1011–1014.

Wise RA. Dopamine, learning and motivation. Nat Rev Neurosci. 2004;5:483–494.

Chapter 17

Research and Redemption

by Doris Sommer-Rotenberg

Does
memory
become
mere
fear
and fantasy?
　Did I
　really
　have
　a son
　　　　one
　　　　with gifts
　　　　more than
　　　　usual
　　　　　　　and
　　　　　　　demons
　　　　　　　unusually
　　　　　　　numerical?
Time
energy
　　suspended
　　by grief
dedicated
to fulfil
his unfulfilled
promise

finding
resource
ashes
dust
    allot
    to his
    extinguished
    life
To ensure
his existence
lived
in pain
shall never
perish

    into anonymous
    oblivion

His achievement
commitment
    prelude
    to study
    devastating
    self-destruction
His spirit
now free
    penetrates
    motivates
    careers
    of strangers

Redemption
through
research
    uncover
    reason
    for
    self-extinction
        why
        desire
        to die

before
pleasure
pain
naturally
expire
understanding
psychic
genetic
uncharted
criteria
comprehending
defenselessness
against
nothingness
counselling
when
perception
withholds
direction
weakness
predicated
strengths
negated
comforting
when
compass
lost
finding
newly
freed
focus

Stimulus
from
a past
presence
creation
inspiration
from
his
existence

Some
remission
of loss
    through
    service
    he could
    give
        granted
        impetus
        to live

September 1996

Section II

Benefactors and Beneficiaries

Chapter 18

Art to the Rescue:
Michael Alzamora, Flat Surrealist

*"Men have called me mad, but the question is not yet settled, wheth-
er madness is or is not the loftiest intelligence – whether much that is
glorious – whether all that is profound – does not spring from disease
of thought – from moods of mind exalted at the expense of the general
intellect. Those who dream by day are cognizant of many things which
escape those who dream only by night "*
Edgar Allen Poe

The ancient Greeks believed creative inspiration was achieved through divine madness or altered states of mind. Irrationality may be the artistic fuel that some artists need, but Michael Alzamora, a Toronto artist, has found the opposite to be true
– his art makes him rational.

Michael Alzamora invented flat surrealism in 1995 by accident. He explains:

There are three basic components of a Flat Surreal Painting. They are: objects,
symbols, and juxtapositions. All these components co-exist in a single plane.
Objects are used as symbols. In flat surrealism, relationships between objects are
made by color, shape, size, and meaning. Juxtapositions are realistic meanings
derived from surreal objects when they are compared. These objects are only a
piece of a puzzle. Alone, their meaning is vague.

Flat surreal paintings are flat in appearance, yet very symbolic. In my case, the
symbols are expressions of symptoms of schizophrenia. I use *fossils*, symbolizing

entrapment by illness. People with schizophrenia, like *fossils*, are helpless, trapped by circumstances.

I use clouds in the shape of predatory fish, symbolizing delusions of persecution. My clouds are just about to swallow the Sun. My fish clouds smoke cigarettes and represent damage to the environment; in a schizophrenic mind, damage is always translated into personal harm. My clouds, sometimes in the shape of egg clusters, feature one egg detaching from its cluster and cracking open to reveal the Sun (as in my painting, called "The Crack of Dawn"). The Sun symbolizes a new beginning and freedom from illness. Since 2003, my paintings have taken on a joy and lightness – celebrating the dawn of a healthy and happy life. Figurative shapes of human and plant elements fused together represent this state of rejuvenation.

In a book called *The Price of Greatness: Resolving the Creativity and Madness Controversy*, author Arnold Ludwig concludes that members of the artistic professions or creative arts as a whole suffer from more types of mental difficulties and do so over longer periods of their lives than members of the other professions. This may be so but, in Michael's case, art has helped him to recover.

Michael Alzamora's paintings and text about art and schizophrenia can be seen on the Internet at http://www3.sympatico.ca/michael.alzamora and his work "Light Headed Dancers" is the frontispiece of this book. This talented artist was born in Bogotá, Colombia in 1964. His earliest memories are of mountains and the cloud formations perched over the mountains of his native city. But the beautiful surroundings of Bogotá remain associated in his mind with crime-ridden, fear-inspiring streets. The duality of beauty and fear informs his paintings.

With his mother and elder brother, Michael immigrated to Toronto in 1975, at the age of ten. He began painting in 1994; it was initially a form of therapy. He has struggled with schizophrenia for a very long time but now considers himself essentially recovered, in large part due to his art. His life, he will tell you, is in good shape.

Michael is of the opinion that people do not understand schizophrenia and that such misunderstanding leads to stigma. Many still seem to think of schizophrenia as a form of multiple personality. He would like to be a spokesman for people with schizophrenia because many of his friends with the same diagnosis are unable or unwilling to speak out.

When talking about his recovery, he stresses the importance of early treatment.

When I first became ill in 1987, my doctor said: "Look Mike, you have to go to a hospital, you are very ill." I didn't listen to her, I didn't want to give up going to school – I was in Seneca College, a three year electronic technology program – "No, no, I'll take therapy and medication, but I'm not giving up school," I said. Terrible mistake. If you go to early treatment intervention, the doctors, with therapy and medication, can curtail the frightening thoughts. In my case, the delusions decided to become more elaborate and believable inside my mind. I kept on making things up that I thought were going on with me. Early treatment stops that kind of thinking from starting. Very, very, important. In fact, Dr. Zipursky at CAMH has an early intervention program going that's helping a lot of people.

When asked about interactions with people, Michael responds that his art has really helped him make conversation. He can talk for hours about art whereas, before becoming a serious artist, he felt as if he had nothing interesting to say. All he could focus on was the pain he was going through – the torture of living with delusions. Not only was he ill, but he was noticeably ill. He was taking medications that made him twitch and stutter and move his arms without wanting to, a form of tardive dyskinesia. People would notice and would think he was odd. Now he takes one of the newer drugs. Not only does it work better but the twitches and stutters are gone. Drug-induced tardive dyskinesia (TD) affects approximately 20% to 30% of patients with schizophrenia. Usually it is mild, but it can be severe, as it was in Michael, in 1% to 8% of patients. The antipsychotics used today are less likely to induce TD than older drugs did. Michael takes clozapine, one of the newer antipsychotics, and that has made his TD disappear.

In the early days of illness, Michael felt all alone, rejected by society and tortured by illness. His self-esteem plummeted and he became depressed. He describes himself at that period as very down, with no ambition and lacking drive. Nowadays, this has all changed. Now he feels on an equal footing with everybody else; people are starting to admire his art. That makes him feel that he has a profession like everyone else.

Michael was first drawn into the art world when he was hospitalized in the early 1990s. He had finally agreed with his doctor that he needed to be in hospital. Art therapy was part of his treatment. He started with ceramics; then went on to drawing and painting. He loved it so much and was so naturally good at it that he kept it up on his own, his technique constantly improving. It took about ten years for him to develop his signature style but, now, many people who have seen his work recognize an Alzamora painting instantly. He is no longer frightened to approach the galleries. He feels that Toronto is the Mecca for contemporary art in Canada and he considers himself lucky to live there.

He is also lucky in being part of a very supportive family – his mother, his brother, Eduardo, his sister-in-law, Suzanna, his six-year old nephew and baby niece and nephew (who are twins).

They are a little tough on me but are very supportive. A lot of times, a family with a person with mental illness treats that person very gently, but my mother gets on my case and notices if anything is wrong. She makes sure I iron my shirt, clip my nails, shave, and keep my apartment clean. They are very tough on me, but, in a way, that helps me because it gives me, to use an expression, almost a "stealth existence" where people don't notice that I'm different from anyone else. I look normal. It was my family who encouraged me to get out of the house and find work.

Since 1997, Michael has been working part time at the Schizophrenia Society of Ontario, Toronto Chapter. He usually works one day a week. He feels that his illness has made him a fighter. At first, being ill undermined his self-esteem but now, paradoxically, he feels it has made him strong. Now he feels driven to get ahead and not to give up and not to let the illness "take a hold of me." He has become less shy, more assertive. He goes to galleries and conducts his business, all by myself. He has designed his own website; he has taught himself computer skills. He recognizes that it is a paradox to feel that schizophrenia, an illness that can be so debilitating, has actually made him stronger. He attributes this to a good support system, a good doctor, a family that is tough but caring. He feels all this has helped him develop a thick skin.

Michael has also developed a belief system that sees him through the hard times. Essentially it is a belief in himself and his ability to weather storms. Whenever he is feeling down, he says to himself; "Wait a second; I've lived through my illness, so I can live through this. I now know that *every problem has a solution*. That's my belief."

His worst memories are the times he was in hospital and the group home experiences he lived through. His worries are that, no matter how well he has recovered, the stigma attached to his type of illness will always interfere with relationships, especially intimate ones. He worries that he may never get married and that, in this way, his life will never be complete.

Michael counsels people not to fear mental illness. "Mental illnesses are all around us. No one is invincible. Everyone is vulnerable; no one is immune. But it's not something to be feared. It's something to be overcome." Because he works at the Schizophrenia Society of Canada, Michael is very well informed about resources, especially in Toronto. He advises everyone to stay informed – about clinical services, housing alternatives, recreational choices, employment options. He is a proponent of psychotherapy.

> Most people with schizophrenia are mentally alert enough to benefit from psychotherapy. Do you remember the movie "A Beautiful Mind"? Remember when Dr. Nash sees the little girl and realizes, "she's a hallucination because every time I see her she never ages." Doctors can help patients see things realistically by exploring beliefs that that don't hang together. Doctors need to be guides. Comprehensive treatment is key because it includes medication, psychotherapy, and community rehabilitation. In Ontario, we have teams that are multidisciplinary and they help the patient live in the community, even helping with legal issues.

Through his association with the Schizophrenia Society, Michael is also familiar with how schizophrenia is treated in other parts of the world. He feels that the public is totally misinformed in some corners of the world and treats sufferers as if they were possessed by devils. He also knows of a place in Europe where, instead of hospitalization, families adopt those with schizophrenia and welcome them into their home and help them become fully functional members of the community. He thinks Canada does relatively well vis à vis other countries. He rates the Canadian mental health system high, giving it a ten out of ten. The general public, though, needs to catch up. If he were in charge, Michael would put resources into films and print media in order to combat the stigma of mental illness. He would encourage people to be mental health volunteers, to meet individuals with mental illness face to face and really get to know them. He would pour funds into research, into community organizations, and he would make it more profitable for pharmaceutical companies to produce psychiatric drugs. He feels that most of the research effort goes toward pharmaceuticals for cancer, and heart and stroke and that psychiatric diseases are, by comparison, poor cousins.

Michael believes in role models and one person he especially admires is the Lieutenant Governor of Ontario, The Honorable James K. Bartleman, an advocate for the mentally ill, a patron of the Schizophrenia Society of Ontario and the Canadian Psychiatric Research Foundation.

James Bartleman, born in 1939, is a member of the Mjnikaning First Nation. After receiving his BA in history from the University of Western Ontario, he joined the Foreign Service where he was considered exceptionally proficient. Nevertheless, James Bartleman has lived with depression and knows how it feels to not want to live. Writing about his experiences has helped him to recover. Mr. Bartleman's first book, *Out of Muskoka*, is a memoir of his early life and his struggles with poverty, adversity, and depression. The proceeds of his second book, *On Six Continents*, support the Munk Centre for International Studies, because, among other things, this centre hosts public lectures on topics concerning mental health.

In an address to the Canadian Mental Health Association in November, 2002, the Hon. James K. Bartleman said the following:

> The decision to seek professional help for depression is a difficult one, because our society has done little to understand and accept those with mental illness. Although as many as three million Canadians suffer from depression, social stigma prevents many from seeking treatment.
>
> It is estimated that as many as two-thirds of all people with mental illness do not seek treatment, largely because of the stigma associated with ......mental disorder. This is a shameful statistic, especially when advances in medical research have made treatment increasingly effective ....there is still a long way to go before we will see the stigma of mental illness wiped out.
>
> For this to happen, people need to accept that mental illness is one of the most common ailments in our society today. As many as one in every five Canadians will have some type of mental health problem at least once in their lives. And whether they realize it or not, every Canadian knows someone who has been, or will be, affected by mental illness.

In an address to the Hong Fook Mental Health Association, in September 2002, Mr. Bartleman said:

… there is the belief that mental illness is the sign of a character flaw. Or that mental illness is a single, rare disorder. Or that people with depression can just snap out of it or pull themselves together.

Those are the myths, but the facts tell a different story. It is a fact that mental disorders are not character flaws but are legitimate illnesses. It is a fact that there are many mental disorders, including anxiety, depression, schizophrenia, personality disorders, eating disorders, and organic brain disorders. And it is a fact that, while mentally ill people can play a large part in their own recovery, they do not choose to become ill and so cannot snap out of it. And yet, these facts are so much harder to disseminate than the mythology.

Mental health is high on Mr. Bartleman's list of priorities. Besides the Schizophrenia Society of Ontario and the Canadian Psychiatric Research Foundation, he is also a patron of the Autism Society Ontario, the Canadian Mental Health Association (Ontario), the Centre for Addiction and Mental Health, the Hincks-Dellcrest Centre, the Integra Foundation, Kerry's Place Autism Services, the Mood Disorders Association of Ontario, and Moods Magazine.

James Bartleman is Michael Alzamora's hero. Michael wants to be not only a well-known artist but also a role model for Canadians who battle psychiatric disease, just like the Lieutenant Governor of Ontario. His illness may have originally fueled his art but his wellness has readied him for further challenges.

Further Reading

Jamison KR. Touched with Fire: Manic Depressive Illness and the Artistic Temperament. New York: Simon and Schuster; 1993.

Lauronen E, Veijola J, Isohanni I, Jones PB, Nieminen P, Isohanni M. Links between creativity and mental disorder. Psychiatry. 2004;67:81–98.

Louza MR, Bassitt DP. Maintenance treatment of severe tardive dyskinesia with clozapine: 5 years follow-up. J Clin Psychopharmacol. 2005;25:180–182.

Paulson GW. Historical comments on tardive dyskinesia: a neurologist's perspective. J Clin Psychiatry. 2005;66:260–264.

Chapter 19

Chair in Schizophrenia Research: Don Tapscott and Ana Lopes

"Some regard private enterprise as if it were a predatory tiger to be shot. Others look upon it as a cow that they can milk. Only a handful see it for what it really is – the strong horse that pulls the whole cart."
Winston Churchill

Mental health problems cost North Americans $80 million (US) a year. Two-thirds of the cost is due to diminished productivity in the workplace. For instance, an estimated 13% of net annual operating profits of all businesses in Canada is compromised by mental health problems. Mindful of opportunities lost, Don Tapscott, authority on business strategy, and his wife Ana Lopes, endow a University Chair in Schizophrenia Research.

The Tapscott Chair in Schizophrenia Studies, currently occupied by the same Dr. Robert Zipursky mentioned in the preceding chapter, was endowed by Don Tapscott and Ana Lopes and named, in the words of Don Tapscott, "in memory of my brother Dave and in honor of our parents Don and Mary Tapscott who worked tirelessly for 15 years to keep Dave healthy."

My brother Dave, two years younger than me, became ill in the early 1970s. We'll never know the real diagnosis – at the time, he was diagnosed as drug-induced schizophrenia. Dave was a bright and kind person, a contract bridge master and a talented pianist and oboe player. He was funny and fun to be with and we all, as a family, had so many great times together. Despite early symptoms, Dave graduated from Trent University – a good place for him to be because the emphasis on student-centered learning didn't allow him to get lost in the crowd. But after a 15-year battle with disease, he gave up – dying under circumstances suggestive of suicide.

Don Tapscott is an internationally known authority on business strategy and methods of transforming organizations to keep them in pace with changing technology. The Washington Technology Report has called him "one of the most influential media authorities since Marshall McLuhan." He is President of New Paradigm Learning Corporation, which he founded in 1992, and Adjunct Professor of Management, Joseph L. Rotman School of Management, University of Toronto.

He is also the author or co-author of ten widely read books on the application of technology to business (See Further Reading). His wife, Ana Lopes, is his partner and the founder of Saralex Communications in 1995. Her interest in communications came after a ten-year career in government and a subsequent stint as Executive Assistant to Premier Bob Rae of Ontario between 1992 and 1995. Ms. Lopes is one of Ontario's quarter million Portuguese-speaking Canadians and a community leader. She established the first linguistically sensitive counseling service for Portuguese women and children in crisis. She is actively involved in raising money for the Chair in Women's Mental Health at the University of Toronto, a Chair currently occupied by Dr. Sarah Romans and named after the late, brilliant Toronto lawyer, Shirley Brown.

> Shirley Alexandra Brown was a successful corporate and commercial lawyer at Blake, Cassels, and Graydon. She was the gold medalist of her graduating class at Branksome Hall and, later, of her graduating class at the University of Toronto Law School. Active in the community, she served for several years on the board of Nellie's, a shelter for women and children. In the fall of 1996, while in the midst of a severe clinical depression, Shirley began to feel that she could not live up to her high standard of excellence. At the age of 39, and in the midst of the most productive period of her career, she took her own life. The Chair was established by her family and friends in an effort to better understand the intersection between gender and mental illness.

Ms. Lopes is also a Director of the Sunnybrook and Women's Foundation and its Vice-Chair of Fundraising, Director and member of the Executive Committee of the Toronto Symphony Orchestra and on the Board of Governors of Trent University. Ms. Lopes and Mr. Tapscott have two children, both presently attending university. Despite their very busy lives, Don and Ana are deeply committed to the cause of mental health. Don is a former member of the Board of Trustees at the Clarke Institute of Psychiatry and was Chair of the Centred on Hope Campaign for the Centre for Addiction and Mental Health Foundation. He is a founding member of the Committee of Advisers of the Business and Economic Roundtable on Addiction and Mental Health. Before he became interested in technology and business, Don Tapscott actually began his career as a psychometrist; he later became a psychologist. His first job after graduating in psychology in 1970 was at the Penetanguishene Mental Health Centre in the Oak Ridge Division for the so-called "criminally insane." (See Chapter 6). "I remember touring the now closed basement rooms – essentially dungeons, complete with metal shackles on the walls to restrain and punish difficult patients." Don wants to dispel a destructive and widely held myth about mental illness: "There is a pernicious notion that mental illness is somehow a flaw or failure in a person's character, rather than a treatable disease. As a society we pay a very heavy price for this false perception." He calls the stigma of mental illness the greatest roadblock to advancement in finding treatment for diseases of the brain. He is quick to point out some of the statistics:

- According to the landmark Global Burden of Disease study, commissioned by the World Health Organization and the World Bank, four of the ten leading causes of disability for persons aged five and older are mental disorders.
- Among developed nations, mental illness is the leading cause of disability.
- Mental disorders contribute to mortality, with suicide perennially representing one of the leading preventable causes of death worldwide.
- In Canada, 300,000 people will be diagnosed with schizophrenia alone at some point in their lives.
- Schizophrenia accounts for one of every 12 hospital beds in our country – more than any other medical condition.
- Four of ten schizophrenia victims attempt suicide.
- No one is immune. Most victims come from families with no history of the disease.

In 2000, Don Tapscott was the keynote speaker at the Canadian Psychiatric Research Foundation annual awards luncheon. He gave an inspiring talk during which he imagined what life would have been like for his brother, Dave, at various times in history.

If Dave had become psychotic circa 1900, he would have been placed in an asylum – likely the Toronto Lunatic Asylum – a horrific setting of chronic illness, isolated from the mainstream of medicine and society. He would have spent his life there under nightmarish conditions. If he did not somehow recover spontaneously, his incarceration would have been life-long. Circa 1950, Dave would probably have been sent to one of the Ontario Provincial Hospitals. If he were lucky, he could have gone to the tiny Toronto Psychiatric Hospital founded by Dr. C.K. Clarke. While barbiturates were used widely to sedate patients, there were no antipsychotic drugs at the time. In the U.S. and Canada, the main focus of investigation and treatment of mental illness was psychotherapy.

In a wonderful book entitled *A History of Psychiatry*, Toronto's Dr. Edward Shorter writes that, at mid-twentieth century, psychiatry became enraptured with the notion that psychological problems arose out of unconscious conflicts over long past events, especially those of a sexual nature. For several decades, psychiatrists were glad to adopt this theory of illness, he writes, especially because it gave them a way out of the asylum and into private practice, a higher income, and a little social respect. Later in the 1950s, electroconvulsive therapy (ECT) came to be used as an effective treatment. Although portrayed as inhumane in popular culture (Jack Nicolson in "One Flew over the Cuckoo's Nest") ECT has brought symptomatic relief to many suffering from depression and psychosis. By 1970, when Dave did become ill, science had overtaken Freud and mental illness had returned to the fold of other medical specialties. Drug therapy was the treatment of choice for psychosis, based on early systematic experimentation into the chemistry of the brain. Researchers investigated the pathology of neurotransmitters like dopamine – the chemicals that transmit the nerve impulse from one neuron to another across a gap or synapse. (See Chapter 13) The big breakthrough had occurred earlier with the invention of chlorpromazine – the first drug to eliminate the symptoms of psychosis, though not necessarily curing the underlying brain disorder. According to Shorter, chlorpromazine initiated a revolution in psychiatry comparable to the introduction of penicillin in general medicine.

But my brother wasn't a big beneficiary. After his first psychotic attacks, we tried to get him into the Clarke but it was full. At 11 p.m. one winter night he ended up in a general hospital in Toronto that was visited, infrequently, by psychiatric professionals. Various new medications were tried, but in hindsight the doses given to him were likely 5–10 times greater than necessary. Such overdoses caused terrible side-effects for him and so he didn't stick with them. As he told me one day, "when I'm off the drugs I might feel crazy but that's better than feeling pulverized."

Now let's consider the present situation. What if Dave were in his early 20s and today became ill? Things would be very different for him. If he were fortunate and lived in a handful of cities like Halifax, London or Calgary he would be admitted into the first episode psychosis clinic of a hospital. In Toronto, where Dave lived, this would be the Centre for Addiction and Mental Health. Clinicians now know that early intervention is critical – and that with it most people can have an effective remission. And with appropriate long-term treatment, there is no reason for many people to have a relapse. A multidisciplinary team of medical, psychiatric, and psychological personnel would conduct an extensive evaluation into the nature and causes of his illness. For starters, one would have much more faith in the correctness of the diagnosis. Was it schizophrenia? Or was Dave the victim of a psychotic depression? Or was he psychotic because of his use of amphetamines?

Diagnosis in mental illness and, for that matter, in all of medicine, is important because it is the basis of effective therapy and prognosis. There has been tremendous progress in the standardization of psychiatric diagnoses since 1970 and this is an important factor in effective treatments for specific psychiatric illnesses. Systematic and reliable approaches to diagnosis have facilitated the development of an evidence base on which current psychiatric treatments are founded. A correct diagnosis would enable the development of an optimal treatment plan, without the trial and error techniques of the 1970s.

A second multidisciplinary team consisting of medical, social work, and occupational therapy professionals would be available to meet his needs and orchestrate his integration back into the community. In the 1970s, community integration meant sending people to the street or to unsupported families who had little chance of coping with the illness. Today there is a much greater appreciation that people need to be engaged on their own terms and treated in a comprehensive way that meets their complete individual needs.

But, by most accounts, even this year 2000 scenario – available to a small proportion of Canadians – pales in comparison to the improvements in the care of people with other diseases. A new patient at the Princess Margaret or Sick Kids has access to resources and a level of care that is almost infinitely better. Even today.

Now flash forward to 2010. We have learned more about the brain in the last decade than in all of human history. I am optimistic we could make far more progress in the next few years. Someday in the not-to-distant future the following scenario will occur. Someone like Dave would simply never have a first episode. His illness would be diagnosed and prevented before it became manifest.

Current medications really only treat the psychotic symptoms (paranoid thinking and hallucinations). They don't in any way address the underlying abnormalities in the brain (caused by obstetrical trauma, genetic abnormality, or other factors) that appear to develop during adolescence or earlier. Soon, there could be ways to help the brain follow a more normal developmental course. For example, there is a theory that schizophrenia results from excessive elimination of nerve synapses (connections between nerve cells) during adolescence compared to the rate of elimination seen in healthy individuals. If this turned out to be true, then it might be possible to develop medications that would slow this process down to a normal rate. Along the same lines, if schizophrenia is due to reduced functioning of inhibitory neurons in the brain, there may be medications that could enhance inhibitory function and prevent the emergence of psychotic symptoms.

In another future scenario, the evaluation of a blood sample after birth would identify a genetic predisposition to brain disease; or a vulnerability to amphetamine-induced psychosis or some other pathology and an effective preventative treatment would be implemented. This might involve some kind of gene therapy by which some genes could be modified to insure that a critical step in the development of schizophrenia does not take place. It might involve advising against exposure to particular forms of substance abuse.

Or perhaps in his early teens Dave's GP, or a teacher or parent would identify pre-symptom evidence that he was having trouble coping – which we know today is often an advance warning of the onset of illness. A full preventative program could be implemented and Dave would have a great shot at a happy and fulfilling life, just like the rest of us.

Don Tapscott told his audience that the future was not something to be predicted but something to be achieved. He pointed out that achieving it means funding it and, right now, mental illness is not attracting sufficient funding. He wants to understand why.

Why have we been capable of marshalling the resources of society to attack other diseases but not those of the brain? To say the brain is more complicated is too easy. I believe we are paralyzed by an all-pervasive stigma that goes back centuries. We fear what we don't understand. And fear gets in the way of doing the right thing. Perhaps we reject people whose behavior is outside the norm. Perhaps the people with diseases of the brain are disorganized, and almost by definition can't lobby for themselves. Because these diseases often strike early in life, victims have no adult children, as in the case with many other diseases, to fight for them – to raise funds for research and to provide proper care. Stigmas die hard. I'm told of cases in Canada and the United States where wealthy parents have offspring tormented by mental illness, yet they turn around and bequeath their sizeable estates to an art museum or other charity rather than to combat psychiatric illnesses.

Perhaps the term mental illness is itself a misnomer – a throwback to the days when scientists thought there was a mind-body distinction. It was not Dave's mind that needed effective treatment, it was the biochemistry of his brain. He didn't need mental help – he needed a healthy brain free from disease, no less than he needed a healthy heart. He did not have a failing of his mind, or personality or character; he had a failing of his brain.

Don Tapscott, speaking in December 2000, reminded his audience that the brain was no longer viewed as the backwoods of medicine, but its vanguard. On October 9, 2000 the Nobel Prize in Medicine was given to three brain researchers – two molecular biologists and a psychiatrist – for pioneering discoveries into how disturbances in signal transduction inside nerve cells can give rise to neurological and psychiatric diseases.

This work has already led to the development of important new drug treatments. The widespread popularity of Prozac has begun to make it acceptable to discuss depression. Many people have begun to tell their personal stories of mental problems and to help change public perceptions. I cannot overstate how important these initiatives are. Consider, for example, the courageous Michael Wilson who lost his son Cameron to illness (please see Chapter 24). Under his leadership, the Centre for Addiction and Mental Health raised an unprecedented $12 million. The value of Michael Wilson's work goes beyond just the money. He is helping create a climate where diseases of the brain can be discussed openly. We need a sea change in the public perception of these illnesses. Let's stop whispering about mental health. Let's start talking loudly and often. And there is a role in these discussions for every individual and every institution in this country. Governments, businesses, community groups, unions, and not-for-profits should all participate. Governments at all levels need to provide the kind of leadership they have shown in mobilizing support to combat HIV and AIDS.

I spoke earlier of the Blair government in the United Kingdom, which is doing great work to raise the profile of diseases of the brain. The government recently committed more than $1.5 billion in new funding for research and treatment of mental illness. In establishing goals for the national health care system, the government gave mental illness the same priority – which is to say top priority – as coronary heart disease. The government has established clear benchmarks of success, such as a 20 per cent drop in the national suicide rate within a decade.

In the United States, the first ever White House Conference on Mental Health in 1999 called for a national anti-stigma campaign. And the first ever Surgeon General's Report on Mental Health noted that nearly half of all Americans who have a severe mental illness do not seek treatment. Most often, the reluctance to seek care is a direct result of the stigma.

Today we have nowhere near the proper level of funding. Research into schizophrenia, depression, bipolar disorders, and other psychiatric disorders has been maintained at a paltry level compared to other major disease groups, such as cancer, heart disease, stroke, AIDS, or Alzheimer's. Quantum leaps in understanding illnesses of the brain will only come if funding is brought up to the level available for the study of these other diseases. If we are really serious about addressing these problems, then funding has to be brought even higher so that the most capable scientists will gravitate to this research area as has been done in the case of AIDS research. There is simply no excuse for the meager number of research dollars currently made available.

Perhaps government funding suffers from the stigma of mental illness. The false assumptions that are always made about mental illness being a personal weakness have tainted government policy on whether research could help understand these illnesses. Our political decision makers simply don't believe that mental illnesses are as preventable, treatable or curable as diseases that attack other parts of the body. But they are. And since these illnesses arise from dysfunction of the most complicated part of the human body – the brain – enormous research efforts will be required to advance our knowledge.

Speaking as a management guru, Don Tapscott understands that mental health is the responsibility not only of government. Private companies need to appreciate that mental illness is not just a social or ethical challenge but also a business one. The Canadian Business and Economic Roundtable for Mental Health, initiated by Bill Wilkerson, estimates that Canadian businesses could save up to $7 billion over five years in prescription drugs and wage replacement costs if even one half of their employees who needed help for depression actually received it. Business cannot call for tax cuts on the one hand and ignore its responsibilities to shoulder the cost of social needs on the other.

What are the Business Stakes in Mental Health?
Don Tapscott

Mental disability is a business cost.

In Canada alone, all forms of mental illness costs the country $16 billion a year, which represents about 14 per cent of the net operating revenue of all Canadian businesses combined.

The Royal Bank Financial estimates that more than a third of all short-term disability stems from mental health problems.

It is foreseen that the percentage of disability insurance and group health claims related to mental health will climb to more than 60 per cent of the total number of claims administered through business-employee plans over the next three to five years.

The average number of workdays lost to one case of depression is about forty, or $10,000 per absent employee for wage replacements and the company's share of drug therapies under a group health benefit plan.

Depression is projected to be the leading source of work years lost through disability and premature death in developed economies by the year 2020.

The societal and economic costs of mental illness and chemical dependencies are three times the actual cost of treatment.

The next generation will be under even greater pressure, facing an uncertain, competitive and dangerous world – academic pressure, information overload, choices, broken homes, downsizing, recession, terrorism, war.

This is Tapscott's advice to employers:

> Think of employees as investors of their intellectual capital. Is your company a good investment for them? Will you work to keep them creative, stress-free, and promptly treated if they develop signs of mental illness? Brains – the new capital – need to be treated at least as well as we treated the capital of money or machines of industrial capitalism. Let's take the same approach to our employ-

ees' mental well-being as we do to their physical well-being. We run workplace health and safety campaigns to cut down on the number of injuries. We put out big yellow caution signs when the floor is wet and slippery. Yet when it comes to creating a healthy workplace for the most important employee asset of all, as a country, we often do little.

Tapscott believes that the antidote for ignorance is knowledge and that the Internet is the right tool for demolishing stigma.

As a stellar example of what can be done, a number of individuals and companies came together to create the "Open the Doors" Campaign and teamed up with the World Psychiatric Association – closerlook, Inc. (www.closerlook.com). For the last four and a half years, closerlook, Inc. has been working to fight the stigma and discrimination associated with schizophrenia. To date, the program has been initiated in 14 countries, including Canada, Spain, Austria, Egypt, Italy, India, and Brazil. A key component of the program is the website www.openthe-doors.com where program participants can access the truth. Measurable results have been achieved in the countries where the program was pilot tested. These results included: changing admission procedures for emergency rooms nationally in Canada and changes in knowledge and attitudes among high school students in Canada and Spain.

This is a great initiative harnessing the power of the Net. I'm an admirer of the French novelist and philosopher Victor Hugo, who said: "There is nothing so powerful as an idea whose time has come." Perhaps the time has finally come for a fundamental change in public attitudes about brain disorders. The time has come for another $12 million and $120 million and $1.2 billion to give the resources our brilliant researchers urgently need to understand the real causes of illness and develop truly effective prevention and treatment programs. And hopefully the time has come for each of us to redouble our energies to make that future scenario for the young Daves of the world a reality.

Further Reading

Cavoukian A. Tapscott D. Who knows: safeguarding your privacy in a networked world. New York: McGraw-Hill; 1997.

Robinson M, Tapscott D, Kalakota R. e-Business 2.0: roadmap for success. Upper Saddle River, NJ: Addison-Wesley Pub. Co.; 1999.

Tapscott D, Caston A. Paradigm shift: the new promise of information technology. New York: McGraw-Hill; 1992.

Tapscott D. The digital economy: promise and peril in the age of networked intelligence. New York: McGraw-Hill; 1996.

Tapscott D. Growing up digital: the rise of the Net generation. New York: McGraw-Hill; 1997. Available at: http://newparadigm.com/books.php

Tapscott D., editor. Creating value in the network economy. Boston: Harvard Business School Press; 1999.

Tapscott D, Ticoll D. The naked corporation: how the age of transparency will revolutionize business, Free Press, October 2003.

Tapscott D, Ticoll D, Lowy A. Digital capital: harnessing the power of business webs. Boston: Harvard Business School Press; 2000.

Tapscott D, Ticoll D, Lowy A, Klym N, editors. Blueprint to the digital economy: wealth creation in the era of e-business. New York: McGraw-Hill; 1998.

Chapter 20

Coast Foundation Society: The Story of Ross Taylor

"It is not the strongest of the species who survive, not the most intelligent, but those who are the most adaptive to change."
Charles Darwin

The etymology of "chiropractics" and "surgery" comes from the name, Chiron, the centaur poisoned by the arrow of Hercules who learned first hand about pain. Doomed to suffer, he became a great healer, the prototype of the wounded healer. As illustrated by the story of Ross Taylor from Vancouver, personal hurts attune a person to the pain of others.

Ross Taylor is a Resource Development Associate with the Coast Foundation Society in Vancouver, B.C. He fund raises for Coast's community mental health services and can be described as a wounded healer.

Coast Foundation Society began in 1972 to serve patients on the point of being discharged from long-term psychiatric facilities. It began as a small activity centre with its own bus service that transported former inpatients from their new boarding homes to the centre. Coast was recreated and incorporated in 1974 when it purchased a staff-supported 24-unit apartment block to house former psychiatric patients.

Since the beginning, Coast's mission has been to promote recovery from mental illness. Today it provides high quality housing, employment programs, basic supports for the poor and homeless and other psychosocial rehabilitation opportunities for people with serious and persistent mental illnesses

Currently, Coast houses 540 people. Its credo is that, without decent housing, other rehabilitation efforts are stymied – recovery starts with a home of one's own, a special challenge in Vancouver where housing costs are higher than anywhere else in Canada. As homelessness, addictions, and poverty have increased in Vancouver, more and more people are coming to Coast for support.

Coast also provides employment opportunities. A landscaping business that hires consumers is one example. Coast has over 200 employees in 30 different work sites. It serves over 2,000 clients a year and has an operating budget of $13 million.

Coast employee Ross Taylor reports personal psychiatric problems dating from the early 1980s when he was a teenager. He describes religious experiences that led him to believe that the end of the world was coming. He lived through periods of what he calls "incredible elation and grandiose dreams" and also periods of great sadness "where I felt like crying all the time. I had no idea what was going on and was never able to discuss these things with others." He slowly came to the realization that he was gay. And that he was an alcoholic.

> I was withdrawn but, when drinking, became argumentative and angry. A lot of people have said that I appeared aloof and arrogant. I was very isolated and many people at school saw me as the intelligent student (I was in gifted programs) who smoked cigarettes, was stoned all the time, and skipped school a lot. Even at home I was isolated, my bedroom was in the basement and I usually missed dinner as I would get stoned at lunch and my family could not wake me up. Most of my report cards said "good work but you can do way better."

He finally told his family that he believed God wanted him to drop out of high school. Speaking of that period, Mr. Taylor says:

> I was suicidal. I had used drugs daily for a period of years, I suffered blackouts when I was drunk. I realized that I was an alcoholic and went to self-help groups to try and gain control of my addiction. I was involved in psychological counseling and saw my general practitioner for counseling as well, but I was not diagnosed with a mental illness by anyone I saw. Most discussions revolved around my homosexuality.

It is now thought that lesbian and gay youth experience higher rates of major depression, generalized anxiety disorder and substance use or dependence than straight youth and that discrimination may help to fuel these higher rates. Lesbian, gay, and bisexual teenagers report high levels of peer harassment in high school.

> It took me seven years to finish high school and my final two years were in an independent study program. I worked about 20 hours a week as a lifeguard, lived at home, stayed sober, attended church regularly and went to support groups. I still had periods of depression and planned a number of suicide attempts and spent a lot of time alone. A number of times I would talk to myself out loud around

strangers when my mind was racing and I thought that God had some great mission and purpose for me in life. I would fantasize about being interviewed on television and being famous and thought that I would be a Prime Minister or a Billy Graham.

Most of my friends were people from support groups. And then I also met people from a church summer camp I worked at and developed some close friends. I got involved with the church's young people's group and had a stable period for a time. I went to a private Christian liberal arts school but, in my third year, I became depressed, withdrawn, wanting to drop out of school, started smoking again and eventually started drinking. In my fourth year of school I hardly slept, lost lots of weight and drank on the weekends.

Rates of alcohol use differ in different countries – see Chapter 16. In Canada, they are highest among men, younger people, and those with higher incomes and education. Rates vary among the provinces, from a low of 59% in Newfoundland and Labrador to a high of 78% in Alberta. Approximately 50% of individuals who have a mental illness also have problems related to the misuse of drugs and alcohol and, conversely, 50% of those with alcohol and drug dependency suffer from a mental illness. Aware of these statistics, the Coast Foundation offers three levels of staff training in concurrent disorders. For clients, Coast provides a program called Clean Start that includes educational and support groups, a Healing Circle facilitated by Hey Way Noqu Aboriginal Services Society, individual appointments with staff and monthly educational presentations by service providers. Coast has supported the development of Dual Diagnosis Anonymous (DDA) – a 12-step peer support program for people with an addiction issue and a mental illness. Currently there are six DDA meeting places in the Lower Mainland of Vancouver.

Mr. Taylor recalls:

I had periods of sobriety in my life ranging from six months to almost three years. During both the periods of sobriety and of active alcoholism, I experienced bouts of great sadness, fatigue, elation, and delusions. I saw a psychologist and at one point an addiction counselor and talked about drinking and other problems, but nothing really related to my mood disorder. Around every new project at work, every new relationship or a breaking news story in the media, I always imagined myself doing great things. After the 1995 referendum in Quebec I thought I had to save the country and designed a concept to have a great Canadian history test with a million dollar prize. When my company was doing a presentation for a client in Calgary, I thought that God was sending me there to run against Preston Manning in the next election.

In 1996 I transferred to Vancouver with my company with the intent to just drink and party and then kill myself when I got fired. To my surprise, I got a new job in 1997 in fundraising but still had the same plan to drink and die. Sometime in 1997, I heard a speech from the President of the institution I worked for and conceived grandiose concepts for the future again. My mind raced, I had a thousand ideas, talked all the time to myself out loud in public, and got nothing accomplished. I usually went to the bar right after work and often would be up the whole night. If I wasn't at a bar, I was at work or sleeping.

In early 1998, I still had racing thoughts and grandiose ideas, walked for miles even in the rain and was still drinking. Then I had a panic attack at work one Saturday and went to a hospital emergency room the next day. The psychiatrist asked me if I wanted to go to detox or go in the hospital but I was too scared to do either. He gave me some Ativan. I went on sick leave from work. I had been drinking heavily and was paranoid and delusional. I thought at work that they engaged in non-confrontational intervention and that I had a great benefactor who had been helping me get through life. I thought I was being followed and that everything around me meant something – an ambulance meant that they were going to take me away – an overheard snippet of conversation was a scripted message.

I eventually stopped drinking, met with an Employment Assistance Counselor who referred me to a doctor; I attended self-help groups and got sober. I had a high level of energy because I wanted to go back to work and implement my grand plans. To stay sober, I followed the basic approach: ask for help from a higher power in the morning to stay sober, don't drink, go to support group meetings and just focus on getting to bed each night without drinking. I went to two or three meetings a day. The EAP Counselor and the GP wanted me to go to addiction treatment but I had no money as my credit cards were all maxed out and I was living from pay cheque to pay cheque. I really did not want to go as the thought of treatment scared me.

I had heard people at meetings talk about getting addicted to prescription drugs so I flushed the Ativan down the toilet. I felt weak taking pills anyway and usually was reluctant to take anything even when I had a cold or a headache.
I returned to work after six weeks. My work clothes did not fit as I had gone from about 180lbs to 155lbs. At work I felt very uncomfortable. I thought my phone was bugged, my e-mails read, and that everybody I spoke to was scripted. Everything seemed staged and surreal. I told one of the PhD students whose office was across from mine that I thought three Vice-Presidents did not want me to succeed and were plotting against me. I broke down in tears one time and called the Employment Assistance Program line and then snapped out of it when someone knocked on my door. I went to my GP and told him that people were trying to get me but I did not explain the extent of the paranoia or delusions. He thought that I should just look for other work.

When sick leave and short term Employment Insurance ran out, my roommate helped me sell or get rid of my limited belongings and he let me sleep on his couch in his new apartment. I stopped all contact with friends, family, doctors, and self-help groups. For months I did nothing but sleep, walk around at night longing to die. I planned to kill myself, wrote a note, but did not follow through.

In early 1999 my friend took me to the GP and he gave me an anti-depressant called Zoloft, identified me as catatonic and sent me for an assessment. The psychiatrist formally diagnosed me with depression.

My friend also helped me apply for welfare. I declared bankruptcy, got on welfare, the GP filled out the forms and I was quickly put on disability benefits. I think it took about three weeks. I really did not want to get well. I did not take my medication regularly.

My GP met with me each week and referred me to an outpatient program for people with concurrent disorders. It was a drop-in intake process and it took months before I went. My friend used to yell at me to get up and get on with it. I did finally go, filled out the forms and was re-assessed again by a psychiatrist and an occupational therapist.

This time I was diagnosed with depression and obsessive-compulsive personality disorder. I dragged my feet about getting into a group program after the first introductory sessions. When I attended the day program, I hated it. The psychiatrist seemed hostile and I felt very uncomfortable talking about my emotions. I was put on 400 mg of Zoloft and other medications such as buspirone and trazadone. I became psychotic and thought all the members of the group were actors and that everything was scripted. I used to walk down the street with my fingers in my ears and hum to myself so I could not hear what others were saying. In group, I never talked about those things but felt defensive most of the time. I had an angry outburst one day and I blacked out and then remember running down the stairs to get out of the therapy room.

I told my friend that I knew what they were up to and he asked what I was talking about. I told him I knew a film company was organizing all the people and cars and conversations around me. I was trying to figure out the pattern of car doors slamming, fire engine sirens, people wearing backpacks and the conversation of people on the street. I quit the group and met with my occupational therapist. I had another angry blackout and the psychiatrist called me at home and put me on an antipsychotic. I can't remember the name of it but, when I took it, I had to move all the time for about two hours after I took it. It felt as if I had ants in my pants. For a while I would just sleep it off with a nap but eventually stopped taking it. I then saw the psychiatrist about a month later. He put me on risperidone and I went to a less stressful group but never felt comfortable.

I took a vocational rehabilitation program for people with a mental illness, which was called Gastown Vocational Services and found it helpful. I think it was a twelve week program, four half days a week. An occupational therapist took the group through different modules such as stress management, medication management, social conversation, goal setting and other life skills. A Vocational Rehabilitation Worker taught courses about workplace behaviors, occupational research, interview practice, and résumé preparation. I also took aptitude, psychological and vocational tests and had a two-hour session with a psychologist. The Rehab Worker then found me a volunteer placement at Coast Foundation working in the fundraising department. A few months later they gave me a final report with recommendations and results of the tests.

By this time, Coast had hired me to work on a few projects but I was still suicidal and stopped taking medications. I was working again, I wasn't drinking but I did not really feel any better. The only place I really went to was work. Even then I would miss periods of work for up to two or three weeks because I was depressed or felt like a complete failure. My boss and other managers and staff were supportive and encouraging. Coast was my lifeline – without work, income and the ability to pay for housing I do not think I would have made it. Coast is a unique organization to work for as they understand the cyclical nature of mental illness, the time it takes to recover. They accommodated my time off due to illness, hospitalization, and attendance at treatment programs.

Before Christmas in 1999, I admitted myself to a small community hospital in the interior of B.C. after a halted suicide trip out into the wilderness. I only stayed overnight but at the beginning of each shift the nurses asked how I was doing and said, "You know there are all sorts of different medications and sometimes it takes time to find the right ones."

I did not go to the doctor but I started to get a lot of energy and have racing thoughts a few months after this. I had had seven beers over Christmas but was not taking drugs or drinking at this time. I felt I had really important work to do, did not sleep much, lost weight, and either paced a lot or had jittery legs all the time. I went to a new GP and talked about doing something about my mental illness but did not want to take medication. One weekend I remember feeling extra outgoing, sociable, and full of energy. While out walking, I got lost and disoriented. I felt out of control and went back to the GP and got some antidepressants. I took the week off work and only felt worse. All the messages and paranoia returned. I was afraid to leave my apartment as I thought "they" would change my locks. By the next weekend I felt completely out of control. Messages were coming from TV and radio and in phone conversations. The way my blinds were hanging, pictures I saw and old letters I read – everything seemed scripted, accusatory. I thought it was a big puzzle I had to figure out. I tried to admit myself to the hospital but they sent me home twice.

Then I saw a cartoon on television that had two lions in it and that meant I had to go to Lions Gate Hospital. I put a few pieces of clothes in a knapsack and rushed out in the middle of the night. I walked around for six or seven hours, finally found a cab and went to Lions Gate.

They admitted me and then I wanted to leave but they talked me into staying. All the paranoia I thought I left at home was now at the hospital. They said they gave me risperidone but it was a different color than I was used to. I thought it was a trick. They kept asking if I had the hospital super bug and I thought I had it and was afraid to go near anyone. When I got to the ward I thought all the patients and nurses were actors who searched my stuff and took my money. I put my coat on and was going to run away but the door was alarmed.

After taking medications and being injected with antipsychotics at night, I got better. I met a psychiatrist named Dr. Pedro Paragas whom I respected and liked. He told me what was going on, he reviewed my files, talked to my family, and asked me questions to help me get insight into what I was thinking and feeling and how distorted or exaggerated thoughts and emotions were related to my illness. While in the hospital, I went to small and large group sessions, education groups, watched videos about addiction and negative coping techniques. The nurses observed that I was stiff across my arms and shoulders from one of the medications and gave me Cogentin. One of the nurses told me that he had noticed some inflection in my voice for the first time. I was diagnosed with bipolar 2, with mood congruent psychosis. It explained my depression, mania and psychosis. I took Risperdal, clonazepam, benztropine, and Effexor. I was in the hospital for almost two weeks.

I continued to see my psychiatrist weekly and he then gradually reduced the frequency of my visits. He supported my involvement in the Dual Diagnosis Program run by Vancouver Coastal Health. The program requires an intake interview. You had to attend ten orientation sessions that began with a check-in, a video, and then a discussion about the video. After this you met with a GP who did a drug and alcohol use history. A counselor then met with you and developed a care plan. I took anger management, relapse prevention (for mental illness and addiction), and rational emotive therapy. I found the program incredibly helpful and still use skills that I learned there.

Apparently my experience is not unusual. It takes time to get a reasonably accurate diagnosis, find a psychiatrist that you connect with and get on the right medication combination. I have also learned how to communicate with others. I did find the help that I needed and I learned to talk about what I was experiencing. I no longer said, "They are trying to get me" in group therapy – I learned to say – "I do not believe what you are saying. I feel that you are meeting in another room and getting your lines before you come in here and that you are all actors and none of this is real." I had to say what was going on in my mind because how could I get the right type of help if no one knew what I was feeling?

Currently, Mr. Taylor describes his mental health as pretty good. He works 32 hours a week, continues to attend peer support groups, takes psychiatric medication (Effexor, Wellbutrin and clonazepam) in small amounts, and sees his psychiatrist occasionally. He has been sober for over four years and has only had seven beers in the last six years. He no longer takes antipsychotics; his psychiatrist gradually reduced them as he and his psychosocial environment have become more stable.

I am now at the point where talking about having a mental illness and my experience in a general way is not difficult. I am learning to communicate more intimate details about my life to friends and mental health professionals. Part of getting well has been learning to open up about my thoughts and feelings in therapeutic settings. Over time, I have also found it is important to have boundaries around what I share and where. Work, social life, and other environments are important to my mental health but they are not therapy. Besides, it's boring to talk about mental illness all the time.

Mr. Taylor wanted to be part of this book so others could learn from his experience.

I believe that one part of reducing stigma is for people with mental illness to say, "I have bipolar disorder" to family, friends, work colleagues, and others. The "crazy" guy is not so scary when people can put a face, story, and relationship to mental illness. It is easier for me as I work for a mental health agency but, unless we identify ourselves, the stigma will not end.

I have also found that hearing stories of people who manage their illness well is encouraging. It is important to know that you can go from walking down busy public streets, humming, with your fingers in your ears to leading an okay life. It is important to know how to describe what you are thinking and feeling to mental health professionals so that they can have a sense of what is going on and can organize effective treatments. I did not become compliant with taking my prescribed medications until I found ones that demonstrated what a difference they could make in my life. It is important to know that you can tell your doctor about side effects and discuss various options. Many people think, "if only he took the medication he would be okay" – but what if the medication is not okay?

Asked about recommendations for improving mental health care, Mr. Taylor suggests better coordination of the medical and community sectors.

For me, recovery was and is managing my illness, education about my illness, a diagnosis that makes sense and a good psychiatrist. But recovery is also work, income, volunteering, stable housing, socializing outside "therapy," and all the elements offered by or taught about by psychosocial rehabilitation-focused agencies. I wish society knew how much us patients need both types of support to maximize our own mental health. If you are homeless why would you take medication?

Coast has understood that one of the greatest needs for people with a mental illness is safe and affordable housing backed up with appropriate support.

[Without appropriate housing, people with a mental illness] use the highest cost public systems – emergency rooms, hospital psychiatric beds, detox, residential treatment programs and, in some places, jail cells.

The 2004 Coast Annual Report describes the key components of the Coast Supported Housing Program for the mentally ill as: affordability, privacy, a stigma-free environment, access to skilled community mental health support workers, a service plan unique to each resident, a strong sense of community and mutual support and links to other mental health programs.

Here's the nagging problem for the patient, Mr. Taylor explains:

Psychiatric symptoms don't matter if you have no housing, no job or meaning, no friends and no hope. Why bother taking medication if your life consists of going to group therapy and back to a ten foot by ten-foot room in a downtown hotel? Why bother taking medications if they do not work? Under such conditions, why not get wasted or self-medicate or jump off a bridge?

The Coast Foundation Society tries to ensure that its members do not run out of resources. It has developed a Trust Program for people who receive B.C. disability benefits and administers trust funds for people with mental illness. Since the money is held in a trust, it prevents impulse spending and protects individual assets.

Coast also offers employment services through individual employment counseling and career exploration, a specialized program for school re-entry, a supported job search, and post-employment support. The Coast Clubhouse program offers volunteer positions and transitional employment for those who want it. Coast is also developing a number of social businesses that employ people with a mental illness and eventually will become self-supporting.

Through a Mental Health Resource Centre in Downtown Vancouver, Coast offers meals, showers, free laundry. Coast's recovery-focused approach to psychosocial rehabilitation provides hope, respects individuality, informs and educates members about how to make their own decisions, encourages the formation of support networks, and reintegrates members into their communities through school, volunteer work, or employment.

Mr. Taylor would like to see a national action and awareness plan that educates people about mental illness and about the services that are available in their communities. "People need to know that there is hope and that you can recover."

As a Coast employee, Mr. Taylor's life reflects the life of the centaur, Chiron, who, after much personal struggle, shares his suffering and advances the cause of healing.

Further Reading

Coast Foundation Society. Available at: www.coastfoundation.com

Chiron. Available at: http://www.godchecker.com/pantheon/greek-mythology.php?deity=CHIRON

Currie SR, Patten SB, Williams JVA, Wang JL, Beck CA, El-Guebaly N, Maxwell C. Comorbidity of major depression with substance abuse disorders. Can J Psychiatry. 2005; 50:660–666.

Chapter 21

Consumer Advocacy: Beva Dudiak – The Insider Perspective

"The reward of suffering is experience."
Aeschylus

Mental health and illness can be studied from two perspectives – that of the insider or that of the outsider. The "etic" perspective is the one adopted by the scientific observer. The "emic" focus is the one that is meaningful to the mentally ill. Beva Dudiak illustrates the insider emic viewpoint.

Beva Dudiak is a consumer advocate. Her experiences with mental illness have given her the authority to speak out about issues that are important to patients or consumers of mental health services (sometimes also called survivors or clients). The first time Beva was asked to sit on a mental health committee, she wondered what she would say. Then, once she was there, she realized that, as an insider, she had a great deal to contribute. Since that first time, she has taken her place on a number of committees and boards. "I think it is really important for consumers to get involved."

Ms. Dudiak was interviewed for this chapter on her 42nd birthday, by which time she had lived with schizoaffective psychosis (a cross between mood disorder and schizophrenia) for more than half her life.

I got ill first at 18 and after 35 hospital admissions I stopped counting; I'm sure I've had 50 by now. The longest one was eight months and the shortest was two weeks.

In the last few years, Beva has gradually won the battle, a victory she attributes to the antipsychotic drug, clozapine (please also see Chapter 18). She remembers her struggle first starting in High School, although she kept it hidden for many years. She suffered from hallucinations for two whole years before she told her parents. Beva describes herself as a very driven teenager. She came to Hamilton at age 18 to be a nurse at Mohawk College. She was the top of her class. "I had A pluses and nobody knew I was ill." Until, ultimately, she could not hide her illness any more.

> For the first 12 years of my illness, my hallucinations involved two characters, I called them my imaginary friends. They lived in my brain and talked to me constantly, all the time. My parents belonged to the Evangelical Friends Church, colloquially called the Quaker church and I thought my parents would think the devil had invaded me. The voices would tell me to cut, they would tell me to hurt; I have cuts all over my tummy and arms, and I've cut my forehead. A big thing with them (the voices) was blood, they were always asking to see blood. They had names, Kelpy and Luwissa. Kelpy was the one who talked me into doing things. Luwissa was the mean one, she'd call me names and tell me I was fat or ugly and I needed to hurt myself and Kelpy would say: "don't listen to her, you are pretty, but you should still cut yourself because it is really important to see blood." He'd make me feel better about the bad things Luwissa would say to me but he would still want me to do bad things to myself. Besides the hallucinations, I would feel responsible for bad things I heard on the news. Once when I was in hospital and I was watching a horse race, one horse broke its leg and had to be euthanized. I felt I was responsible for that, so I went around for weeks sobbing and saying: "why did I let the horse break its leg and it had to be killed and it was my fault." It made me want to hurt myself even more. I thought I was an evil person so that if I touched someone or looked at them in a certain way, I'd send them to hell. All those psychotic symptoms faded out with the clozapine.

As a consumer advocate, Ms. Dudiak has been critical about some aspects of mental health care and has been vocal about speaking out for change. Most of all, she feels mental health professionals should be better screened and better trained.

> There are nurses who have damaged me. One of them in particular, a male nurse, sexually abused me. I worked through it; it turned out two other girls had been sexually assaulted as well, and he left.

Because nurses often feel powerless in the hospital hierarchy, they do not always protect patients as well as they might want to. When they observe offences, they do not always report them. Sometimes they close ranks to shield the offender. Even when an offense is reported, management may not do anything, which further undermines trust between staff and patients. Better education about legal protections for whistle blowers may make staff less afraid of losing their jobs and, therefore, more forthcoming. The visible presence of consumer advocates in mental health facilities is another potential remedy.

Issues about medication, physical restraints, and the use of involuntary treatment elicit strong negative feelings among consumers and can lead to massive distrust of the whole mental health system. Consumers want to participate in treatment decisions and not be browbeaten into taking medications they do not feel they need. Too often, consumer opinions are ignored or considered delusional. It is important for health professionals to understand why some patients refuse medication. Some have advocated the use of advance directives, in which consumers specify choices about treatment when they are well in the event of future incapacity. Because of bed shortages, only the very ill are hospitalized nowadays, so, in fact, more involuntary treatment may be being used now as compared to earlier times. This is due to the increasing illness acuity of hospitalized patients.

> A lot of patients think the nurses are trying to hurt them by forcing them to do things like take pills, but I thought they were there to help me and I trusted them until I had that experience with the abusive nurse.

Lack of time spent with patients on a psychiatric ward is a serious complaint of many former inpatients, including Beva Dudiak. It takes time to establish relationships, but time given to one patient can come at the expense of another patient, a dilemma for nurses and doctors. Sometimes so little time is spent with a patient that a diagnosis cannot even be established.

> During the first couple of years, my parents took me home from hospital and were wondering what was wrong with me and no one knew what was wrong.

Ms. Dudiak now talks to women's groups at churches and to others interested in mental health. She answers the questions that keep surfacing. What to call someone with a mental illness is a frequent question. Most consumers prefer a "people first" language, i.e., "a person with a mental illness" rather than "a mentally ill person." People first emphasizes the fact that patienthood is only a small part of a person's identity. Patients may be mothers, girlfriends, opera singers, skiers, lawyers, or university professors and they want their primary identities recognized. Some consumers very much want their nurse or doctor to not only spend time but also to be a friend – while the professional prefers, for legal and ethical reasons, to maintain boundaries. Discussing such discrepant views is important to a relationship of trust. Consumers and professionals often speak different languages and may not share a common world vision. Stepping into each other's shoes and adopting the perspective of the other can help the professional as well as the patient. Efforts need to be made to encourage consumer-professional dialogue. Consumer advocates also feel that efforts are needed to develop treatment plans from a strength-based perspective, e.g., based on what individuals are able to do rather than on their deficits.

> The treatment I had at Hospital X, I would consider that humane treatment. I was treated as a human. Treated as a person. At Hospital Y, every Tuesday and Friday one of the nurses would bring me in for ECT [electroconvulsive treatment] and I honestly felt like an animal, or a number, or a piece of junk. There was no personal attention. They treated me just like an animal. It didn't matter how many patients were there, the first treatment I had I remember there were seven of us and I was last and I had to listen to each person have their treatments. There was just a curtain between us and the other patients.
>
> During my last treatment, my blood oxygen level went way, way low and they were scared I was going to die and I could hear them talking about me dying.
>
> Only once there did someone, a student, come up to me and introduce herself and tell me her name. Out of 11 ECT treatments I only got the impression that this one person cared. When I compare that to Hospital X where you were in a room with 4 walls and there were eight or ten staff members there talking to you and putting you at ease, it was completely different.

ECT is a much-maligned form of treatment. Was it warranted?

> Yes, it was warranted both times. The first time I was 21, I hadn't eaten in three months and before that I had been eating very sparsely. I was emaciated and I weighed 91 pounds. They just didn't know what to do. I was too depressed to even think about eating. They said: "let's try ECT." and I was scheduled for 12 treatments but, after eight, I was so much better that they cancelled the rest. I started eating.
>
> The last time I had one was two years ago today, because I can distinctly remember that it was my 40th birthday. I had 11 treatments, it was supposed to have been 12 but then the SARS [severe acute respiratory syndrome] broke out and, because I was being transferred from one hospital to another for the treatments, that was stopped. Transfers between hospitals were prohibited during the SARS epidemic in Ontario. It did work, it lifted my mood, but within a week and a half I was just as depressed as before the treatments.

Consumers often speak of stigma about illness and its treatment even on the part of close relatives. It was different for Beva.

> You know what helped? I resented it at the time, but it was my mother taking a real interest in educating people about depression and schizophrenia. If she met someone on the street and they mentioned something about mental health, she would talk to them and she knew everything. She read as much as she could. She

joined the Friends of Schizophrenics, which is now the Schizophrenia Society of Ontario, and my family became really involved in that. At the Hamilton Program for Schizophrenia here, they were involved in a family group. Mother immersed herself in the information and shared it with everyone – people at church, people in the neighborhood.

I remember I used to get mad and say: "if she met somebody in the mall, a stranger in a coffee shop, the first thing she'd say is that her daughter has schizophrenia." It irritated me, but I realized it meant she was not ashamed and that it wasn't a bad thing to her. She wanted to educate people, she had had no idea I was becoming ill, and she wanted to help people know more about the disease so maybe, if someone close to them got ill, they would know.

So I realized what she was trying to accomplish and how she touched people. When I'd go home for a weekend, it took me a while to get back to church, but when I went back, they didn't treat me like a freak – my mother had pre-educated them and I thought: "my gosh, this education thing really works." So that's how I became comfortable talking about it.

Many questions from consumers and their families revolve about the future – will my son be able to marry, will my daughter be able to have a child, will I ever find a job? Each person has to find his or her own answer. "I've seen people in every state of the illness, from sick, sick, sick, to those who are successful and go back to university and get a degree and succeed." In Beva's case:

I've had two marriages and both were to men who had schizophrenia. My first husband and I were each other's very first love. Neither of us had ever had a boyfriend or girlfriend before. We met at the Hamilton Program for Schizophrenia and we were married for about 5 years. I was in hospital more often than I was out and he found that very difficult. It was very hard for us to break up because we did love each other so much. After we broke up, he stayed in the city for over a year, but then his mother died and he disappeared. Nobody knew where he was. A couple of years later we found out he had killed himself.

In the meantime I had married again; that would be nine years this February. His name is Jeffrey, we've been divorced four years and were married four years before that. We still celebrate our anniversary because we are still each other's best friend. He lives about a block and a half this way. We were very happy. Jeff and I were very happy, both of us having symptoms and trying to live together in a small apartment with three pets.

We tried to get pregnant and went up to Motherisk at Sick Kids in Toronto to discuss which meds I'd have to stop. We tried for 8 months and decided then that it really wasn't for us. So we got a puppy instead. I knew I needed something to nurture. Now I thank God that we didn't have a baby because, not just because we broke up, but I see, by observing my brother and his wife, how difficult it is to raise a child.

But I'll always have that sorry feeling in my heart for not having a child, I'm not sure if every woman feels that, I feel I haven't really done my duty as a woman in not having a child.

Beva works at a Daily Grind coffee shop, run by mental health consumers. She is one of three managers. Everyone working there suffers from a mental illness.

It's really, really good even though we don't make much money. We started at 33 cents an hour and now we are up to around a dollar. At the end of the month we total up all the earnings and the hours everyone has worked and divide it up and it doesn't matter if you are a server or a janitor or a manager, you get the same hourly wage. It is a great job and I've been there for three years, one year as a manager. We are going to be doing some more advertising. This May is the third anniversary of the coffee shop. I love my job. I talked to the manager who hired me the other day and he and I have a vision for the shop and we have committed to five years. We are going to, five years down the road, make more money, so we're thinking about some philanthropic kind of thing we could do if we are making enough money.

I don't make much money, but it is something to do and gives me self-esteem. When I finally gave up on University, I really started to make some differences in the world. I started talking about my illness and teaching, even though I didn't have a university degree, I go to women's groups and churches and explain that there are people out there who are suffering.

What families worry about most, and sometimes are too frightened to ask about, is suicide.

. At the time, I thought I was doing what God wanted me to do. I thought that, somehow, if I was gone, the world would be a better place and that God would prefer to have me with him and not screwing up everybody's lives. I saw myself affecting my parents and my brother and some friends from high school. I thought they were suffering because of me. I thought that the world would have been a better place if I hadn't been born. I was absolutely sure I shouldn't have been born, it was some accident or fluke that I came into this world and it just wasn't meant to be.

The suicide attempts stopped when I had a visit from someone who, now looking back, I have decided was my guardian angel. I don't know her name or who she was. She came to my bed when I was in the hospital and made me promise that if I ever felt like committing suicide again that I would talk to someone before I acted. After that, I did, I'd go to my doctor or my worker and say: "Look, you know, I'm really desperate here and you have to help me or I'm going to die."

Is there any joy for people with mental illness? Is there anything to look forward to in a life that is buffeted by mood swings and false perceptions? This is a core concern that consumer advocates need to address, whether someone asks or not. For Beva, her greatest joys have been:

Falling in love with both my husbands, at different times of course! Falling in love has been wonderful, but falling in friendship with my ex-husband has been the best, best thing. He is the best thing in my life, my best, best friend and he knows more about me than anyone. Years ago in my first marriage if I had a problem I would call my mother first, now I call Jeff first. He is my rock, that's what I tell people. We were so close when we were married and we are apart now – in terms of a physical relationship and living together – but our spirits are joined. I have a friend that I know will be there for me no matter what. He would help me through anything and I'd do the same for him. That is a joy, a great joy, having such a loyal friend.

For Beva, her religion and her church community are vital.

I am a born again Christian and James Street Baptist is my church family. It took me years to find this church. There was a time when I couldn't get up and dress myself so I would watch ministers on T.V. and that was the way I worshipped. I really wanted to go to church but I couldn't. Whenever I am in hospital, my church is very supportive. I get cards and the Pastor comes to visit. I sit on the Pastoral Care Committee at my church, which means I help visit the elderly who are shut in. When I finally gave up on my worldly ambitions of going to university and becoming a great researcher, I began to become much more content with myself. I had to come to the conclusion that there were things in this world that I could do to help people and reach people, to spark God's love, to be a good example of how Christ can shine through someone with a mental illness and they can have a good earthly life besides – my own apartment and a job. I don't think I would be where I am today if it wasn't for Christ.

Beva Dudiak has overcome many of her disabilities and she thinks this is due to her medication. She believes that the hand of God has led doctors to the medications that work for her. If she were a researcher, she would go through the country with a fleet of research assistants to find people in out-of-the-way places who have conquered their problems with mental illness. She would locate people who were content being who they were, not necessarily making large amounts of money or working eight hours a day or owning a BMW, but content. She would study such people, people much like herself, and try to figure out what has made it possible for them to overcome pain, stigma, discouragement and loss. Speaking from an insider's point of view, she feels that research of this kind would really benefit humanity.

Further Reading

Hamilton Program for Schizophrenia. Available at: http://www.inform.hamilton.ca/details.asp?RSN=409/3

James Street Baptist Church, Hamilton, Ontario. Available at: http://www.inform.city.hamilton.on.ca/details.asp?RSN=66599&Number=83

Motherisk. Available at: http://www.motherisk.org/

Psychiatric Consumer Advocacy. Available at: http://www.cccinternational.com/InvoluntaryTreatment/advocacy.html

Schizophrenia Society of Ontario. Hamilton Chapter. Available at: http://www.neurosurvival.ca/LocalResources/resources/schizohamilton.htm

Chapter 22

Depression: Sandra Sharwood's Story

"Although the world is full of suffering, it is also full of the overcoming of it."
Helen Keller

Narratives of illness can take many forms. When narrated by physicians, they are stories of diagnosis, treatment, and cure. When told by protagonists such as Sandra Sharwood, they are more evocative accounts of identity disruption and continuity, of challenge, loss, exploration, survival, and victory.

Those with a story of illness to tell often speak of losses they have sustained, of unfulfilled dreams. But many speak instead of survival and self-discovery and it is in this context that Sandra Sharwood understands her life. She has trouble with the phrase "mental illness." She experiences her own psychiatric illnesses as physical, every bit as physical as arthritis or asthma. She does not understand why the distinction is made between physical and mental illness. For Sandra, the conventional dichotomy between physical (organic) and mental (functional) is purely linguistic since distress is simultaneously biological and psychological. Brain events, she would argue, produce psychological events.

> I have a lot of trouble with even the phrase "mental illness." To me it is a physical illness, why do we keep talking about mental, mental, mental? It is a physical illness or we wouldn't be taking pills for it. It is physical. There is something in there that isn't working.

Sandra suffers from depression, as does one of her sons and a sister. She believes that there is no question but that some physical entity has been transmitted genetically in her family that causes her to experience severe recurring attacks of depression. Individuals with depression often report a history of depression in immediate family members. It is estimated that genes account for one third to one half of the risk for major depression. It is thought that variations in certain genes can decrease the production of growth factors needed in the development of the brain or alter the release of a synaptic neurotransmitter such as serotonin. The gene for the serotonin-uptake protein, for instance, exists in several variants; its short form is associated with depression and an increased vulnerability to stress. From the point of view of brain function, neuroimaging studies have identified neurophysiologic abnormalities in specific areas of the brain, notably the amygdala, in individuals carrying the short form of the serotonin-uptake protein gene. It has recently been reported that mutations in the gene that controls serotonin synthesis in the brain may also predispose to mood disturbances. The current evidence suggests that several genes probably act in combination with environmental factors to produce complex diseases such as depression.

The onset of mood disorders usually occurs during adolescence. For Sandra, the episodes started approximately at age fourteen when she entered grade nine. She was placed in the A class, as her grade eight marks were high. Her first term grades were in the eighties but her second term grades plummeted to the forties! She was then downgraded to the B class, with no one pausing to wonder what had caused this remarkable drop in grades. Sandra remembers feeling humiliated and angry.

Her next memory is of being treated with electroconvulsive therapy:

> I was in and out of the Wellesley hospital when I was a young woman, I couldn't tell you how many times. I went through shock therapy; so did my sister. It was certainly not like it is now, you'd have headaches for days and days; you wouldn't know who people were and couldn't remember anything.

Sandra is not alone in suffering from depression. The lifetime prevalence of major depressive disorder is 17%. Depression accounts for 18 million office visits per year in the U.S. One hundred million prescriptions are written per year for depressive disorders and the economic costs amount to U.S. $44 billion a year. Two-thirds of those who suffer do not at first seek treatment but this is a mistake because one bout of major depression strongly predicts future ones. More than 50% of individuals who have one attack of depression experience a recurrence. It is estimated that only half of all depressions are accurately diagnosed and only 10% are appropriately treated. Sandra Sharwood was fortunate. She was diagnosed accurately and, while some may argue that electroconvulsive treatment should not have been used for her type of depression, she first became ill when few other effective options were available (she is now 70). Accurate diagnosis and treatment are essential for health and for survival. It must be remembered that one out of seven patients with recurrent depression suicides. Seventy percent of those who take their lives suffer from a depressive illness.

Depression takes many forms. Most common is a feeling that life holds no joy; all interest in activities or people that make life meaningful is lost. Sadness and tearfulness are signs of depression but apathy is present more often than acute unhappiness. The lack of interest extends to vital activities such as eating. Depressed people take no interest in food; they shed pounds without noticing it. Sleep is fitful, sometimes non-existent. No matter how tired she was, Sandra could not sleep. Movements and speech are slowed. Talking is so much of an effort that telephone calls go unanswered; it seems easier to remain mute than to explain why you are depressed or to be told by a well-meaning caller that: "when I get down, I just pull myself together, and that is what you should do."

Sandra used to work at the Canadian Imperial Bank of Commerce and numbers come easily to her. However, when depressed, she is unable to focus. Her thinking is distorted and her mind goes numb. Summing one-digit numbers becomes impossible. Reading novels is too hard a task. The centre of attention becomes one's sense of failure – a mix of hopelessness, helplessness, worthlessness, guilt, and regret. Decisions are impossible. A simple decision such as what to wear is enough to make her give in to her apathy and stay in bed all day.

Worry and rumination are part of the mix of depression. Everything becomes a source of worry and the worries keep going round and round no matter how one tries to stop them. Pain is another constant companion – so much hurts: it hurts to breathe, to chew, and to move. Headaches can be unbearable and add to the already deep concern about health. Depressed individuals often feel they are dying of a malignant disease. In fact, several generally considered physical conditions, such as stroke and heart disease, Parkinson's disease, epilepsy, arthritis, cancer, AIDS, and chronic obstructive pulmonary disease (COPD), may contribute to the overall prevalence of depression.

Many areas of life are affected: social, occupational, and educational. Sandra could not complete her last year of High School due to illness and was unable to go to university. Does she regret that? No, because she started to work early in life, at age nineteen.

> I wanted to be financially independent because I hate having to depend on other people and, as the old saying goes, "He who pays the piper calls the tune." My first job was as a doctor's receptionist – very boring! I then worked in advertising, which I enjoyed but there was little opportunity for women in those days. I left to work for the first pay TV company in Canada, writing and interviewing people. The company was poorly managed and subsequently folded.
>
> A short time after this I attended a dinner party that changed my life. I was by chance seated next to the president of the Bank of Commerce. After a chat about banking in general, about which I knew little or nothing, I suggested that the service in all the Canadian banks was very bad. He fortunately was of the same

opinion and offered me a job on the spot, and I accepted. I developed a training program for female staff, which was very successful and the first of its kind in Canada. I was appointed a superintendent, the first female to have this position and worked in the Bank, in Human Resources, until my marriage. I tell this story to highlight the fact that many people who suffer from a mental illness can work and do a good job.

As was the case for Sandra, many individuals with depression function very well indeed in life. But this "smiling depression" requires extraordinary effort and becomes more difficult to sustain with time.

Depression

The diagnosis is made when depressed mood or loss of interest in usual activities lasts at least two weeks and is accompanied by at least four additional symptoms from the following list:
- Feeling worthless, helpless, or hopeless
- Loss of interest or pleasure (including hobbies or sexual desire)
- Change in appetite
- Sleep disturbances
- Decreased energy or fatigue (without significant physical exertion)
- Sense of worthlessness or guilt
- Poor concentration or difficulty making decisions

Major depressive disorder is a recurrent illness with frequent relapses, but full recovery from any one episode is possible for most people. The stressors in life that provoke depressive illness frequently have to do with loss. In Sandra's case, she lost her father when she was nine. He was a sniper in World War II. His job was to cross enemy lines before a battle to see if the passage was safe for troops. He was killed in Holland just before the end of the war.

> He went over the lines and then the story came back that he tried to help a wounded man and tried to swim the Maas River in February when it was freezing cold. The body was never found. I was very upset…my mother sold my father's business (Maple Leaf Milling Co.) and she took my sisters and me to live with her parents in Rosedale.

Sandra had a teacher who functioned in the capacity of an extra surrogate parent.

> I had a wonderful teacher in First Grade. I was there first thing in the morning and I'd stay to help her clean up. I was a child who didn't want to be home and she knew it. She was important in my life. I can't explain it, but we kept in touch until she died. She played an important role.

Social supports of this kind are important for those with a vulnerability to depression. So is education for family members who need to recognize early signs and ensure that treatment is started early. Effective treatment usually means antidepressant medication and psychotherapy. Society needs to recognize that mood disorders are eminently treatable.

Sandra Sharwood does not hide the fact that she suffers from depression. She has been on the Board of the Canadian Psychiatric Research Foundation for many years and serves on its Psychiatric Awareness Committee and its Youth Project Committee. In 2003, Sandra's two committees were awarded an Ontario Trillium Award for outstanding volunteer services.

> I'm very quick to tell people I suffer from mental illness. I know I don't look as if I'm totally nuts and I don't have any trouble with it. As a result, a lot of people talk to me about it. I think the interesting thing is the number of people in the arts who suffer from depression. I've asked people what profession has the most mental illness and I've been told that the highest rate is in poets.

As often happens, Sandra believes that her experience with depression has made her more sensitive to the needs of people with mental illness. She can empathize with those who are suffering and they, in turn, feel that and confide in her. She values this and, as she grows older, she is thankful for the extra sensitivity that has become part of who she is. Hers is not a story of loss but, rather, a story of victory.

Further Reading

Blazer DG, Kessler RC, McGonagle KA, Swartz MS. The prevalence and distribution of major depression in a national community sample: the National Comorbidity Survey. Am J Psychiatry. 1994;151:979–986.

Davies K. "Silent and censured travellers?" Patients' narratives and patients' voices: perspectives on the history of mental illness since 1948. Soc Hist Med. 2001;14:267–292.

Dowman J, Patel A, Rajput K. Electroconvulsive therapy: attitudes and misconceptions. J ECT. 2005;21:84–87.

Hariri AR, Drabant EM, Munoz KE, Kolachana BS, Mattay VS, Egan MF, Weinberger DR. A susceptibility gene for affective disorders and the response of the human amygdala. Arch Gen Psychiatry. 2005;62:146–152.

Chapter 23

Establishing an Award:
The Life of Edward Bronfman

> *"A great hope fell. You heard no noise. The ruin was within.*
> *Oh cunning wreck that told no tale and let no witness in.*
> *A not admitting of the wound until it grew so wide.*
> *That all my life had entered it and there were troughs beside."*
> Emily Dickinson

Wealth does not provide shelter from mental illness. In fact, affluence can work against close ties, can engender unfulfilled ambitions and can elicit envy – all risk factors for depression. Edward Bronfman's sister died by her own hand at the age of 26, the tragic outcome of postpartum depression. His family foundation perpetuates her memory.

Edward Bronfman, a man known for his towering generosity, died on April 2005, before the interview for this chapter could be completed. In 2001, through the Edward Bronfman Family Foundation, he had created a $750,000 endowment fund [in partnership with the Canadian Psychiatric Research Foundation (CPRF), the Centre for Addiction and Mental Health (CAMH) Foundation, and the Canadian Institutes of Health Research (CIHR)] to support a Postdoctoral Fellowship Award in mood disorders. Named the Mona Bronfman Sheckman Post-Doctoral Fellowship Award, it commemorates the life of Edward's sister Mona who, in 1950, at age 26, suffered from severe post-partum depression and took her own life. At the time of the endowment, Edward said:

> I felt it was time to talk about this and bring it out into the open and help people face their own inner devils.

We now know that between 10% and 15% of new mothers experience depression after the birth of a child. The wealthy are not immune. This kind of depression is often described as a "confused sense of inadequacy" and lasts six months and, sometimes, longer. What often determines how long the depression lasts is the time it takes to seek and receive treatment. The faster treatment begins, the shorter the depression. An enquiry into maternal deaths in England in the years between 1997 and 1999 found that suicide was the leading cause of such deaths, accounting for 28% of them. The findings from this enquiry highlighted the severity of postpartum mental illness and the high risk of recurrence with each subsequent childbirth. The first 42 days after delivery were found to be the period of greatest risk for suicide. Four thousand Canadians suicide each year, and this is probably an underestimate. Throughout the world, about 2,000 people kill themselves each day (please see Chapter 30). Men suicide at about four times the rate of women. Female rates are at their maximum during middle age. Compared to other causes of maternal death, the women who suicide following childbirth are relatively older and, like Mona Bronfman, are relatively well off. Wealth and social advantage does not shelter them from depression.

A recent review of 15 clinical trials of altogether over 7,600 women has come to the conclusion that psychosocial interventions do not *prevent* postpartum depression. Identifying at-risk mothers and providing intensive postpartum support, however, does help the problem once it surfaces. Unfortunately, postpartum depression frequently goes unrecognized. Especially among the affluent who feel they have no right to be depressed, depression can remain hidden. And antidepressant drugs are underused because of concerns about breast-feeding while on medication.

The aim of the Mona Bronfman Sheckman award is to foster research into the causes of mood disorders. The first awardee (2001–2004) was Dr. John Strauss for work carried out in the laboratory of Dr. Jim Kennedy (please see Ch 26 for more on Dr. Kennedy) on brain-derived neurotrophic factor or BDNF. BDNF is a nerve growth factor that is present in several regions of the brain. It is needed for nerve cells to survive, for messages to cross the gaps or synapses of brain cells, for the formation of neurotransmitters, and for the brain to be able to modify its nerve cell networks in response to experience. This ability is called brain plasticity. The BDNF gene is located on chromosome 11 and is present in human populations in several forms or polymorphisms. Some variants of this gene have been associated with an increased risk for bipolar disorder (please see Chapter 4 on the genetics of bipolar disorder). Dr. Strauss found that the odds of carrying one variation of the gene were 3.94 times greater in adults with a history of childhood-onset mood disorder than in those without such a history, a promising lead for future investigations. He looked for but did not find any association between variants of the BDNF gene and aspects of memory. This had previously been suggested as a possibility. Nor, in other work, was he able to confirm a previously reported association between a variant of the tryptophan hydroxylase (TPH2) gene and suicidal behavior. Dr. Strauss' research illustrates both the promise and the frustrations of genetic research. It is not uncommon for one laboratory to fail to replicate findings from another. The reasons for this are not fully understood.

Edward Maurice Bronfman (1927–2005) was the grandson of Mindel and Yechiel Bronfman, refugees from Czarist Russia who brought their family to Canada in 1889. Yechiel was a tobacco farmer who first settled near Wapella, Saskatchewan, and then moved to Brandon, Manitoba, where he started a wood business. Yechiel and Mindel had eight children: Abe, Harry, Laura, Samuel, Jean, Bessie, Allan, and Rose. The three eldest were born in Russia, the younger ones in Canada, and Samuel (1889–1971) may have been born at sea on the way to Canada.

Some Members of the Legendary Bronfman Family

Yechiel and Mindel Bronfman
- Abe Bronfman (1882–1968)
- Harry Bronfman (1886–1963)
- Laura Bronfman
- Samuel Bronfman (1891–1971) and Saidye Rosner (1897–1995)
  - Minda Bronfman de Gunzburg (1925–1986)
  - Phyllis Bronfman Lambert 1927–
  - Edgar M. Bronfman, Sr. 1929–
    - Sam Jr.
    - Edgar Jr. 1955–
    - Matthew
    - Holly
    - Adam
  - Charles R. Bronfman 1931–
    - Stephen R. Bronfman
    - Ellen Bronfman Hauptman
- Jean Bronfman
- Bessie Bronfman
- Allan Bronfman (1895–1980)
  - Mona Bronfman Sheckman (1924–1950)
  - Edward Bronfman (1927–2005)
    - Paul Bronfman
    - David Bronfman
    - Brian Bronfman
  - Peter Bronfman (1929–1996)
- Rose Bronfman

In 1903, the Bronfmans purchased their first hotel in Manitoba. From there, they took over more hotels and expanded. Liquor was a best seller in their hotels so they decided to move into the liquor business. Sam Bronfman bought the Bonaventure

Liquor Store Company in Montreal in 1916. He sold liquor by mail, which was legal at the time, and later, during the American Prohibition (1920–1933) smuggled alcohol over the border to customers in the U.S. In 1924, Sam and Allan opened Distillers Corporation, Ltd. in LaSalle, Quebec. Four years later, the company acquired Joseph E. Seagram and Sons, went public, and changed its name to Distillers Corporation-Seagrams Ltd. Knowing that prohibition was coming to an end, the Bronfmans began storing whiskey in the late 1920s. By 1933, Seagram had put aside the largest reserves of aged whiskeys in the world. They established now classic brands of smooth, blended whiskeys, including Seagram's 7 Crown, V.O., and Crown Royal. In the decades that followed, the company acquired a string of distilleries in the U.S. and the West Indies and diversified with the purchase of a variety of liquor brands, among them Mumm and Perrier-Jouet S.A. champagne and Chivas Brothers scotch. The Seagram Company burgeoned into one of the world's richest business empires.

Edward, his older sister Mona, and his younger brother Peter were Allan's children and bore witness to a bitter split between their father and uncle. Older brother Sam is said to have never forgiven Allan for sitting at the head table (in preference to Sam) during a dinner honoring the British Queen Mother. To keep Allan's children from having a say in the running of Seagram's, Sam forced Allan to sell a large amount of the stock at below-market rates. The breach between the two brothers never healed.

Like the rest of this eminent family, Allan and Lucy Bronfman, Edward's parents, were open-handed philanthropists. Edward reflects:

> From the Jewish General Hospital, which my father helped found in 1934, to Israel Bonds and the Hebrew University, my parents were deeply committed to Jewish – and non-Jewish – causes. Giving came naturally to me – for which I am fortunate and deeply grateful.
>
> The gift that our family has given in Montreal is a way to give back to the city where I grew up. It was a way to return, in some small measure, the richness that I enjoyed in that remarkable community.
>
> The gift that our family has given in Toronto sustains a solid foundation for the outstanding city in which I now live.
>
> Our family is committed to the philanthropic tradition my parents handed down to me. We hope to provide to our children and their children a testament to our family values. We want to contribute to this diverse, exciting and growing population well into the future.

Edward attended Selwyn House High School in Montreal and Bishop's College in Lennoxville, Quebec. In 1950, he received a degree in Business Administration from Babson College, in Wellesley, Massachusetts. He served in executive positions in a string of Canadian Companies and, along with other members of his family, played an important role in the expansion of the Canadian economy. After their father's death, Edward and his brother Peter (who died in 1996) sold their $25-million stake in Seagram stock and reinvested it in undervalued Canadian firms to create Edper Enterprises in the late 1960s. By the late 1980s, Edper's 40 publicly traded companies accounted for more than 10% of the value of the Toronto Stock Exchange. Its holdings included Noranda Inc., Trizec Corp. and MacMillan Bloedel Ltd. At one time, Edper controlled approximately $100 billion in Canadian corporations.

Edward was an athlete who ran, skied and loved hockey. From 1971 to 1978, Edward and Peter owned the Montreal Canadians hockey team. The team won the Stanley Cup four times during that period. In the early 1990s, Edward sold his interest in Edper and, from then on, devoted his time entirely to philanthropic causes. Until his death, he was intensely involved in many charitable organizations among which were the Canadian Council for Christians and Jews and the Canadian Psychiatric Research Foundation. In 1989 he formed the Edward Bronfman Family Foundation, a member of Philanthropic Foundations of Canada (PFC).

PFC Members

- 96% of members are family foundations
- Total number: 82 (as of January 2005) from across Canada
- PFC members collectively manage $4.7 billion in assets
- PFC members granted over $200 million in 2002
- 38% of members are foundations with assets under $10 million

In recognition of his eclectic philanthropic interests, Edward received the Order of Canada in 2000. Bronfman created a research clinic for Multiple Sclerosis at Mount Sinai Hospital, built a strong relationship with the Hebrew University in Jerusalem and was always deeply committed to the Jewish community of Toronto. He created several endowment funds that supported the Jewish poor and trained leaders for generations to come.

Edward's way of donating has been described as "all about looking after the little guy" – giving start-up funds to service groups. He wanted his gifts to have a direct positive impact. He donated funds to every synagogue in the city that was interested in starting an "out of the cold" program. He personally went out in street vans that distributed food to the homeless. Edward Bronfman was known as an especially kind, soft-spoken person, a gentle soul. He is survived by his wife of 14 years, Marsha Noik Bronfman, three sons, Paul and David of Toronto, and Brian of Montreal, a stepdaughter, Lisa Noik Genser, who lives in Washington, and seven grandchildren. The psychiatric community will always be indebted to his foresight in endowing the Mona Bronfman Sheckman award for research into mood disorders. Its message is clear. Everyone, no matter how fortunate or how privileged, can suffer from depression. Depression is a severe disorder. Research is badly needed.

Further Reading

Beck CT. Theoretical perspectives of postpartum depression and their treatment implications. MCN Am J Matern Child Nurs. 2002;27:282–287.

De Luca V, Voineskos D, Wong GW, Shinkai T, Rothe C, Strauss J, Kennedy JL. Promoter polymorphism of second tryptophan hydroxylase isoform (TPH2) in schizophrenia and suicidality. Psychiatry Res. 2005;134:195–198.

Dennis CL, Creedy D. Psychosocial and psychological interventions for preventing postpartum depression. Cochrane Database Syst Rev. 2004;(4):CD001134

Diener E, Biswas-Diener R. Will money increase subjective well-being? Soc Indicators Res. 2002;57:119–169.

Gittins S. Behind closed doors: the rise and fall of Canada's Edper, Bronfman & Reichman Empires. Toronto: Prentice-Hall Canada; 1995.

Luthar SS, Becker BE. Privileged but pressured: a study of affluent youth. Child Development. 2002;73:1593–1610.

Oates M. Perinatal psychiatric disorders: a leading cause of maternal morbidity and mortality. Br Med Bull. 2003;67:219–229.

Postpartum Depression. Available at: http://www.toronto.ca/health/pp_depression.htm

Strauss J, Barr CL, George CJ, King N, Shaikh S, Devlin B, Kovacs M, Kennedy JL. Association study of brain-derived neurotrophic factor in adults with a history of childhood onset mood disorder. Am J Med Genet B Neuropsychiatr Genet. 2004;131:16–19.

Strauss J, Barr CL, George CJ, Ryan CM, King N, Shaikh S, Kovacs M, Kennedy JL.BDNF and COMT polymorphisms: relation to memory phenotypes in young adults with childhood-onset mood disorder. Neuromolecular Med. 2004;5:181–192.

Chapter 24

Making Neuroscience Matter: The Honorable Michael H. Wilson

"The heights by great men reached and kept
Were not obtained by sudden flight,
But they, while their companions slept
Were toiling upward in the night."
Henry Wadsworth Longfellow

The word charisma (from the Greek word charis or gift) describes personal magnetism and a special inborn ability to influence others. The Honorable Michael H. Wilson uses his charisma to raise funds for neuroscience research and, more recently, to advocate for all Canadians.

If you were the dinner companion of Michael Wilson, Canada's ambassador to the United States, chances are he would not talk to you about politics. He is a man preoccupied with topics few people discuss over scaloppini and wine: solving the mysteries of depression, schizophrenia, addictions, and neurological disorders.

Before his recent appointment to Washington, Wilson held a job he considers one of the most important of his long and distinguished career: special advisor on mental health. In this role, he made Canadian workplaces safer and psychologically healthier.

Michael Wilson lost his 29-year old son, Cameron, to suicide in 1995. As a way of helping to overcome his personal grief, Wilson assumed the Chairmanship of the Toronto Centre for Addiction and Mental Health's "Centered on Hope" campaign. His role in the campaign was critical; through his dedication and leadership, the campaign was able to endow its first University Chair, the Cameron Parker Holcombe Wilson Chair in Depression Studies.

The inaugural Cameron Wilson Chair holder was Dr. Sid Kennedy, now the head of Psychiatry at the University Health Network, Toronto. The incumbent is now Dr. Trevor Young, an internationally known expert in neuropsychiatry.

Professorial Chairs have proven to be effective incentives to intellectual innovation – and the need for innovation is something with which Michael Wilson is very familiar. He was first elected to the House of Commons in 1979 and served as Minister of State for International Trade. He was Minister of Finance in the Mulroney government from 1984 to 1991. He also served as Minister of Industry, Science and Technology and Minister for International Trade. When appointed ambassador by Canada's new Prime Minister, Stephen Harper, Wilson was President and CEO of UBS Canada. Beyond that, he is Chair of the NeuroScience Canada Partnership and NeuroScience Canada Foundation. The Partnership of private donors, with the help of leveraged funding from government and other voluntary health organizations, supports the Foundation, which directs 85% of its funds toward research.

In 2003, NeuroScience Canada launched the national Brain Repair Program. Its mission is to fast-track transformative research to accelerate the discovery and development of new treatments for neurological and psychiatric diseases. Neurological and psychiatric diseases are the leading cause of disability in Canada. Brain and psychiatric disorders, including Alzheimer's disease, Parkinson's disease, chronic pain, brain tumors, depression, schizophrenia, autism, and addictions affect some seven and a half million Canadians.

Neurological and Psychiatric Diseases

- Neurological and psychiatric diseases are the leading cause of disability in Canada.
- 7.5 million Canadians are directly affected by them.
- Half of all Canadians (15 million people) have an affected family member.
- The costs to individuals and to the Canadian economy are approaching $30 billion annually – 20% of health expenditures.
- With the population aging, this percentage will increase within the next decade.
- Research funding is totally inadequate.
- 90% of what is known about the brain was discovered in the last 15 years – the pace of research is accelerating.

What differentiates Wilson from other mental health stakeholders is that he does not believe more money is necessarily the first step toward system improvement. He believes in first raising the priority level for mental health. He echoes the Honorable Roy Romanow, author of the Romanow Report on the future of health care in Canada: "mental illness is the orphan child within the health care system." Mr. Wilson thinks that more support for psychiatric research will only come when the public fully understands what it is to be mentally ill. Education needs to come first.

On the morning of the interview for this chapter, Michael had been talking about mental illness to David Miller, the mayor of Toronto. Homelessness has been a major concern of the mayor's. "One known and accepted problem such as homelessness can be used to raise the profile of mental illness," says Wilson. There are approximately 30,000 homeless persons in Toronto, of whom 50% suffer from a diagnosable mental illness.

> People need to understand the magnitude of the problem, the number of individuals and families affected, the way that mental illnesses and addictions affect business and the economy. Only then can you get to research. You won't be successful if you go to Queen's Park or Ottawa and start out saying: "we need more money for research"– that is putting the cart before the horse. Understanding has to come first.

Non-governmental organizations – NeuroScience Canada and the Canadian Psychiatric Research Foundation – are crucial, says Wilson. Organizations such as these are able to support breakthrough areas that politicians may not be able to fund. Their success depends to a large degree on the caliber of the scientific board. Also critical are the communication (to the public) of scientific breakthroughs and their celebration in the press.

One of Wilson's objectives is to eliminate the discrimination and stigma that attach to mental disorders. "It is a roadblock to appropriate funding," says Wilson, "but, most devastatingly, it prevents people from receiving proper treatment." Because of the stigma, many people with psychiatric symptoms simply avoid going for help. Wilson offers the example of a friend, an active volunteer for mental health causes who had raised money for years for mental health but, when he sank into depression himself, didn't go to a doctor. In retrospect, after he felt better, the friend himself could not believe that he had reacted in that way. It was a knee-jerk reaction to deny mental health problems, something no one would consider doing if stricken with a painful back or downed by an infectious disease. Wilson also points out that business people, his long-time colleagues, tend to struggle with psychological symptoms on their own and avoid treatment until matters get serious. Too often this ends in their being fired. The inevitable result: they lose their job and their company squanders a critical resource. Wilson's post as special advisor on mental health allowed him to put regulations in place to prevent this from happening.

> It's important for those who suffer from mental illness to talk about it frankly. The community can then begin to discuss these illnesses openly, and perhaps when they themselves fall ill, they will be more willing to seek medical help.

Michael Wilson started thinking about promoting mental illness research many years ago. He had worked for the Canadian Cancer Society, one of 45,000 annual volunteers. Mental health, despite heavy personal costs, attracts few supporters. It's not trendy to be a mental health volunteer. You don't often hear about ballroom galas for depression research, though they exist in spades for other illnesses (see Chapter 28). Wilson decided, therefore, that this was a place where he could make a difference. So he got involved with what was then the Clarke Institute of Psychiatry. Tragically, fate made sure that he stayed committed to the cause when his son fell ill. Cameron, who had once been energetic and athletic, suddenly took to spending all his time in bed. The family thought he had mononucleosis; he went to see several doctors but it took time to reach the right diagnosis. Initial treatment was not effective enough to prevent Cameron from taking his own life. Michael had left politics at that time but, bravely, took up speaking engagements again, lecturing throughout Canada on the plight and gaps in service for the mentally ill.

Relatively few private research institutions, community organizations, and foundations fund mental illness and mental health research. And university healthcare dollars tend to go toward physical health. Raising funds for mental illness is difficult everywhere but a harder struggle in Canada than in the United States. Michael Wilson believes there are several reasons for this. The first is self-evident: There are more wealthy people in the U.S., and many more of those whom we might call the "super-rich." The second reason is that Americans have a long tradition of private philanthropy while Canada historically relies more on the government. In the case of stigmatized illnesses, this phenomenon exacts a heavy toll: Unless there is political will to fund mental illness, research will die on the vine. Furthermore, there is a distinction between the two countries in terms of tax structure. The top tax bracket in the U.S. starts at a threshold that is about four times higher than in Canada.

> That is a structural impediment to charitable giving because you cannot generate wealth as fast in Canada as you can in the States. It is from that top level of wealth that significant levels of philanthropy spring, particularly when it comes to research.

However, the nature of Canadian charity is evolving. Wilson noticed a significant change in charitable giving during the period he was first in politics. He believes there is a real desire to give in Canada. Canadians are inherently a generous people but the wealth in the country needs to grow. The necessary funding base for basic scientific research cannot be achieved unless the seeds of prosperity and entrepreneurship are planted first.

Fortunately, mental health receives more money now than in times past. Michael Wilson remembers that when some of his predecessors were raising money for mental illness in the late 1980s, they would hear statements such as: "I don't want to give money to you because people will then ask why and I don't want to have to explain that my wife suffers from depression." That isn't so much the case today. People are now more likely to talk openly about mental illness in the family and are more willing to volunteer their time for mental health causes. As Michael Wilson says, "It is better than it was by a good margin but, when compared to diabetes, cancer, heart and stroke, and AIDS, it is still tougher for mental illness."

In the policy community, there has been talk of special tax breaks for charitable organizations that raise money for mental health, but Wilson is not in favor. He says:

> Individual research domains are no longer as separable as they once were. Progress in basic research in one field can benefit another. It is not for a politician or a bureaucrat to decide whether one field of research should get different tax breaks from another. What they should do is set the stage for a level playing field for all medical research. Two important fields of research today are imaging and genetics. Should we be drawing a distinction between imaging focused on Alzheimer's and imaging focused on depression? Should we be drawing a distinction between genetics as it relates to mental illness and genetics as it applies to other diseases? I wouldn't focus on one particular research area anymore than I would focus on mining shares eligible for a tax break but not oil and gas shares. It's not fair.

Wilson uses the example of his son, Cameron. "There was a debate among the doctors over whether he suffered from schizophrenia or depression. My theory is that if they can't figure out that difference, why should I, as a layman, be drawing lines between funding depression or schizophrenia?"

Michael Wilson grew up in a family where people wanted to give something back to Canada, and that played a determining role in his life. It led him into public life, which, he acknowledges, is at times stressful. A long-time student of what generates stress in public life, he knows that the mind is a complex muscle that pulls in one direction and pushes in another.

> It is more difficult than private life because when you make a mistake you are sitting out at the end of the diving board and there is only one way down. There is more stress because none of us like to be wrong, period, but if you are wrong in front of thirty million people, well, that is stress. Stress in itself is not a bad thing. Stress teaches you, it motivates you, and it allows you to do things at a higher level of intensity for a longer period of time than would otherwise be the case. But it must be managed. Does this put undue pressure on families? I've watched the families of colleagues I served with and sometimes the stress of leading a public life has been difficult, and sometimes not. People react in different ways.

NeuroScience Canada recently launched a program to fund excellence in research in the area of brain regeneration and repair. There is mounting evidence that the brain can repair itself. Neurogenesis, the formation of new neurons, has been demonstrated in several regions of the cerebral cortex that mediate cognitive and perceptual function.

The first grants in this program have been awarded to teams led by Freda Miller (central nervous system white matter repair), Michael Salter (research on chronic pain), and Yu Tian Wang (therapeutic strategies to repair brain abnormalities in psychiatric disorders). An international committee of experts selected these projects as having a high potential for achieving breakthroughs. The three awards are valued at $1.5 million each, spread over three years. The researchers will be using new technology to study the ways in which the brain repairs itself and how that ability can be enhanced. The discoveries that result will, it is hoped, lead to new treatments for a wide range of disorders of the nervous system, including Alzheimer's disease, multiple sclerosis, spinal cord injuries, chronic pain, schizophrenia and autism. Each team will receive an additional $60,000 over three years for the purpose of networking and for knowledge dissemination.

Wilson considers this blend of investment and knowledge transfer critical to success: "NeuroScience Canada," he says, "developed the Brain Repair Program with the goal of giving our world-class Canadian neuroscience researchers every opportunity to seek breakthroughs, so that we can alleviate the human, economic, and societal costs of brain disorders."

Politically, Wilson is best known in Canada for brokering the first free-trade agreement with the US during his tenure as Finance Minister. In 2004, he was named to the Order of Canada for serving as a "force for positive change throughout his career." In 2005, he was appointed special advisor to the federal governement on mental health. On February 16, 2006, Wilson was named Ambassador to the United States, one of the most important political posts in Canada. The same qualities that made him an advocate for the mental health of Canadians will allow him to advocate for Canada.

Further Reading

Neuroscience Canada. Available at: http://www.neurosciencecanada.ca

Brain Research Centre, Vancouver. Available at: http://www.brain.ubc.ca/

Canadian Psychiatric Research Foundation. Available at: http://www.cprf.ca/

Miller FD, Kaplan DR. Signaling mechanisms underlying dendrite formation. Curr Opin Neurobiol. 2003;13:391–398.

Nong Y, Huang YQ, Salter MW. NMDA receptors are movin' in. Curr Opin Neurobiol. 2004;14:353–361.

Chapter 25

Peer Support for Social Phobia: Earla Dunbar

> *"Always do what you are afraid to do."*
> Ralph Waldo Emerson

Those who share a disability have something to offer each other that professionals cannot provide. Peer counselors such as Earla Dunbar of Toronto are easy to confide in, have acquired invaluable expertise in problem identification and can forge a unique alliance with peers that serves as a powerful agent for change.

Earla Dunbar is founder of the Social Anxiety Support Group of Toronto where she functions as a peer support worker and group facilitator for individuals suffering from social phobia. She is part of the mental health peer support movement, a collective whose history dates back to 1935. It began with Alcoholics Anonymous, one of whose founding principles was that individuals who had experienced and overcome their battle with alcohol would be more effective than anyone else in guiding others out of the maze of alcohol addiction. Peer support in mental health rests on the belief that those who share similar experiences have something to offer each other that professionals cannot provide. Several aspects of help lend themselves particularly to peer involvement. They are: providing information about appropriate resources, lending emotional support, encouraging self-exploration and skills development, identifying problems, setting goals, planning action, and monitoring the attainment of self-set goals.

By empowering former clients to be peer counselors, a peer support model distinguishes itself from the medical model. Professional medicine draws a dividing line between doctor/healers and patient/sufferers. The peer support model acknowledges that healers are sometimes sufferers and patients can, at times, be doctors. The theory of the effectiveness of peer support fits best with the recovery model of mental illness, peer support workers seeing themselves as sufficiently recovered from their own ills to be now capable of helping others.

Earla's group has a website: http://www.socialphobia.ca/ where the group's mission is explained: "The Social Phobia Support Group of Toronto is committed to provide group and individual support, understanding, educational information and processes to enable individuals suffering from social phobia to control their disorder and achieve greater stability within their communities, workplaces and individual lives."

On the website is an open letter from Earla:

> Most of my life I was terrified of people. They terrified me so much I would hide from them when I could. Life would have been so much easier for me if there were no people in the world. I would not have to worry about what I looked like, what I said and what I did. I always felt people were watching me and being critical of me. I could never relax. I thought people found me boring, stupid and that they knew I had no friends. I was sad, lonely, and in so much emotional pain I really wanted to die.
>
> But in 1998, when I was 44, I found out I was a social phobic. What I was feeling was wrong and I learned I could get well. With cognitive behavior therapy and medication my life has completely changed around. I am outgoing, happy, and, believe it or not, love people.
>
> The struggle to get well was very painful and hard. At times I wanted to give up the therapy. But deep inside me I wanted to live and be like other people. I wanted to be in control if my illness. CBT (cognitive behavior therapy) made me realize that my thoughts were false and these thoughts held me back. It taught me that I was the one in control of my thoughts and feelings, not other people and there is no magic pill. You control your thoughts and feelings. You have a choice. Life should not hurt; it should feel good.
>
> There are ups and downs in life but it should not be filled with anxiety and depression. Each step, no matter how small you think it is, will bring you closer to having control over your anxiety. The anxiety will no longer control your life....
>
> You have a choice: Life should not hurt; it should feel good. Face the fear, face the fight and believe in yourself. You can get well.

Groups are known to exert a powerful effect on their members because of the strong group identity that the facilitator needs to forge. This puts heavy demands on the facilitator.

> My group: it started in 2001, which is four years ago now. We started it in High Park, downtown, with three members, and now we meet three times a week with 65 members. This is my passion, doing this. There are 65 members but they don't come all at once. They come maybe three times a week or once a week or once

a month or once a year just to check in. Usually we have six to 16 members for any group and the ages range anywhere between 18 to 65 and there is a mixture of men and women.

People may be quiet for months in the group but then they'll say: "Hello, how are you?" and it's as if they had given me a gift and it's beautiful. For some of them, it's just a comfortable place to be. They can do and say what they want and nobody will think they are strange. Of course, some will come and find it's not for them.

Earla (an unusual name that was also her mother's name) began suffering social anxiety at the age of five when she first started school. She had trouble interacting with other children and always felt sick.

It was difficult for me to leave the house without my parents. I started school and I was sick all the time with stomachaches. I would have anxiety about going to school, and I didn't sleep very much. Whenever a teacher asked me a question, I'd freeze and I'd get a scolding, or the ruler.

Earla's father, Wallace Clark Dunbar, died when she was ten. As a result of his death, Earla fell into a severe depression.

When my father died, my mom and the psychiatrist I was seeing threatened me and took me up to Penetanguishene, a mental hospital, when I was ten and it was this big huge hospital with big fences and the people there were a little, you know, "strange" and they said: "if you don't straighten up, this is were you'll end up."

So Earla tried to hide her fears, which led directly to the abuse of drugs and alcohol in high school and then to dropping out of school in grade 11.

School was pretty much impossible. I thought everyone was paying attention to me and thinking negative thoughts about me.

Quitting school did not make the symptoms go away.

If I had to go buy milk at the corner store, I would do it the first thing in the morning because my anxiety would get worse in the afternoon and I couldn't do it then. So as soon as I got up, I'd go out to get milk and I'd cross the street to the corner store – all the time I was worried about seeing somebody. If I went into the corner store to get milk I'd have to have it written down because my anxiety was so bad. I'd forget why I was even there. I didn't really spend much time outside. If somebody knocked on the door, I wouldn't answer. I had to hide behind a chair – just so I knew they couldn't see me. At work, even making a phone call was terrifying. I had to make sure that no one was listening. I was terrified of people. I would shake, blush, my stomach would become upset and my hands would sweat.

Everything seemed to get worse for Earla until she was laid off her last job in 1992.

Now I didn't have a routine and I didn't have to go to work, so it just made it worse. For six years it was hard for me to leave my house, even to go in my backyard. I loved to garden, but I'd check to see if anyone was out there and if somebody came out into their backyard, even though they couldn't see me because it was pretty closed in, I'd run back inside. I didn't want them to see me because when you have social phobia you think everyone is judging you. I didn't feel I was important enough to spend time with anyone – my opinions were not important and I had nothing to say. So even walking out my front door, most of the time I couldn't do it.

It was getting really worse, my panic attacks were so severe that I had, I think they call it "disassociation" where you feel like you are above your body looking down. That was happening all the time, I'd wake up from my sleep and it would be happening and I could see myself floating above my body and thought I was going to die and I'd say, my God – it was really terrifying.

When Earla went for help in 1992, she was first diagnosed with chronic fatigue syndrome. Feelings of panic were taking over her life and she thought of suicide, and tried it. Her therapist finally referred her to Dr. Martin Katzman at the Centre for Addiction and Mental Health.

In 1998 he diagnosed me with social phobia, agoraphobia, panic disorder, and depression. With his help and medications and CBT I've become better. I still see him and I am also going for psychotherapy with Kate Kitchen, a social worker, and I've been doing that for over a year and a half.

With the help of her doctor, she began to keep a thought record of her fears and gradually began to face them. (For more on social anxiety, please see Chapter 2).

I've gotten so well that now I want to be a voice for people who are afraid. So now I do that. I've been on TV and I've been interviewed before and I am comfortable in this role.

Earla Dunbar is on the Board of Directors of the Anxiety Disorders Association of Canada and the Chair of its consumer advisory committee. Because social phobia is Canada's third most common mental health problem and often, as in Earla's case,

Rates of Anxiety Disorders in Canada	
Panic Disorder	1.3%
Social Anxiety Disorder	6.5%
Specific Phobia	7.4%
Agoraphobia	2.0%
Obsessive Compulsive Disorder	0.8%
Generalized Anxiety Disorder	2.1%
Any Anxiety Condition	12.6%

Source: Anxiety Disorders Association of Manitoba and Provincial Anxiety Disorders Strategy, BC, 2002. http://www.anxietycanada.ca/
(Post-traumatic stress disorder was not evaluated in this study but falls in the range of two to four percent)

starts in childhood, Earla believes that it is imperative that teachers be educated about it as well as about the other anxiety disorders of childhood and adolescence. The Canadian Psychiatric Research Foundation distributes a handbook for teachers entitled *When Something's Wrong*. The book first appeared in 2003 and is made up of eight sections: Anxiety Disorders, Autism, Depression, Eating Disorders, Control Disorders, Schizophrenia, Tourette Syndrome, and Resources. Each disorder section describes the disorder and lists the behaviors associated with it so that teachers can recognize them early. The book also offers helpful strategies that teachers can use to assist their students. Unfortunately it was not available when Earla Dunbar was a little girl, so her battle was longer than it need have been. But like the legend of the phoenix that rises from the flames, Earla has shown that recovery is possible, no matter how difficult the battle may have been.

Further Reading

Anthony WA. Recovery from mental illness: the guiding vision of the mental health service system in the 1990s. Psychosoc Rehab J. 1993;16:11–23.

Anxiety Disorder Association of Canada. Available at: http://www.anxietycanada.ca/

CPRF. When something's wrong. Ideas for teachers. Available at: http://www.cprf.ca/Order/order.html

Dunbar E. Social phobia. Available at: http://intotem.buffnet.net/mhw/41ed.htm

Hall G, Nelson G. Social networks, social support, personal empowerment, and the adaptation of psychiatric consumers/ survivors: path analytic models. Soc Science Med. 1996;43:1743–1754.

Mead S, Hilton D, Curtis L. Peer support: a theoretical perspective. Psychiatr Rehabil J. 2001;25:134–141.

Mowbray CT, Moxley DP, Collins ME. Consumers as mental health providers: first-person accounts of benefits and limitations. J Behav Health Serv Res. 1998;25:397–411.

Resnick SG, Fontana A, Lehman AF, Rosenhek RA. An empirical conceptualization of the recovery orientation. Schizophr Res. 2005;75:119–128.

Solomon P, Draine J. The state of knowledge of the effectiveness of consumer provided services. Psychiatr Rehabil J. 2001;25:20–27.

Young SL, Ensing DS. Exploring recovery from the perspective of people with psychiatric disabilities. Psychiatr Rehab J. 1999;22:219–231.

Chapter 26

Philanthropy: Joseph M. Tanenbaum Exemplifies Its Meaning

"To give away money is an easy matter, and in any man's power. But to decide to whom to give it, and how large and when, and for what purpose and how, is neither in every man's power – nor an easy matter. Hence it is that such excellence is rare, praiseworthy and noble."

Aristotle

According to Maimonides, the highest level of righteousness or tzedaka is to ensure that the recipient is never again in need. Such philanthropy initiates the process of self-sufficiency. Joey and Toby Tanenbaum, through their ten year provision of an annual Schizophrenia Research Award to the Canadian Psychiatric Research Foundation, exemplify this level of tzedaka.

Ever since Bill Gates and his wife Melinda gave an initial $16.5 million to improve health care for the poor in developing countries, the face of global philanthropy has changed. It has become much more ambitious. Benefactors now address important social issues, not only world poverty but also mental health. Philanthropy has become more strategic. Donors are taking the same planned approach to charitable giving as they have used previously to amass wealth in the marketplace. There is a new hands-on involvement on the part of donors. They want to direct the funds in very specific ways and it may sometimes now be a requirement for the agencies that receive funding to put donors on their boards. The new philanthropy can come with conditions. Increasingly, it demands results. It has become business-like. Recipients of funds must meet pre-selected milestones and produce outcomes that are measurable and competitive. They have to demonstrate efficiency and be transparent (i.e., clearly show how the money is spent) or lose their funding. Many of today's big givers are no longer interested in leaving large inheritances to their children. They believe that the example of a lifetime of hard work and devotion to a purpose is a more valuable legacy than money. Increasingly, they want to be alive to witness the good their money can accomplish, not wait to do good until they themselves are dead.

Joey Tanenbaum first learned the importance of charity from his grandmother, his *Bubbie*, when he was two and a half years old. He learned the lesson well. It was the Sabbath and he was at his grandparents' home where six rabbis were sitting down to lunch with the family. He noticed that his grandmother stayed behind in the kitchen. "Why aren't you eating, Bubbie?" he asked her. "There isn't enough food," she said. He said: "Why should the guests eat and not you?" She answered: "My son, no matter how little one has, one must always share." That lesson has become Tanenbaum's ethic. It is why he and his wife give so generously to charity. They have been major donors to healthcare, to the theatre and visual arts, and to Israel. And for ten years, via the Canadian Psychiatric Research Foundation, they donated $50,000 a year to the Joey and Toby Award in Schizophrenia Research. At the time, it was the single largest award for schizophrenia research in Canada.

The Tanenbaums wanted to support schizophrenia research because one of their five children was given that diagnosis. This son graduated from grade 13 and, like all the Tanenbaum children, went to University in the United States. After one semester, he returned home very distressed, unable to continue his studies. Soon afterward, he was diagnosed with schizophrenia but never accepted the diagnosis and refused, as so many young people with schizophrenia do, the treatment offered him. (For more on schizophrenia, please see Chapters 13, 18, 19, 21, 26, and 27).

It is extremely difficult for a person to accept the fact that he or she has a disorder of the mind. The nature of schizophrenia is such that it fools the person into believing that what he thinking is true and what others tell him is a lie. Usually it takes a long time before a person with schizophrenia accepts the possibility that something may be wrong with the way they think. Almost everyone with this illness initially denies being ill.

Their son's refusal to accept illness and take responsibility for its treatment made the next ten years very difficult for the Tanenbaums – their son disappeared; they didn't know where he was. Friends would report seeing him, his parents would try to have him come home, he refused and they lost him again. There was essentially no contact for ten years. This happened to be a difficult period for the family in other ways as well. Harold, Joey's older brother and business partner, was diagnosed with malignant melanoma in 1977 and passed away nine months later. Joey's father, Max, fell ill and suddenly Joey had to take over the entire family business. At that time, the Tanenbaums were the largest steel manufacturers and distributors in Canada. They had 27 plants across Canada and the United States and 3,650 employees. But, in 1981, interest rates rose and debts started to accumulate. Bankruptcy seemed imminent and only by dint of very hard work did Joey manage to pay off the debt and emerge unscathed. The difficult period was soon to be over. In 1984, Joey and Toby heard that their lost son was working on a banana plantation in Israel. Joey flew there and met with him in Jerusalem's King David Hotel and pleaded with him to return to Toronto. As if by magic, the young man seemed to pull himself out of his psychosis. He continues today to feel somewhat different from others, but he tells his parents that he likes the person he is. He feels at peace with himself. Their son's recovery motivated Joey and Toby to donate funds for schizophrenia research, to reward Canadian scientists who have made major advances in the area, and to inspire young scientists to learn more so that the disease can eventually be conquered.

Their idea, consonant with Maimonides' highest level of *tzedaka*, was to take the lead, to champion a cause, and then to leave it to others in the Canadian Psychiatric Research Foundation to carry the baton. What has disappointed the Tanenbaums is that no other donors have stepped forward to perpetuate the Schizophrenia Research Award after their own ten-year support of it came to an end. They attribute the reluctance of donors to assume this particular challenge to the continuing stigma surrounding mental illness.

The RaMBaM, or Rabbi Moshe ben Maimon, (Maimonides) identified eight levels of charity, or doing justice. They are, from the lowest to the highest:

1. Giving unwillingly
2. Giving cheerfully but little
3. Giving adequately but only when asked
4. Giving to a known beneficiary without having to be asked
5. Giving to an unknown recipient but not anonymously.
6. Giving anonymously to a known recipient.
7. Giving anonymously to an unknown recipient.
8. The highest level of charity is to give in order to prevent another person from ever being poor again (i.e., lending money to start a business, finding a person a job, teaching a person a trade)

As much as he owes to his *Bubbie*, Joey Tanenbaum's hero is his *Zayde*. Grandfather Abraham Tanenbaum arrived in Toronto in 1911 from Parczew, Poland. Parczew is north of Lublin, on what used to be the Polish-Lithuanian border. Grandfather had eight dollars in his pocket and, with that, he bought a pushcart and began to peddle scrap metal. After three years, he had saved enough money to bring his wife and two sons to Canada. (Joey's father was the younger son). By 1917, Abraham Tanenbaum had bought a horse and started a company, the Runnymede Metal and Salvage Company, located at Runnymede and Dundas. He had purchased the property with a $200 down payment and a 3% mortgage. When he sold it in 1921 to the Toronto Railway commission (now the Toronto Transit Company), the newspapers reported that he received $96,000 for it. It was a typographical error. The sum was really $16,000, but the typo made Abraham Tanenbaum's reputation! In 1928, the family business, now called Runnymede Iron and Steel, bought out Reid and Brown and, by 1940, they had become the second largest steel company in Toronto, next to Dominion Bridge. With his two sons, Abraham built a great empire.

I'll never forget my grandfather saying to me in '42 when I was only 10," reminisces Joey Tanenbaum, "remember one thing my son; never forget from whence you came, don't make money your god, there is only one God, the God in heaven. Make business your science and you'll become one of the great men in Canada."

Second of seven children, Joey followed in the family footsteps. He graduated in civil engineering at the University of Toronto and joined the family business at York Steel Construction Limited. "It was the best steel business in Canada," says Joey. Years later, after selling the business, he moved into the art world and built what he calls "the best" art collection. His interests changed from industry to art, but the drive to be the best, learned at his grandfather's knee, remained the same. He feels strongly about always striving for the best, he feels strongly about his family, he feels strongly about his God. He believes that the strife in the world could be overcome if everyone acknowledged that there is one God in heaven.

He also feels strongly about the taboo associated with schizophrenia. He has been amazed about how many people have told him, after he has spoken about his son, that their child also suffers from schizophrenia but that they keep it hidden, and seldom reveal the secret. The taboo has abated since fifteen years ago but is still present. It stands in the way of raising money for mental illnesses of any kind. It helps when prominent Canadians who are role models for others, like the Hon. Michael Wilson (see Chapter 24), stand up and speak about the mental illnesses affecting their own children. Joey feels that more people should make such statements publicly at every appropriate occasion, in every major city across the country. Everyone needs to understand that mental illnesses exist in every family and that secrets need to be divulged before they can be attended to.

"To me the CPRF is the answer to find the solution to mental illness," says Joey Tanenbaum.

Joey Tanenbaum feels that there is more charitable giving in the U.S. compared to Canada not only because of the tax structure (although that too is important) but because Canadians identify with their parents' country of origin and consider themselves British, Scots, and Irish rather than thinking of themselves as Canadian first.

"There is not the same commitment to one's country, to Canada. The Americans are much more active in giving to scientific research. There is enormous wealth in this country but, as a group, we don't seem to want to share it and give it back to Canada. It is absolutely tragic. We have a lot to learn, we Canadians, from Americans when it comes to charitable giving. If I were in charge, what I would promote would be that when you give, whether it be cash or a stock, to a charitable institution, that it be 100% deductible. Not 50%, not 75% but 100% deductible."

Leading Canadian Charitable Trusts	
Lucie and André Chagnon Foundation	$1.3 billion
Vancouver Foundation	$564 million
J.W. McConnell Family Foundation	$464 million
Hospital for Sick Children Foundation	$400 million

Source: The Globe and Mail, Jan. 13, 2005

"Don't count on politicians to do something for mental illness. Politicians don't seem to have a clue as to what is good for the country," continues Mr. Tanenbaum. "I have had nothing but aggravation in dealing with those bureaucrats in Ottawa. Their minds are only focused on getting re-elected. They seem to have no respect for the people who give back to their country. We've been through that, my wife and I, ourselves."

When asked about the highlights of his life, Joey Tanenbaum mentions the Order of Canada he received in 1996. He has received many honors but this one made him truly proud. He had fulfilled his *Zayde's* hope for him. He had become a great man of Canada by contributing at multiple levels of *tzedaka*. On May 22, 2005, he and his wife, Toby, celebrated 50 years of marriage and 50 years of *tzedaka*. The Joey and Toby Tanenbaum Charitable Foundation distributes grants of $185,000 annually. Over the years, the Foundation has donated an estimated $60 million to Canada.

Further Reading

Masterpieces from the Tanenbaum gift. Available at: http://www.cjnews.com/pastissues/01/mar1-01/tab/tab.htm

Sharp R, Abella I, Goodman, E. Growing up Jewish. Canadians tell their own stories. , Toronto: McLelland & Stewart Inc.; 1997.

Tzedaka. Available at: http://www.tzedaka.org/

Chapter 27

Renée Claire Marier: Proceeds to Give Away

"In everything I showed you that by working hard in this manner you must help the weak and remember the words of the Lord Jesus, that He Himself said, 'It is more blessed to give than to receive.'"
Acts 20

Being only on the receiving end of help is uncomfortable. Feeling beholden severely restricts freedom of choice and damages self-esteem. As an artist who has been disabled by schizophrenia, Renée Marier donates a percentage of earnings from every one of her art sales to the cause of schizophrenia research. She much prefers giving to receiving.

Marier (pronounced in English as Mariyay) is an artist who has dedicated her art to schizophrenia research. Schizophrenia research is her cause because she has suffered with this illness from a young age. "It has affected all my life. I no longer hope for a cure for myself but I want to contribute toward one so that children with schizophrenia will be born with hope for a better life." Marier would like to be able to donate large amounts of money to her cause but, unfortunately, does not have the resources. Because of illness, she is unable to maintain a regular job. There are days when she is not even well enough to leave her apartment. She receives approximately $600/month in disability payments and has to support herself, her cat, Muche (a French word that means "shy one"), and her dog, Taffy. As an artist, she knows the importance of establishing routines, but she finds the routine of a typical nine to five job impossible. An artist's work depends on inspiration. Sometimes she wakes up in the middle of the night with an idea and needs to immediately put her idea on paper. "I cannot wait, I cannot sleep, I have to get up and do it." Sometimes she keeps going and going without stop and without sleep for 48 hours. She works from her home, which doubles as a studio.

Leaving the safety of her apartment is not easy for Marier.

> When I go out in public, I get dizzy, I get scared, and I think I will fall. Sometimes I start hearing voices and I don't know if they are real or not and I get paranoid and sometimes I can become aggressive.

She is not able to go to crowded places, like theatres or concert halls, and shopping is a chore. When she travels to Montreal to visit her family, she has to plan a month in advance, and she takes her pets with her.

> My dog is a working dog. Since I have a hard time going places, I bring my dog with me and that makes it better. I have a card that my doctor signed that says I can bring her into the hospital. I have all the necessary papers; rabies, tags, and everything. In Montreal, dogs are not allowed on the bus so I have a card in French to say that I can bring her on. Sometimes I bring her to group therapy.

Marier finds that keeping busy prevents depression. She paints prodigiously – notecards and original watercolors. Once a month she goes to the Centre for Addiction and Mental Health/Clarke Site to sell her art and raise funds for schizophrenia research. Otherwise…

> I would feel there was no point to my life. I would feel that I was trapped in my apartment and could not get out. This is because I am trapped in my mind and I cannot reach out. Sometimes I have trouble speaking. I feel that I might talk funny and people will think something is wrong with me, so I keep my mouth closed.

Marier started painting before she could write.

> But I stopped for twenty-three years. When I was 19, they gave me medication for the first time and I lost my ability to control my hands; I couldn't even sign my name. Then, after that I was given a drug holiday, and I could write again. So I thought, "if I can write, I can probably paint" but I was afraid of colors since I hadn't painted for so long. So I started sketching. But eventually I became more comfortable so I went into a shop and looked at all the colors and noticed what looked like crayons. I didn't want to crayon but I asked what they were and the man said, "They are water-color crayons." Basically, you draw and then you take a wet brush and go over what you have drawn and it looks like a watercolor. I

thought, "That is interesting!" I bought a box and for about six months I used them. Then I moved onto paints and now I use tubes. I tried acrylic but I still like watercolors the best.

To help herself get back to painting, Marier used to go to the Art Gallery of Ontario, bury herself in the sculpture room, and start sketching. Her sketches were elaborations rather than copies of what she saw. For instance, once she saw the sculpture of a woman leaning back with her legs raised in the act of childbirth. She thought, "She can't enjoy this, having everyone staring at her and not being able to move." So, in her sketch, she raised one of the woman's arms, then another arm, then she drew a baby emerging from the womb and put a smile on the woman's face. In other words, she gave life to the sculpture. She began to envisage the sculpted woman in different life situations and to draw what she imagined, creating cartoon people engaged in a variety of life situations (see, as an example, the cover design of this book, entitled "Let Sleeping Psychiatrists Lie").

Marier gives 50% of the profits from her sales to schizophrenia research. She has a sale every four weeks on Thursdays from 8:30AM to 3:30PM, diligently preparing her cards and paintings for many days in advance.

I made a big sign to go with the sale that says: "Mental Health is Music to my Mind." My art reflects the whimsicality of my life. Joie de vivre makes me paint bright colors and light-hearted sceneries.

I am schizophrenic and I've been receiving mental health support since I was 19 from Medicare and I feel that, if you receive something, you have to give something back. I can't hold down a regular job, so I figured since I have all this time and I paint, I might as well do something positive with it. I am also working for the future. You never know if they will figure out a cure. I was born with schizophrenia and maybe, with research, they will be able to figure out which children will develop schizophrenia and maybe they will be able to help them early and prevent the schizophrenia altogether.

I have lived so long with the symptoms that they have become part of me. So it isn't so much for me; I figure if they cured me then I wouldn't be me anymore. I'd rather spend the rest of my life taking medication that prevents me from being in the hospital but keeping things pretty much the way they are. As long as I don't have side-effects.

Gaining weight is Marier's main side effect.

I am not able to shed it. This is not my body anymore and it is hard to live with. If that could be eliminated and I could become a toothpick again, I'd be happy. I used to weigh 112 pounds then, in the first month after the medication, I gained 20 pounds and then 30 in the following month.

eder-Ischia U, Ebenbichler C, Fleischhacker WW. Olanzapine-induced weight gain and disturbances of lipid and glucose metabolism. Essent Psychopharmacol. 2005;6:112–1127.

Among the atypical antipsychotics, clozapine and olanzapine are known to cause significant weight gain. Along with quetiapine, they may impair glucose metabolism and increase the risk for type 2 diabetes. They are also associated with a rise in triglyceride levels and an increased risk for coronary artery disease.

Marier works on keeping a positive attitude in the face of the challenges in her life. This makes it possible for her to see the ridiculous aspects of new challenges and helps her to overcome them. Laughing defuses the difficulties of daily life.

> Days go by easier when I laugh as opposed to days when I think about my situation. Life is funny. My dog is funny. My cat, she is funny. The things they do make me laugh. I feel like I am a profiteer – I get the most out of funny situations.

Stress and coping

How we handle stress depends upon our attitude. Attitude can also affect the way stress handles us. Optimists are able to cope more effectively with stress. Optimism reduces their chances of developing a stress-related illness. When optimistic people do become ill, they tend to recover more quickly.
http://www.uihealthcare.com/topics/stressandcope/stre5136.html

Marier was in a psychiatric hospital (The Douglas Hospital in Montréal) from 1973 to 1976, and remembers being put in isolation and having to go the bathroom on the floor.

> I had no clothes or bed sheets so I slept on the floor naked. I couldn't see through the door because they put paper over the window. That's worse treatment than people get in jails. But there were good parts too. I worked in the greenhouse and took care of the lawn. W.J. Johnstone, the gardener, was my boss; he was so nice. He was so kind to me, he gave such a boost to my confidence. He'd teach me to do things and then allow me to do them creatively and then he'd bring visitors to see what I had done. He was so proud of me.
>
> At the entrance to the grounds, there was a bed of flowers that spelt out "Douglas." One day Mr. Johnstone told me to go with an employee to write "Douglas" with flowers but the man left out the "u." I noticed the mistake and went to tell him but he was drunk and had fallen asleep. So Mr. Johnstone came and said, "Okay, can you do it?" We took the flowers out and then I raked it all smooth again and put the flowers in properly, making sure it was spelled right.
>
> I used to talk about my hospital experiences in the program they had at the Centre for Addiction and Mental Health called Beyond the Cuckoo's Nest where

I'd talk to students about what it was like to be a psychiatric patient. I was even interviewed on CBC radio and television, in the newspaper, the *Sun* and the *Star*, and on CTV. I don't do that anymore.

Marier believes that the future for people with mental illness lies in education and in research. "I did education before when I volunteered for Beyond the Cuckoo's Nest. Now I do research by raising money for schizophrenia research."

Her fundamental beliefs are that everyone has a reason to be here – no one is superfluous on this earth.

I sometimes get thinking what would happen if I wasn't here. Would there be someone to fill my shoes? To do everything I do, and mean everything I mean to other people? I don't think I am useless. Maybe I'm not as productive in terms of tax dollars as somebody else, but I'm useful in other ways."

Marier comes from what former Québec premier Jacques Parizeau would call a "pure laine" family (descendants of the original French settlers of Lower Canada) who have lived in Québec since 1540. The family has now spread beyond Québec and many of her cousins no longer speak French. Her mother, brother, and sisters live in Montréal. She feels that it is important for families to be informed about mental illness, to be told that it is not a crime.

Depression comes once to everyone in their lifetime and they shouldn't blame themselves and think they did something wrong. Our body gets ill every now and again and so does our mind. If they saw it as a normal part of life there would be less stigma. It would be easier for patients and their families.

She began selling her art and giving the proceeds to research two years ago.

It will be two years this July. I feel I have a purpose now that I have started painting again. I feel that, with my cards, I am giving something back. I am not just receiving when I come here to the Clarke anymore; sometimes I come here and give something back. I hope that balances everything out. I'm hoping to be known as someone who gives, and not just as a patient. I have been receiving psychiatric help for 33 years, all covered by Medicare. Raising funds for research is my way of saying thank you.

Further Reading

CAMH Annual Art Show. Available at: http://www.camh.net/News_events/News_releases_and_media_advisories_and_backgrounders/being_scene_exhibit0604.html
Beyond the Cuckoo's Nest. Available at: http://www.camh.net/About_CAMH/Organizational_Publications/Breakthrough/Winter_2004/cuckoos_nest_btwinter2004.html

Chapter 28

Special Ways of Giving:
Ted and Diana Tremain, Toronto
Sandra Schulze, Calgary

"It is one of the most beautiful compensations of life that no person can
sincerely try to help another without helping themselves."
Ralph Waldo Emerson

A state of "helper's high" has been described in the psychological literature. Giving
to others reduces stress, promotes well-being, and can sometimes induce intense
euphoria. A Toronto couple, Ted and Diana Tremain and a Calgary mother, Sandra
Schulze, have found unique ways of supporting mental health research that assist
not only recipients, but donors too.

Torontonians Ted and Diana Tremain shared a philosophy about the projects they
helped to fund. Before Ted's recent death on December 24, 2005, they were interviewed
together and this is what they said:

> If we give money to a cause, we like to learn more about it. The Centre for Ad-
> diction and Mental Health (CAMH) has been wonderful in this respect; they tell
> us specifically where the money goes, they often invite us to discussions, which
> inform and enlighten us about the research they are supporting. So it works both
> ways; we all benefit.

Benefit to the donor can come in many forms. Diana tells the story of the first
Chair auction (in support of funding Chairs in Psychiatry) held by what was then the
Clarke Institute (now the Centre for Addiction and Mental Health – CAMH). Chairs

of every kind were being auctioned: antique, modern, highchairs, garden benches. Among them all was Michael Smith's laboratory stool. Michael Smith (1932–2000), the 1993 Nobel Prize winner, who donated half his award money to Canadian schizophrenia research, was present at the auction and had contributed his lab stool for sale. His signature was there on the wooden top of the stool, alongside the many doodles he had carved over the years. A number of schizophrenia researchers at CAMH coveted that stool. Diana hatched a plan to bid for it against Dr. Jim Kennedy, psychiatrist and renowned genetic researcher. Her plan was to win the bid and then secretly donate the stool to Dr. Kennedy and his team. She won (much to Jim Kennedy's initial chagrin), placed a big bow around the stool and attached a note saying: "I hope whoever sits on this stool will be inspired by Michael Smith from the bottom up." She slipped it into Dr. Kennedy's laboratory when he wasn't there and left it for him to discover. In this case, the benefit to the donors was Jim Kennedy's surprise and delight.

In 1997 and 1998, Diana was responsible for two series of eight concerts called Music for Midwinter, held every Tuesday during the winter months from 5:30 p.m. to 6:30 p.m. in the Clarke Auditorium. Asked why she initiated the series, Diana said:

> I have always felt music to be a great leveler, uplifter, and something with which to stir up the psyche. I noticed there was little or no music at the Clarke and, having seen what wonders music can perform, I spoke to my friend, the remarkable musician and diva, Mary Lou Fallis. She, too, had seen the power of music through her own performances, so we struck a committee of two in an attempt to bring music to the Clarke. Mary Lou arranged for the musicians (all very professional; everything from jazz, folk, percussion, chamber programs, klezmer, R&B, vocal, and more) and I produced the series. We were given a great deal of enthusiastic assistance from every level of the Clarke community. The concerts were free to the public and the auditorium seemed to be filled to overflowing – particularly in the second year. I have many testimonies as to the pleasure those concerts generated. This was a different but enormously gratifying and enjoyable way of giving both time and money.

Diana Tremain thinks that more money could be raised for research into mental illness if it weren't for the stigma that still surrounds psychiatry. A stigma is a stereotype applied to a group – for instance, the stereotype that the mentally ill are dangerous. Ted stated when interviewed for this Chapter:

> When I started at the Clarke in 1986 (as a member of the Board of Trustees), there were people who mentioned they didn't want letters with the Clarke letterhead arriving at their house because someone might see it and think – or learn – there was a psychiatric problem within the family. That's how tough the stigma was. When it comes to capital funding, other hospitals can use their patient database but we are naturally prevented from doing so because of the confidential nature of

mental illness. When we (the CAMH Foundation) had our first capital campaign, getting through to individuals and corporations was very difficult indeed. However, the turn-around and difference in the last ten years has been phenomenal.

The Canadian Centre of Philanthropy and Statistics Canada estimates that, in 2003, Canadians donated more than $8 billion to charities and volunteered more than two billion hours of time. But when it comes to raising funds for psychiatric research, there are many obstacles. One is that the community is generally not aware of psychiatric advances. It was always the belief of Ted and Diana Tremain that research initiatives and discoveries about successful treatments and cures should be better publicized.

As an unusual example of giving, a few years ago, Diana Dunbar Tremain helped raise $30,000 for the Royal Military College in Kingston by paddling a voyageur canoe (with fourteen men) for six days along the Rideau Canal.

According to the National Council for Voluntary Organizations (NCVO), women are more likely to give money to charity than men and the three most popular areas of donation are medical research, children and young people, and animals. This holds true for Diana Tremain who is a registered nurse who has studied anthropology and psychology at the University of Toronto and has had a lifetime interest in human behavior.

Ted Tremain was raised in Montreal, went to Bishop's College in Lennoxville, Quebec and later attended the Royal Military College of Canada in Kingston (graduated in 1957). A chartered accountant by profession, he worked in Toronto since 1971. He was a senior executive with Consumers Gas and then with Hiram Walker Resources. In 1987, he founded his own consulting firm, providing consulting services to small, family-owned companies. Over the last thirty years of his life he increasingly worked for non-profit organizations, attributing this to deeply rooted family values. When he retired as Chairman of the Clarke Institute Board, he joined the Clarke Foundation Board and later became Chair of the now renamed CAMH Foundation. He was a member of the Capital Campaign Committee of CAMH until his death.

Both the Tremain and Dunbar families have been involved in supporting their respective communities (in Montreal and in Guelph) over many generations so it was only natural for Ted and Diana to follow suit. Diana is certain that their daughter Julia, a lawyer and a social worker and their son Tony, a music and English teacher, will carry on the family tradition. Julia and Tony are already greatly involved, taking a personal interest in helping with the decisions and direction of the family charitable foundation. There are approximately 2000 such private foundations in Canada. Together, in 2002, they held almost $12 billion in assets, a critical support for medical research.

The Tremain hope has always been that when people know how much fun philanthropy can be, contributions will flow freely. The funding for medical research has risen sharply in the past 25 years. The next 25 years, Ted always believed, would show comparable increases in specific support for mental health.

***

After her 21-year-old son, Carlos, took his life, Calgarian Sandra Schulze found a unique way to give his life special meaning. She formed a committee to raise awareness (and funds) for schizophrenia research. An extremely good organizer, she has been successful in educating the public about schizophrenia. The Calgary Herald, for one, ran a full-page article on the topic. "We've had tons of coverage. We create awareness about the illness."

The Schulze organization will every year hold a fundraising party or gala, an event that attracts over 200 people every year. The first year it was held at the Riverbend Community Centre, a small community hall. The next year it was at the Delta hotel in Calgary. For the last four years, it has been at the Hyatt Hotel, the Hyatt Calgary.

> This year our theme is Hollywood; it is more of an entertainment theme. My background is creating events – so this helps me in fundraising.

Special events are in fact the most popular form of fundraising in Canada, used by two-thirds of Canadian charities (although such events account for less than 15% of charitable funds raised). The Brazilian Ball in Toronto, whose beneficiary changes every year, gave 2.5 million dollars in 2005 to cardiac care. The Terry Fox Marathon of Hope is probably the best-known recurrent special event. In Canada, the annual Terry Fox Run is held every September, usually on the second Sunday following Labor Day. The first Terry Fox Run in 1981 attracted 300,000 participants across Canada and raised $3.5 million. To date, more than $360 million has been raised worldwide for cancer research in Terry's name. The first Terry Fox Run was organized in conjunction with the Canadian Cancer Society. In 1988, The Terry Fox Foundation became a Trust, independent of the Canadian Cancer Society, and received tax-exempt charitable status under the Income Tax Act. All money raised by the Foundation is distributed through the National Cancer Institute of Canada. Overhead is negligible. Currently, 87 cents of every dollar raised goes to fund cancer research. There are approximately 4,500 Terry Fox runs per year in 50 different countries, making it one of the most successful charities in the world.

The problem with special-events fund raising, however, is that success is always unpredictable. Many charities end up canceling events rather than using hard–to-come-by volunteer time for an event that might end up in the red.

Sandra Schulze was born in Guatemala City. The family moved first to Oshawa, Ontario and then to Kingston. At age 18, Sandra became a graphic designer and at age 21, she came to Calgary, starting her own agency at the age of 24. She currently runs a one-of-a-kind Internet Café, a cross between Kinko's and a high-end coffee shop, called the Hard Disk Café. It features a series of workstations equipped with PCs and Macs, and photocopiers. It also offers computer and business services such as computer upgrades and marketing consultations. At the same time, there is a daily menu of sandwiches, salads, muffins, coffee, and specialty drinks. Sandra and her husband Jerry have two children, Luke (ten) and Katherine (five).

Carlos was Sandra's eldest son. Excelling in sports, he was a hockey goalie, making it all the way to the AAA Bantam League. The hockey scouts were very interested in him but suddenly, at age 17, Carlos decided he did not want to play hockey anymore. He took up golf and started on a Junior Tour but abandoned that as well. He seemed to be losing interest in all his activities, though he continued working at a driving range and golf course in the summers. One summer he worked at The Calgary Tennis Club. After school he was a bus boy at an elegant seafood restaurant. When he graduated from grade 12, he went to live with his dad in the Virgin Islands (Sandra and her first husband divorced when Carlos was 16). Though he said he enjoyed the sunshine and beaches of the Caribbean, he began feeling "not himself." He became withdrawn and told his mother that he was hearing voices. By age 19, he was back in Calgary. He was not a happy person but sometimes, unexpectedly, he would start to giggle. Despite his personal difficulties, he started attending a program at the DeVry Institute.

And then he went to Ontario for the wedding of his father's sister. After the wedding, while the relatives gathered at his grandmother's house in the country, Carlos began to think that his dad was making faces at him. He became convinced that all his relatives were vampires and were plotting to kill him. He fled his grandmother's house in his dad's car, drove to the nearest farm and told the occupants that he was being chased by vampires, that his grandmother was the leader of the vampire clan and that he was going to die. The neighbors called the police, as a result of which Carlos disappeared for two days. He eventually ended up in the Peter Lougheed hospital in Calgary where he was diagnosed with schizophrenia.

After that, Carlos was in an out of the hospital for two years. He received several treatments but, unfortunately, none of his treatments really worked. Nevertheless, he went back to DeVry and seemed to be doing well there.

> One day he drove me to a meeting and, when I came home two hours later, I found him hanging in our garage. We had just spent a nice weekend together as it was Super Bowl weekend. We watched the game at home on the Sunday. He helped me make mashed potatoes for our roast beef dinner after the game. This was his last dinner. He died at about 1:00 p.m. on Monday. My meeting was at 11:00 a.m. downtown. He drove me there and told me he loved me when I got out of the car. It still doesn't make sense.
>
> I had gone to the Schizophrenia Society to try to find information about this illness. The people at the Society kept insisting that I sign up for meetings and that I join programs. I was never given useful information. I was never told that suicide could result from schizophrenia. I never thought that this could happen, although it happens quite often from what I know now. Parents should be made aware of this very important fact. There needs to be more information right away about the potential of people killing themselves.
>
> If I were in charge, I'd create a massive national marketing plan that would allow different bodies like the Schizophrenia Society of Calgary or the Mental

Health Board in Saskatoon or the Society of Red Dear, to have access to specific funds to print educational material about the symptoms and risks of schizophrenia so parents and teachers would recognize them. What is needed is a unified Canadian marketing plan. We need to catch these things earlier and make sure that parents don't feel that they can't approach their doctors if they feel those symptoms are there. You need to let parents know what the symptoms are and it would be helpful if parents knew what to do right way. We need an association, a Canadian association like the Canadian Cancer Board. We have fragmented organizations and there is no overall co-ordination. There is no "body" that I can see that oversees all the awareness functions. Cancer raises millions of dollars because of their awareness and because they plan similar events across the country.

Altogether, Canada hosts about 75,000 dispersed, disconnected charitable organizations. A Chamber of Charities modeled on the Chamber of Commerce, with national, provincial, and local branches, could link these charities, foster specialization and eliminate unnecessary duplication. A centralized organization would also improve visibility with the public. Until then, individuals like the Tremains and Sandra Schulze create their own unique ways of contributing to the well-being of society and, in so doing, experience the satisfaction of seeing something important take shape as a direct result of their efforts. By making a difference in the lives of others, they give special meaning to their own.

Further Reading

Hard Disk Café. Available at: http://www.world66.com/northamerica/canada/alberta/calgary/internetcafes/hard_disk_cafe

Luks A, Payne P. The healing power of doing good. New York: Fawcett Columbine; 1991.

Michael Smith autobiography: Available at: http://nobelprize.org/chemistry/laureates/1993/smith-autobio.html

Michael Smith autobiography. Available at: http://nobelprize.org/chemistry/laureates/1993/smith-autobio.html

The Michael Smith Awards for Research in Schizophrenia. Available at http://www.cihr-irsc.gc.ca/e/22374.html

Dr. James Kennedy. Available at: http://www.student.cs.uwaterloo.ca/~mblanktr/Kennedy.htm

The Rideau Canal trip: http://www.forces.gc.ca/site/community/MapleLeaf/html_files/html_view_f.asp?page=Vol3_38___16backcover

Picard A. A call to alms: the voluntary sector in the age of cutbacks. Available at http://www.andrepicard.com/Atkinson%20Fellowship.html

The Terry Fox Run. Available at: http://www.terryfoxrun.org/english/home/default.asp?s=1

Tremain, Edward. Obituary. Available at: http://www.whughes.ca/RMC/RMCTremainTed.htm

Chapter 29

Transcendence: Jack Barr and his "Triple Whammy"

"Sorrows come not single spy but full battalion."
Shakespeare

The example of Jack Barr, a Halifax senior, illustrates the phenomenon of gerotranscendence – how adaptive development can take place with age. His story is one of gradual rescaling of goals, closer connections to family, new understanding of the spiritual dimension of life, discovery of non-material and unselfish sources of happiness; in short, the achievement of wisdom.

Jack Barr, now in his late 60s and living in Halifax, suffered for much of his adult life from what could be called "a triple whammy" – bipolar disorder, alcoholism, and the secondary effects of a burst brain aneurysm.

The origins of these troubles are somewhat obscure to him. His childhood was difficult, perhaps because his father went away to fight in World War II when Jack was five and did not return until he was ten. Mr. Barr senior was in the Royal Canadian Navy and took part in the Battle of the Atlantic. Jack's mother, nervous for her husband's safety, was "rough" on her two sons. Jack remembers "a lot of beatings." Soon after his father returned from the war, another brother was born and family dynamics made Jack a rebel by the time he reached his teens. Drinking began when he was seventeen and got serious by the time he was 21.

> I began drinking alcoholically and everything became pure hell. At first I loved it and I'd play poker with friends and go square dancing. Then, as it does with every

alcoholic where it starts off fun, it turns on you. Once it turns on you it makes your life horrible. I was unhappy but it had a grip on me and, like all alcoholics, I couldn't stop drinking."

Mr. Barr is right. Regular use of alcohol over time induces tolerance so that the desired effect (euphoria, sociability, energy) can only be achieved through higher and higher doses. Heavy use over long periods of time disrupts everything – social, family, and working life. Once started, it is not easy to stop. There are uncomfortable withdrawal symptoms. Trying to stop drinking means jumpiness, sleeplessness, sweating, nausea, and vomiting. In some instances, people experience physical tremors, convulsions, and hallucinations. Abrupt withdrawal can even result in death. (Please see Chapter 16 for more about alcoholism).

Being a radio announcer was what Jack had always wanted to do and he achieved his ambition at age 21, even as his drinking spiraled out of control. He held on to his radio job for over 20 years despite his drinking. On top of that, he developed a bipolar disorder at age 24. His ability to work says something about his strength and determination but life, needless to say, was not easy.

It is an offence in Canada to drive with a blood alcohol content of 0.08% or greater. Mr. Barr was arrested five times for drinking and driving.

It [jail] doesn't help, because as soon as you get out, you start doing it again. Unless you get alcohol out of your life nothing helps. You can use fines, jail, but unless you deal with the alcoholism, nothing the government says or does to you will help the problem. Wives leave [Mr. Barr has been married and divorced four times], families are taken away, but alcohol is the most important thing. That was the case in my life from the age of 21 until 1995. There was nothing more important than alcohol.

Jack Barr tried getting help early on, in his mid-twenties, but his attendance at therapy programs was sporadic. The message didn't take, probably because he was hit by his second strike, psychotic symptoms first diagnosed as schizophrenia. For two years, Mr. Barr was treated for schizophrenia; only after two years was the diagnosis changed to bipolar disorder. The differentiation between the two disorders in their initial acute stage can be very hard to make – it is often the longitudinal course of illness (whether people recover fully or partially, whether they can go back to work or not) that distinguishes the two diagnostic categories. Some researchers wonder if the two illnesses (schizophrenia and bipolar disorder) are perhaps different expressions of a common underlying genetic predisposition. In the case of Mr. Barr, as with many others, there was no prior family history of either disorder. Though diagnoses are hard to make in psychiatry, a diagnostic label can, however, wield a very powerful influence on recovery: "Knowing I wasn't schizophrenic helped," states Mr. Barr, unconsciously reflecting the different degrees of stigma attached to the various psychiatric diagnoses.

He experienced stigma when first admitted to hospital for manic depression.

> Maybe there wasn't any (stigma), and it was just me feeling it. I felt degraded. I
> don't think there is any stigma anymore. I don't go around telling people I'm a
> manic-depressive or have been in hospital, but people who find out don't seem
> to treat me any differently. They care about me, they don't let the disease affect
> the way they feel about me. They care about how it affects me, but that's because
> they care about me.
>
> I've been lucky to not have been particularly stigmatized and I'd like to em-
> phasize the fact that it is very important that they don't put stigma on people
> with mental illness. It is like a physical illness, nobody goes and breaks their leg
> off on purpose.
>
> Discuss it more, talk about it on talk shows. People with mental illness could
> put together a weekly show, or have one program a month on people who have
> mental illness and they could explain it. That might help."

At the age of 46, Mr. Barr suffered the third medical strike (the word "strike" is in-
apt in this context, he feels, because it didn't put him out; paradoxically, he feels it led
to his recovery... although not immediately). A berry aneurysm burst in his brain; he
hemorrhaged into the brain and had to undergo emergency surgery.

According to autopsy data, an estimated 5 million individuals in North America
live with intracranial aneurysms. Every year, 28,000 rupture, either because of high
blood pressure or because of a congenital defect in the artery. The artery balloons out
at the site of the defect but this takes years to develop, explaining why rupture occurs
in middle-aged adults. Approximately 50% of patients whose aneurysm ruptures die
or become permanently disabled.

> The doctor who operated on me said it was a miracle that I lived and wasn't in a
> coma. I was the fifth one to be operated on [for this condition], the first success-
> ful one. Three died, one was in a coma. I came out of it more or less normal, but
> seemed to lose my short-term memory in later years as my doctor had predicted.
> Because my short-term memory was shot, it forced me out of radio. I couldn't
> remember details when I covered a story. So I had to get out of the business and
> that disappointed me very greatly. I did not want to retire. I got into car sales and
> I discovered you need a good memory for that too. That lasted a year, and then I
> retired altogether at 48. The only woman that I truly loved, my last wife, parted
> company with me right after my operation in '83. But when I was saved from
> death from the aneurysm is when I first began to develop faith in God.

His faith was strong for four months afterwards but then, he says, "I forgot about it."
Mr. Barr went through significant depressions, with frequent thoughts of suicide
and frequent admissions to hospital. Although he had first sought help for his drink-

ing when he was 24, it took a long time and many experiences before an Addictions Program worked for him. He attributes the delay to being an atheist and "not having any spirituality." Mr. Barr feels he needed to develop a lasting faith and belief in God before he could embrace the kind of help that would work for him.

Ten years ago this week I decided to give an Addictions Program one more chance. I caught onto it. I haven't had a drink since February 18th, 1995. I could say that all but one of all of my friends is either in church or in recovery.

Today, Mr. Barr believes in complete abstinence.

If you don't abstain you can't stop, you'll get worse. The longer you drink, the worse you get and you are locked up or you die from drinking. I have been locked up. I've been arrested for drinking and driving several times. It is my manic depression that put me in the hospital, but I feel myself that my drinking has aggravated my depression. I've never been told that by a doctor but I definitely feel that way.

As he gets older and wiser, his faith continues to evolve.

I was an atheist up until three years ago. I have a friend who had been taking me to various churches trying to get me to change my views. I didn't like any of them. Then he took me to a church I liked, and I got baptized. I have a firm belief in God now. I read my bible. I have a bible class that meets here at my place every Tuesday and then I also meet on Wednesdays at a high school. Wednesday there is a class there. I go to that one. Last year I went to a bible class and I feel I am learning a lot and what I am learning is helping me to relax and get along better in life and get along better with people.

Mr. Barr feels his alcoholism is over:

I am sure in my heart, that I will never drink again. And my church has helped me with the rest of it and my problems aren't that great anymore. Without big problems, I don't get shaky or feel that I am going into a manic depressive episode. I used to feel them [the episodes] coming on and couldn't do anything about it. I don't know how many times I've been in the hospital in the last eight years, a great number of times, but not in the last three years. Five years I was in and out and in and out. I think an Addiction Support Program and church are the main things that helped. I can't recommend strongly enough the importance of getting help for alcoholism.

Jack Barr's mood disorder has also considerably improved.

I don't get depressed anymore, maybe a little tiny bit once every three months. I'm usually in an up mood, I do a lot of laughing with my friends and I am just a happy person and I wouldn't want to go back to the other way, it would be foolish. I always wanted to be happy, as we all do, but I really couldn't when I drank. I'm not special, when I say these things. I'm speaking for every alcoholic in the world. Alcohol ruins our lives.

He also recognizes the importance of being alert to fluctuations in mood.

It is important that you be on the lookout for signs that an episode is coming on. I'd get confused, irritable, I would get worried, I knew when an episode was coming on and I'd let it go so far I couldn't control it. If I had gone for help sooner, I'd have been better off. Although we see it coming, we think somehow we'll get a hold of it. Once you begin sinking into that mire, you are shot.

Mr. Barr's priorities have changed. The glory of being a radio announcer is no longer what counts. Faith and the maintenance of a support network have become more important. In the last several years, the Seniors' Mental Health Outreach Team (Capital Health Mental Health Program, Halifax) have become part of Mr. Barr's support system. At first he was in a 24-hour residential support program but now he has opted for greater independence. He moved into his own apartment in October, 2002. A combination of resources helped this transition to greater independence. These included a community agency, friends, the church, the Victorian Order of Nursing (VON), Mr. Barr's family physician, and the Seniors' Mental Health team.

The Seniors' Mental Health Team of the Capital Health Mental Health Program, Halifax, Nova Scotia includes psychiatrists, nurses, social workers, recreation therapists, and occupational therapists specialized in helping seniors with mental health, cognitive, and medical issues. The philosophy of the service is to help support seniors in maintaining their independence, and to help them stay at home and out of the hospital whenever possible. The team works with seniors to bolster their choices and decisions. The service includes outreach to the community as well as a specialized inpatient service, outpatient clinics, and a day program that offers group treatments for people with depression and anxiety disorders.

Mr. Barr credits his family doctor, Dr. Cameron, for helping him with his mood problems, as well as his psychiatrist, Dr. Cassidy, and his social worker, Heather Rea. Another great help has been a close and supportive best friend. In the main, however, it is Mr. Barr's determination and tenacity that have made his current independent living situation possible.

Over time, he has acknowledged and taken responsibility for his problems, accepting the help he needs. For example, he knows that he has difficulty with his short-term memory, particularly when it comes to names and numbers.

That is the one thing that bothers me now, because it curtails so many of my activities. I must learn to live with it, I guess I have.

Mr. Barr handles his memory problems by writing down all the important things he has to remember in order to live alone safely.

I have a calendar book on the desk, which is full of appointments and times, I write absolutely everything down. I have to check it twice a day, but I keep track of my appointments and that's how I stay on top of things. I taught myself to do it and I do it religiously. If I didn't, I'd miss 95% of my appointments.

He has also studied the bus schedule and practiced taking different routes in order to learn how to use the public transportation system, and he made the effort to increase his cooking skills by attending a cooking course for seniors in the community. He knows he has to repeat things many times so that they become automatic. He knows he has to find ways to accommodate to his memory problems. Successful aging means being increasingly selective about what really matters. It means optimizing your chances of getting things right by being extra-prepared for all contingencies. (For more on memory and aging, please see Chapter 7).

Getting older does not mean never trying something new. Not long ago, Mr. Barr took part in a clinical trial of a blood-thinning drug, coumadin, that he believed had a potential to help short-term memory, although "they did tell me not to get my hopes up." He tried the drug for a year, but it didn't work for him. "It worked with some people I know, not that I know personally, but I've been told."

Jack Barr has some suggestions on psychiatric research, particularly for psychiatric diseases:

I think psychiatric illnesses are still somewhat of a mystery. I guess it is because the mind is such a complicated thing. If it were possible, I don't know if it is, if the government would spend more money on research, it would help. I don't feel they spend enough money on research. Research is just as important [as treatment] if not more so because it is the way of stopping it – if there were a way of stopping it then we wouldn't need treatment. A lot more on research, a little more on treatment. Set up committees that take care of mental illness amongst the politicians, talk about it more in Parliament. I'm sure there are some politicians who have friends or family with mental illness and they could set up committees to work on it.

Today, Mr. Barr has found ways of adapting to his losses. He has been lonely since his wife left in 1983. For a full ten years he could not stop thinking about her.

But I don't miss her any more. I don't think I'd get married now if I could. I am independent now. I don't know if I could get along with anyone. I was taking a young lady out who thought I was much younger than I am. When she found out my age, she said: "that's it."

He has also lost contact with one of his daughters.

She wants nothing to do with me. I searched for her for a long time and then contacted her five months ago. She was civil with me on the phone. I said, "If you don't want me to call anymore then I won't." She never called me after so I decided to give her a call three months ago and said, "if you don't want to talk to me then don't answer this call" and she didn't call me, so I guess that is over.

But he has made a connection with his younger daughter, Heather, and his grandson, Zach, who live in Indiana. Heather is his daughter from a common-law relationship – her mother is American and Heather has dual citizenship. They talk on the phone once a week and Heather and Zach came to Halifax two years ago.

He [Zach] was eight at the time, he is ten now. I went to Indiana last summer; I get along well with all of them, including her husband.

Jack has also re-established contact with his two brothers, Harry and Ronald. They live in Ontario and keep in touch by email. His family, remaining sober, and his faith in God "are the most important things in my life." Another companion for Mr. Barr is his cat, Tina.

She's three last October. She was a stray and they nursed her back to life and adopted her out. She sleeps on my chest when I'm on the couch. She sleeps in my bed. I bought her a little bed; sometimes she sleeps in there.

Material possessions no longer matter to him.

I get enough money from my government pension. Car sales and broadcasting didn't have unions when I was in them, so I live strictly on my Canada Pension Plan (CPP) and Old Age Security Income Supplements and I get enough to be able to save some money. I went on vacation to Indiana last year. I came back with money in my pocket. I hadn't spent it all. I make enough money to live comfortably.

Not being able to drive because of his memory problem is a disappointment, but not a major one.

I'm limited in what I can do. I can't take people out with me or join committees because by bus it is too difficult to go, especially in winter. But I can go to local programs and meetings and help set up and greet people at the door. I go out to eat with my good friend. We go out once a week after church, maybe twice a week. He lives just down the street. He picks me up when he's not working on Sundays and takes me to church and then we usually go out to get something to eat. Usually two of us, but sometimes six or seven.

Jack's plans for the future:

I want to continue to grow spiritually. I want to go to church. I want to stay away from alcohol. I can't speak highly enough of the help they give me when I ask for it.

Mr. Barr was recently nominated for the first annual "Inspiring Lives Award" of the Mental Health Foundation of Nova Scotia. The award celebrates Nova Scotians who have been inspirational in their ability to cope with the challenges of serious mental illness and/or addictions. Gerotranscendence, or overcoming the burden of aging, includes learning to lean occasionally on others, accepting help when needed, and achieving wished-for goals even if the agency of others is sometimes necessary. This means that, rather than being subjected to help, rather than being made to feel obligated and dependent, one orchestrates one's own assistance network, retaining control of the situation. Expectations alter as one gets older and emotionally wiser. Jack has learned to reappraise his circumstances so that they appear in his eyes not *less* good than they were but "good in a different way."

Further Reading

Albanese MJ, Pies R. The bipolar patient with comorbid substance use disorder: recognition and management. CNS Drugs. 2004;18:585–596.

Brandtstadter J, Rothermund K. Self-percepts of control in middle and later adulthood: buffering losses by rescaling goals. Psychology & Aging. 1994;9:265–273.

Goldsmith RJ, Garlapati V. Behavioral interventions for dual-diagnosis patients. Psychiatr Clin North Am. 2004;27:709–725.

Levin FR, Hennessy G. Bipolar disorder and substance abuse. Biol Psychiatry. 2004;56:738–748.

Pagano ME, Friend KB, Tonigan JS, Stout RL. Helping other alcoholics in alcoholics anonymous and drinking outcomes: findings from project MATCH. J Stud Alcohol. 2004;65:766–773.

Poage ED, Ketzenberger KE, Olson J. Spirituality, contentment, and stress in recovering alcoholics. Addict Behav. 2004;29:1857–1862.

Polcin DL, Zemore S. Psychiatric severity and spirituality, helping, and participation in alcoholics anonymous during recovery. Am J Drug Alcohol Abuse. 2004;30:577–592.

Powell J, Kitchen N, Heslin J, Greenwood R. Psychosocial outcomes at three and nine months after good neurological recovery from aneurysmal subarachnoid haemorrhage: predictors and prognosis. J Neurol Neurosurg Psychiatry. 2002;72:772–781.

Ruigrok YM, Rinkel GJ, Wijmenga C. Genetics of intracranial aneurysms. Lancet Neuro. 2005;4:1791–1789.

Tornstam, L. Gerotranscendence: the contemplative dimension of aging. J Aging Studies. 1997;11:143–154.

Chapter 30

Doris Sommer-Rotenberg: Transmuting the Tragedy of Suicide

I Once Had a Son
by Doris Sommer-Rotenberg

I once
had
a son
Yes
I really
had one
  Now untrue
  So long
  since
  that
  maternal
  sense
  had
  valid
  existence
My son
no longer
is

gone
from
his
world
of sorrow
and despair
he
took
his life
without
warning
spite
or hate
I grieve
every
minute
second
never
heart
beat
passes
unaware
of his
loss

I
cry
yearn
question
whisper
he will
never
return
to the world
I still
inhabit
I
try
to inhibit
pain
through
burning

of consciousness
  fire
  of activity
Time
and
my soul
cannot
be
stilled

Never
is
sorrow
excised
  crushed
  into being
  beyond
  sentient
self
  beyond
  bruised
  clutch
  of eternity

August, 1993
First published in the U. of T. Bulletin, Jan. 6, 1996

Sublimation is the psychological process by which the energy of strong emotion is turned into action. Doris Sommer-Rotenberg has coped with the suicide of her son, Arthur, by spearheading an endowment fund for a Chair in Suicide Studies at the University of Toronto.

Arthur Sommer Rotenberg was the son of Doris Sommer-Rotenberg and Kenneth Rotenberg, a founding member of the Canadian Psychiatric Research Board. Arthur was a successful, well-respected family physician who took his life at the age of thirty-six. He had struggled half his life, in his mother's words, with the "discomforting highs and unbearable lows" of bipolar illness. His mother remembers two aspects of Arthur:

one [aspect] was full of passionate energy and promise...... skiing, cycling, tennis, sailing, mountain climbing......chess, calligraphy, carpentry (he built many pieces of furniture for his house as well as constructing alone the large terrace and railing of a balcony into his garden); gardening, – there is a wonderful picture of him up a tree as he pruned off an unwanted branch; photography (I have some beautiful scenic pictures he took of water and mountains); music – both listening to classical and modern music as well as playing the guitar; an eclectic taste in art...... [Arthur won] five annual merit prizes at Upper Canada College, and the Lieutenant Governor's Award when he graduated from the University of Toronto.

Arthur was both a loving son and a devoted brother to his four sisters, the only boy in the family. I have a delightful memory of Arthur and his younger sister walking hand in hand in the garden, aged approximately seven and two. They were both wearing hand-knitted wool suits and from my view in the window, they looked like Christopher Robin and Winnie the Pooh. In the way they were holding hands, Arthur/Christopher Robin appeared to be looking carefully after Winnie the Pooh!

One year, the family spent a Christmas Holiday skiing in Switzerland. At the time, Arthur was a student at Atlantic College in Wales. Both Arthur and I wanted to have a "night on the town." So I tried to look like an attractive, older woman dating a handsome younger man and off we went to a local night club. We pulled it off and had a lot of fun. Even after all these years, I still remember what I was wearing!

However, the other side of Arthur, manifested by his illness, caused his emotions to turn inside out – the pain, rather than the pleasures, taking over his life and vitiating all the usual irrepressible energy and activity. Whereas, when he was well, the strength of his feelings and interests enriched his life, with the same strength, those feelings turned negative, depleted his energy and darkened his existence. When this dark side predominated, Arthur was enervated, withdrawn, the cheeks of his face pulled back into his head, lacking the confidence to carry on... Tragically, the dark side defeated the bright side ...

Suicide is a leading cause of death for Canadians between the ages of ten and forty-nine. Over three and a half thousand Canadians kill themselves every year, and an estimated hundred times that number attempt to do so but fail. The World Health Organization reports that Canada's suicide rate is higher than that of many industrialized countries, perhaps because of the very high rate of suicide in Quebec (twice that of Ontario) and in aboriginal communities. Suicide attempts and deaths cost the Canadian economy over $14.7 billion annually, according to the Canadian Association for Suicide Prevention (CASP), which has recently developed a blueprint for a Canadian National Suicide Prevention Strategy.

Physicians are at high risk for suicide, perhaps because of the extraordinary challenges they meet in their work and their reluctance to seek help from colleagues. Rates of burnout, depression, and emotional exhaustion are high among doctors. Doctors demand a lot of themselves – too much by ordinary standards. One of Arthur's friends wrote of his "endless capacity to give audience with quiet, fascinated attention." Another friend wrote:

> Arthur was a man of great inner force. He lived with the intelligence of the heart … From Arthur I learned that life is to be lived with brio; that is, with intensity, purpose, passion for romance and adventure and most of all, compassionate communication. Arthur was one who saw far and deeply. His mind was incisive, original, capable of grasping so much, yet never solely on a material level. He always sought to penetrate to the heart of matter. He could receive with sensitivity and appreciation the full beauty of music, literature, and the visual arts.

Yet another friend, to whom Arthur left a bequest the night before he died, wrote:

> That he considered the welfare of others despite his own suffering, so that their lives could be lived out in greater abundance. This is astounding.

"In a short space, he cast a long shadow," wrote another of Arthur's friends.

Knowing too much about medicine can be a problem for physicians, thinks Doris Sommer-Rotenberg. Her son, for instance, stopped taking the lithium that had stabilized him because he knew that serious side-effects could potentially ensue. Psychiatrists treating physicians may not insist on compliance with their prescriptions (as they would with non-medical patients). They may assume that the physician/patient is more rational than, in actuality, anyone can be about their own state of mind. During Dr. Rotenberg's final episode of illness, hospitalization was suggested, but he refused. Perhaps, had he not been a physician, his psychiatrist would have been more adamant. That may, or may not, have saved him. Doctors are reluctant to hospitalize their fellow doctors against their will even when it is necessary. Doctors, when they are patients, are treated more diffidently than other patients. And doctors' knowledge about drugs and other means of death can be dangerous. Determined to take their lives, they know how to ensure that the attempt does not go awry.

Physicians who do reach out for help when depressed or overwhelmed often make great efforts to hide it, according to Dr. Michael Myers, a Vancouver psychiatrist who specializes in treating physicians. He reports that physician/ patients come to him from all over Canada and the U.S. "parachuted out of their home communities, [afraid to be] found out." (see Further Reading: Myers and Fine). The majority are self-referred and do not want a letter sent to their family physician. "Some drive a distance of 200 miles to get their serum lithium checked," Myers says. (Lithium blood levels have to be regularly re-assessed).

A Canadian study reports that 40% of physicians anonymously acknowledged being clinically depressed at some time in the five years preceding the study, but only

16% sought help from a physician and only 13% took antidepressants. Most studies fail to report the numbers treated with psychotherapy because psychotherapy can be hard to define on a questionnaire survey.

Mrs. Sommer-Rotenberg has thought deeply about the potential of psychiatry to help people in distress:

> Despite whatever reservations I may have as a result of the tragic loss of my son, I believe psychiatry is an important component in medicine. Initially, psychiatry dealt only with the psychological part of the brain, using psychoanalysis, to find the roots of the dysfunction. It also endeavored to give support, enabling the patient to deal with past trauma, often hidden from the patient's conscious thoughts yet still inhibiting normal functioning. Today, the importance of psychopharmacology has entered into the psychiatric domain. It must, therefore, become increasingly challenging to determine not only the nature of the illness, but the means to treat it: psychotherapy or medication or both?
>
> Another element has entered the current practice of medicine and psychiatry in Canada: the financing of patient care has been taken over by the government. While providing help to greater segments of the population than before, it has the disadvantage of limiting the options of physicians to practice their skill. Often, vital decisions may be made by the physician on a financial basis [the most economic use of health dollars], rather than on the basis of benefit to the specific patient. I have sometimes wondered about the consequence if the medical profession rebelled, and decided to give certain services, without payment, in order to more fully honor their sense of responsibility to both the patient and the integrity of their profession. This suggestion is a quixotic alternative arising out of a consumer's frustration and desire to reinstate medicine on its idealistic foundation.

A widely publicized case of physician suicide was that of Dr. Suzanne Killinger-Johnson in Toronto, who was suffering from a postpartum depression and took her infant's life as well as her own. The editors of the *Canadian Medical Association Journal* were rebuked by a reader for even mentioning the cause of Dr. Killinger-Johnson's death. They responded:

> Several editors debated whether our obituary should refer to the tragic circumstances surrounding Suzanne Killinger-Johnson's death. One proposal was simply to announce her death and ignore these facts. In the end, we decided that this would do no one a service. Shrouding such events in silence in our view perpetuates the stigma that still, unfortunately, accompanies mental illness and suicide. We also felt that omitting any reference to the death of Killinger-Johnson's child would be disrespectful of the importance of that young life. Physicians experience medical problems every bit as severe as those faced by their patients. We

hope that acknowledging such incidents, when they occur, will raise an awareness that may, perhaps, help to prevent future tragedies.
CMAJ. 2001;164(7):965

Whether within or outside the medical profession, depression and suicide continue to be associated with shame, guilt, and secrecy. Doris Sommer-Rotenberg points to the use of the phrase, "commit suicide," analogous to commit burglary, commit adultery – as if suicide were a sin or a felony. The "connotation of illegality and dishonor intensifies the stigma attached to the one who has died as well as to those who have been traumatized by the loss.... Suicide ....has been demonized as a metaphor for moral weakness and failure. Many people consider any form of psychological vulnerability, including depression, to be a moral lapse."

To honor the memory of her son, Mrs. Doris Sommer-Rotenberg led a fundraising initiative that raised $1 million for the study of suicide. The University of Toronto matched these funds, creating a $2 million endowment for the first university chair in North America dedicated to suicide research. In 1997, Dr. Paul Links became the inaugural head of the Arthur Sommer Rotenberg Chair in Suicide Studies and launched a program of research to better understand the agony that can lead to suicide.

When raising funds for the Chair, Doris Sommer-Rotenberg hoped to achieve victory over two interrelated problems – the lack of systematic research into suicide and the scourge of shame that attaches to suicide – still a taboo subject in the 21st century. She describes her motivation in establishing the Chair in her son's memory:

> To keep alive the vitality of my son's life and spirit, and to help prevent similar tragedies, I initiated a campaign to establish in his memory a research chair in suicide studies at the University of Toronto – the first of its kind in North America. This fact in itself attests to the silence that has historically surrounded the issue of suicide. As the campaign progressed I realized that raising awareness about this act of despair was as important as raising money.
>
> A large corporation whose president had taken his life declined to make a donation to our fund-raising campaign for fear that such a contribution would open the door to unwanted, deprecating publicity. Such responses only serve to exacerbate the stigma of suicide, to preclude open discussion about it and to discourage research that may help prevent it.

Doris Sommer-Rotenberg has sometimes heard suicide described as a selfish act but, she says:

> Often the decision to kill oneself is taken out of a distorted consideration for those one loves; the dislocation of emotion is so immense, the feelings of unworthiness so overwhelming, that the suicidal person believes that loved ones would fare better if he or she were no longer part of the world.

Although guilt and regret can arise after any death, suicide leaves the bereaved with especially acute feelings of self-denigration and self-recrimination. The continual weight of the unanswerable and relentless inner refrain – "If only I had done this, or if only I had not said that" – can become unbearable. ....Hence the impulse to assign blame to the victim of suicide, who thus becomes a scapegoat so that others may rid themselves of uncomfortable emotions.

Ninety percent of those who take their lives suffer from a mental disorder at the time of death. But simply treating illness is not prevention enough. Real prediction and prevention of suicide await a time when mechanisms of both depression and impulsivity (translating thought too quickly into action) are better understood. The suicide program made possible by the endowment of the Arthur Sommer Rotenberg Chair will improve this understanding and make intervention more effective. Its mission is to reduce suffering by advancing scientific understanding into causes. Research domains include epidemiologic studies of high-risk populations, the neurophysiology of suicide, the development of clinical protocols and therapeutic intervention strategies.

Doris Sommer-Rotenberg believes that the most effective antidote to emotional pain is being able to share it with others (the least effective is to try to hide it). One of her motivations for initiating the research fund that led to the creation of the Arthur Sommer Rotenberg Chair was the importance of not hiding how Arthur died – to assure the dignity of his memory and to be able to share the pain. Instead of turning inward in her grief, she reached out to create something of value, "to fulfill the unfulfilled promise of Arthur's shortened life." In so doing she also succeeded, to some extent, in alleviating her grief, sustained by the knowledge that her actions could prevent the sorrow of others. The Chair is visible proof that the life of a young man with so much potential, ended by a self-inflicted death, had not been lived in vain. Arthur's life, though difficult, had been a rich one; his family and friends consider themselves blessed through having known him. His mother says, "I try to concentrate on my life having been enriched by his presence – if only temporarily – rather than the everlasting desolation of his loss." Now others who had not known him will be able to benefit from his life. Doris Sommer-Rotenberg's efforts to endow the Chair have raised public awareness to the tragedy of suicide and have helped to remove the taint of shame. "Sensitized awareness," says Doris Sommer-Rotenberg, "cauterizes the shame and replaces it with a respect for the dignity of the life that had been lived."

Doris Sommer-Rotenberg has some concluding thoughts on the fundamental questions of living and dying.

What is the purpose of life? Being a gardener, I have found the answer in the life of trees, plants, and flowers, whose purpose is simply to grow. Each stage of life has its rewards. Older years balance the vitality and activity of youth with the freedom, born of necessity, to prioritize. A more advanced age, due to limitation of energy and concomitantly of time, can be compared to modern art. One pares interests and activities down to their essential significance in one's life. The increasing awareness of mortality allows a certain freedom to say "no," together with opportunities to explore new vistas, often unavailable with the responsibilities of a younger age. Mortality gives meaning to life. I believe our mortality can also be a metaphor for the ephemeral nature of our lives' experiences. The acknowledgement of the existential transient quality of both pleasure and pain facilitates our acceptance of the death of pleasurable experiences and of our ability to endure painful ones.

Further Reading

Arsenault-Lapierre G, Kim C, Turecki G. Psychiatric diagnoses in 3275 suicides: a meta-analysis. BMC Psychiatry 2004, 4:37. Available at: http://www.biomedcentral.com/1471-244X/4/37

Leenaars AA. Suicide: a multidimensional malaise. Suicide Life Threat Behav. 1996;26:221–236.

Lesage AD, Boyer R, Grunberg F, Vanier C, Morissette R, Menard-Buteau C, Loyer M. Suicide and mental disorders: a case-control study of young men. Am J Psychiatry. 1994;151:1063–1068.

Links PS. Suicide and life: the ultimate juxtaposition. *CMAJ* 1998;158:514–515.

Milne C. Doctors and suicide. February 13, 2001 37:(6) Medical Post.

Myers M, Fine C. Suicide in physicians: toward prevention. MedGenMed. 2003;5(4):11.

O'Carroll P. Suicide causation: pies, paths, and pointless polemics. Suicide Life Threat Behav. 1993;23:27–36.

Rotenberg AS. Bilateral meralgia paresthetica associated with pelvic inflammatory disease. CMAJ. 1990;142:42–43.

Schernhammer ES, Colditz GA. Suicide rates among physicians: a quantitative and gender assessment (meta-analysis). Am J Psychiatry. 2004;161:2295–2302.

Sommer-Rotenberg D. Suicide. The Globe and Mail. 1993 Sept 29.

Sommer-Rotenberg D. Suicide and language. CMAJ. 1998;159:239–240.

Chapter 31

Participanting in Research: Volunteering

"Ethics, too, are nothing but reverence for life. This is what gives me the fundamental principle of morality, namely, that good consists in maintaining, promoting, and enhancing life, and that destroying, injuring, and limiting life are evil."
Albert Schweitzer

This chapter addresses potential risks to research participants and how to minimize them. It covers such topics as confidentiality, consent, competence, placebo trials, challenge studies, and oversight.

Section I of this book highlighted the achievements of research and researchers. Section II has celebrated the benefactors and the beneficiaries – those who fund science and those who have experienced mental illness and have been the subjects, directly or indirectly, of clinical research. Direct participation greatly benefits science but participants can incur risk because the outcome of an experiment is, by definition, unknown. Psychiatric experiments gone wrong have been referred to in the Introduction to this book. They do happen, making safeguards essential.

A central issue is whether volunteering to be a subject in an experimental protocol is, in truth, voluntary? If I am ill, beholden to my care providers, and I agree to be part of a research study, is this a free decision? Am I truly informed (even when the study has been thoroughly explained to me) if my mind is clouded by distress or chemical sedation? These are important questions because, as a rights-based society, we place higher value on the principles of protecting the vulnerable, respecting autonomy, and defending privacy than we do on the benefits that may eventually accrue from research. Participants in research are guaranteed many safeguards, which this chapter will review. But questions of ethics are never settled once and for all. Times change. Attitudes change. What is always critical, for both researchers and research participants, is to think through decisions carefully, to examine motives, to seek consultation, to be open about every individual step of the research process.

A study protocol must always be submitted to a hospital or university research ethics board before research can begin.

Coercion

The worry about coercion applies, in the main, to patients in hospital. They are, in some sense, prisoners – do they really have a choice?

Choice is protected in several ways: A) Review boards will only allow patients to be approached for research if their personal physician has judged them "competent," i.e., able to understand what they are consenting to and make dispassionate, knowledgeable decisions. Competence, however, is not a black and white concept. There are degrees of competence – more on this later. B) Review boards will not allow care providers to approach patients for consent to research (it is felt that patients would find it hard to say "no" to physicians on whom they are dependent and to whom they feel indebted). The approach needs to be made by a neutral party, by someone not involved in the patient's care. C) Written assurance must be provided to the patient stating that refusing to take part or withdrawing from a study before it is finished will have no effect on the subsequent provision of care. D) Research boards also consider the incentive provided (paying a subject a large amount of money to take part could constitute coercion). That is a difficult call, however, because, while research participants deserve to be paid for their time and effort and while all participants in a study are generally paid the same amount, what seems a small amount to one person may be seen as undue incentive to another.

All subjects of clinical research are vulnerable in the sense that they can potentially be swayed to volunteer when they don't really want to.

Are psychiatric subjects potentially *more* vulnerable to coercion than others? A physician may consider me mentally competent but my cognitive processes may be compromised in a subtle way. One cognitive error to which many research subjects are prone has been called "the therapeutic misconception." Participants are inclined to think that the results of a study will be of immediate benefit to them when, for the most part, the aim is to benefit persons with a similar diagnosis at some time in the future. For instance, I may think that taking part in a brain imaging study will alleviate my brain symptoms, whereas medical imaging is an assessment tool, not a treatment. In fact, in psychiatry, medical imaging does not even aid assessment, at least not as of now. In other words, although a study may be thoroughly explained, wishful thinking may cloud perception and influence decision-making. It is the responsibility of the researcher to disabuse would-be research participants of the notion that a research study will benefit them directly. There are, of course, instances where volunteering in a clinical trial of a new psychiatric drug could give me quicker access to a treatment that may prove beneficial but, as with any new treatment, risks sometimes outweigh benefits.

It is important not to treat persons suffering from mental illnesses as necessarily more vulnerable than other patients. This is unfair and unduly stigmatizing.

Most psychiatric patients, even when hospitalized, understand clear explanations of research studies, especially when they are repeated more than once. An important function of the research review board is to look at consent forms that participants are asked to sign and ensure that the language is simple, lucid, and intelligible. Recent work has shown that techniques such as repetition and feedback of information allow patients who may initially be compromised in their understanding to finally grasp in full the details of research protocols. It is, of course, the responsibility of the researcher to ensure that this is done.

It would be unfair to individuals suffering from mental illness to exclude them from clinical research on the basis of a supposed extra vulnerability. Women used to be excluded from clinical trials because of the risk that they might become pregnant and expose an unborn child to an experimental medicine. But women protested, rightly, that medicines were being put on the market and prescribed universally without ever having been tested on women. Women protested that they were being both overprotected and discriminated against. They insisted on being included in clinical trials. HIV patients also lobbied for more inclusion in clinical trials of new drugs for HIV. They wanted to take the risk of being given a new, perhaps not totally safe, drug on the chance that newer drugs were likely, on balance, to be more effective than older ones.

No group should be deliberately excluded from taking part in research.

It is often the case that, by volunteering for research, a person receives the most up-to-date and beneficial treatment that is otherwise not yet available. All individuals should be able to participate, should they want to, in psychiatric research as long as there is no deception, as long as nothing about the study is hidden, and as long as they know and appreciate what they are saying "yes" to.

A very powerful motive for those who volunteer is the help they are providing to future generations. They do not feel like guinea pigs; on the contrary, they often feel like courageous heroes or heroines who may be taking chances but doing it for a good cause. They may do it for altruistic purposes and, as a result, feel better for it. They see it as a gift they give to others and, as is true for much gift giving, the donors derive the principal benefit. They describe it as a boost to their self-esteem. It is important not to deprive persons with mental illnesses of such opportunities.

Study Protocol vs. Individualized Treatment

There is evidence that individuals treated in study protocols have better outcomes than those in "treatment as usual." This has been attributed not only to researchers having access to new and superior treatments but also to the extra attention and rigor with which study participants are treated. Nevertheless, many people do not like the concept of the "cookie cutter" approach of research interventions where, indeed, all subjects usually need to be treated identically. They prefer individualized treatment where their own particular needs are recognized and addressed.

Three particular types of study designs in drug research trials have been criticized from an ethics point of view: Placebo-controlled trials (where about half the participants who require treatment are, in fact, given a sugar pill), washout designs (where there is a drug-free period for participants prior to the beginning of the study), and challenge designs (where participants are given a drug that can provoke or worsen pre-existing symptoms).

The concern in placebo trials is that some research subjects will be prescribed no therapeutic drug at all. Critics argue that the control group could, instead of placebo, be given an older treatment with proven efficacy. Ideally, all comparison groups in any research should be given treatments that the researcher considers to be equally effective (the researcher should be in a state of no prejudice, or what epidemiologists call "equipoise"); only the outcome of the trial should decide which treatment is, in reality, best. It can be argued that no one should forego clinically effective treatment by agreeing to a placebo. For instance, a depressed person receiving nothing but a sugar pill may, over the duration of the research study, become more and more depressed, and may even suicide. This is always a theoretical possibility in placebo trials but, in practice, study subjects are very closely monitored and a person whose depression was intensifying would be withdrawn from the study and treated with a known antidepressant.

A more problematic case (in placebo or washout designs) would be a patient suffering from paranoia being discontinued from a medication that had kept his paranoia in check and subsequently becoming so suspicious that he or she effectively stops treatment, refusing further contact with researchers or caregivers. This would argue for very careful subject selection for placebo or washout designs and a clear protocol indicating what steps researchers need to take if unsafe situations arise.

Many patients welcome a legitimate reason to be drug-free for a period of time. Most long-term patients dislike having to take medication and an incentive to clinical trial participation may, in fact, be the opportunity to have a drug holiday. Such a motivation needs to be explored. Like paying subjects to take part in research, the prospect of being drug-free may be seen as undue incentive, i.e., coercion. Research review boards may, and should, demand a higher level of mental capacity on the part of a subject consenting to a placebo-controlled study than for one entering a drug study involving an active comparison drug.

The higher the risk, the more the research participant should be protected.

The issue of the ethics of placebo-controlled trials has divided the research community. Some feel placebo trials should never be done. Some feel they are actually *more* ethical than trials with a comparator drug because the sample size needed in a placebo trial is relatively small. Because the sample is small, *overall,* fewer patients are exposed to the risk inherent in taking a new medication (even though the risk for those in the placebo arm is relatively higher).

More of a problem is challenge studies, where symptoms are deliberately provoked in order to study the neurochemical pathways involved in the expression of symptoms. The "challenge" need not be a drug. Sometimes a psychological stressor like public speaking or solving a math problem or recalling a traumatic event is used to trigger symptoms. Challenge studies may also require that participants be only partially informed about the details of the protocol (because if someone knows she is being deliberately stressed, her response may not be authentic). This heightens the ethical concerns.

But, again, some participants in challenge studies feel that the risk to themselves is minimal while the potential for good to others is substantial. They opt to do the study, which is their right – as long as they know what it is that they are deciding for or against.

Conflict of Interest

The researchers highlighted in this book all have as their primary concern the well-being of those who take part in their research. They want to do good science, but never at the expense of patients. These are, of course, their *conscious* motives, but oversight committees such as research review boards are also concerned about unconscious motivation. Investigators, unconsciously, may be motivated to do science because it is a route to tenure, promotion, and a salary increase. They may want to publish papers not only to disseminate knowledge but also to elicit the admiration (and envy) of colleagues, to see their name in print, to achieve fame. These are *competing* interests that *could,* but usually do not, interfere with the process of scientific inquiry.

The most blatant conflict of interest is when a researcher has a financial interest in the product he or she is researching or is receiving payment for recruiting subjects into a study or is allowing sponsors (who have a direct financial interest in the outcome of the study) to direct the design of the study or to run the analysis of the results or even to decide what is published and what remains secret.

Pressures such as these can result in inadequate sharing of information and may undermine the carefulness with which selection of appropriate research participants is carried out. Conflict of interest issues are increasingly preoccupying research review boards and researchers are being asked to detail their other interests on the consent forms that participants sign.

Confidentiality

Another issue that review boards monitor is the privacy and confidentiality of the information that research participants share with researchers. Research information is never kept in the patient's clinical chart but is stored separately. How and where it is kept is detailed on the consent form that potential subjects sign. With the advent of electronic research databases on password-protected computers, it may become more difficult to explain where exactly the data reside. Participants have a right to know where the information is being kept, who has access to it, and how long after the completion of the study it will be destroyed. Review Boards usually mandate that the files be numbered and therefore not identifiable by name. The subjects are never identified in research presentations or in publications because the data are grouped and presented as statistical frequencies: medians and means and standard deviations. The results of qualitative research rely on direct quotes from statements made by a participant and are therefore harder to mask. Those taking part in qualitative research always need to ask how their identity will be obscured when the results of the work are eventually published.

In an effort to protect research subjects, several authors have suggested using "arm's distance" participant advocates.

Such advocates could determine whether a would-be participant were competent. They could help in the explanation of research risks and/or lack of benefits. A three-part consent process involving participant advocates has been proposed for individuals with severe mental illness who want to take part in research: (1) an informed consent discussion takes place with the research recruiter, (2) a psychiatrist reviews the person's competence and, (3) a designated participant advocate ensures that the person understands the risks and benefits, and is volunteering freely. The advocate can also act as an educator – he or she can teach basic research concepts, explain how research differs from treatment, and how and why research designs use randomization and placebo controls. Another role for an advocate is to monitor the participant over the course of a study to ensure that initial competence is not lost along the way.

In conclusion, there are several ethical requirements of clinical research studies that participants need to insist upon: a) that the research not be trivial, that it have a specific scientific purpose, b) that the research be conducted rigorously, c) that subject selection be even handed (no special treatment for anyone), d) that benefits significantly outweigh potential risks, e) that there be arm's length and continuing oversight of the study, f) that participants be thoroughly informed about the methodology and purpose of the research, g) that their consent be wholly voluntary and, h) that their privacy be protected. There may be discomforts and burdens associated with being part of any research study but individuals have the right to undertake such risks for outcomes they value. This includes the possibility that being part of the study will facilitate access to therapies that would not otherwise be available, i.e., enhance life for the participating individual. It also includes the pride that comes from doing something selfless, the hope that participation will ultimately benefit the larger society.

Further Reading

Appelbaum PS. Missing the boat: Competence and consent in psychiatric research. Am J Psychiatry. 1998;155:1486–1488.

Appelbaum PS, Roth LH, Lidz CW, Benson P, Winslade W. False hopes and best data: Consent to research and the therapeutic misconception. Hastings Center Report. 1987;17:20–24.

Appelbaum PS, Roth LH, Lidz C. The therapeutic misconception: Informed consent in psychiatric research. International J Law & Psychiatry. 1982;5:319–329.

Carpenter WT Jr, Gold JM, Lahti AC, Queern CA, Conley RR, Bartko JJ, Kovnick J, Appelbaum PS. Decisional capacity for informed consent in schizophrenia research. Arch Gen Psychiatry. 2000;57:533–538.

DuVal G. Ethics in psychiatric research: study design issues. Can J Psychiatry. 2004;49:55–59.

Emanuel EJ, Wendler D, Grady C. What makes clinical research ethical? JAMA. 2000;283: 2701–2711.

Flory J, Emanuel E. Interventions to improve research participants' understanding in informed consent for research: A systematic review JAMA. 2004;292:1593–1601.

Fried E. The therapeutic misconception, beneficence, and respect. Account Res. 2001;8:331–348.

Freedman B. Equipoise and the ethics of clinical research. N Engl J Med. 1987; 317:141–145.

Hall LL. Medication discontinuation and symptom provocation in research: a consumer and family perspective. Biol Psychiatry. 1999;46:1017–1020.

Lemmens T, Miller PB. Balancing ethical research issues in psychiatry. Psychiatric Times 2000 17:#6.

McNeill P. Paying people to participate in research: why not? A response to Wilkinson and Moore. Bioethics. 1997;11:390–396.

Morreim EH. By any other name: the many iterations of "patient advocate" in clinical research. IRB. 2004;26(6):1–8. Available at: http://www.medscape.com/viewarticle/496529_

Roberts LW, Geppert CM, Brody JL. A framework for considering the ethical aspects of psychiatric research protocols. Compr Psychiatry. 2001;42:351–363.

Vogel-Scibilia SE. The controversy over challenge and discontinuation studies: perspective from a consumer-psychiatrist. Biol Psychiatry. 1999;46:1021–1024.

Wendler D. Deception in medical and behavioral research: is it ever acceptable? Milbank Q. 1996;74:87–114.

Chapter 32

Conclusion: Emerging Themes

Several important themes emerge from the interviews: Mental illnesses occur in all families. They are widespread and impose a significant emotional and financial burden on society. The burden is intensified by the stigma of psychiatric illness, which persists despite there being no rational distinction between physical and mental disorders. In both public and private sectors, stigma acts as an obstacle to appropriate levels of research funding, a major problem because hope rests on research.

Mental illnesses are a daily fact of life for twenty to twenty-five percent of Canadians. They are more widespread than heart diseases, more pervasive than cancer, arthritis, and diabetes combined. On a global basis, mental health problems constitute 8.1% of the burden of disease. Depression alone is currently the fourth leading cause of Disability Adjusted Life Years and is projected by the World Health Organization to become the second leading cause by the year 2020.

No family is protected from mental illness. Everyone is vulnerable.

Psyche in the Lab is divided into two distinct sections; the first showcases the accomplishments of researchers, the second explores the roles and motives of funders and patients. We read (Chapter 9) that actual experience of mental illness can be a strong driving force in research whether the illness is one's own, that of a close relative, or that of one's patients. In the opinion of many, the research of clinicians who deal with patients daily is more immediately relevant to treatment than that of non-clinicians, even though clinicians' research time is much more limited than that of full time researchers. There is no doubt after reading these chapters that mental illness closely observed or personally experienced has profoundly influenced the lives and careers of the men and women profiled in both sections of the book. Though individual biological predispositions hidden in our genes and massive social forces to which some humans are exposed are powerful risk factors for psychiatric illness, in the end no family is spared, no matter how affluent and educated, no matter how warm and cohesive, no matter how harmonious and supportive. No distinction can be made between "them" and "us."

The fundamental lesson is that we do not yet know, for the most part, how to prevent psychiatric illnesses. While governments are eager to put preventive programs in place, the science for doing so is not yet available. This is best illustrated in the chapter on child psychiatry where the implementation of large-scale programs that *should* work, don't always produce the expected results (Chapter 5). For this reason, an expansion of all domains of psychiatric research is urgently needed: neuroscience, genetics, infection and immunity, brain imaging, gender, minority status and health, human development, psychotherapeutics, health systems and policy, substance abuse, trauma, population and public health, stigma, and neuroethics.

Psychiatric researchers face many obstacles, the main one being the continuing stigma surrounding mental illness. Queen's University social scientist, Heather Stuart (Please see Further Reading), writes that the word stigma comes from the branding (*stig*) that slave owners in ancient Greece inflicted on their slaves to signify ownership. Today, stigma refers to an invisible mark of social disapproval and rejection, which in turn elicits in the stigmatized person feelings of guilt, shame, inferiority, and the wish for concealment. Its pervasiveness with respect to mental illness is surprising given that no family is spared. It envelops the sufferers and the professionals who try to help them. It discredits the very services that are meant to assist and it contributes to the persistent under-funding of psychiatric research. Stigma impedes recovery and promotes disability. It adds to the burden of illness and detracts from the appeal of mental illness research as a career option.

Many of our interviewees suggested solutions to the problem of stigma. Self-stigmatization can be overcome by the telling of personal stories, as has been done in this book. Education is a powerful tool with which to eradicate social stigma based in lack of knowledge, mistaken attitudes and hurtful practices. It is important to disseminate the fact that mental illnesses are ubiquitous, that they occur in essentially all families, that they are not a result of moral weakness or sin, that they are not self-induced, and that they are treatable. Recent anti-stigma work has targeted key groups such as landlords, employers, health care providers, criminal justice professionals, policy makers, and the media. The Institute of Neurosciences, Mental Health and Addiction is currently targeting mental health in the workplace. Heather Stuart from Queen's University is examining the role of newspaper stories about the mentally ill. Stigma campaigns have also addressed structural or institutional discrimination and attempted to change the laws and policies of private and governmental institutions that restrict opportunities for persons with mental illnesses.

One approach is to develop positive models of mentally ill individuals, public champions such as many of the individuals interviewed for this book. Another strategy worth investigating is to reward and publicize exemplary antistigma and antidiscrimination efforts. Estroff et al. (please see Further Reading) have done a U.S. review of such programs. They report the results of a national survey of noteworthy efforts to reduce the negative consequences of bearing a psychiatric label. Their sample consisted of nontraditional, innovative local efforts as well as better-known programs. Nominations of exemplary antistigma and antidiscrimination efforts were solicited from a national database and, from among 102 nominations, an expert consensus panel selected 36 exemplary programs. This exercise could and should be replicated in Canada.

Addressing the issue of stigma, Sandra Sharwood (Chapter 22) raises a perennial philosophical question: Are psychiatric illnesses different in kind from illnesses of the body? Since physical risk factors exist for most psychiatric illnesses and many are treated physically (by drugs for instance), why does the distinction remain? What is the essential difference between depression and multiple sclerosis, between epilepsy and schizophrenia, between anxiety disorders and Parkinson's disease? This complicated theme is explored in the two psyche and soma chapters (Chapters 10 and 11). Cardiovascular stroke, a physical event, can, depending on the area of the brain it occurs in, result in depression, a psychological event. Streptococcal infection, an infective agent, is thought capable of inducing obsessive-compulsive (cognitive /behavioral) symptoms in children (see Chapter 2). Breathing exercises (see Chapter 10) can protect against the return of depression. Is it rational to make a distinction between the physical and the psychological? Would stigma be reduced if the distinction were abolished? The answer is probably "no" since physical illness can become tainted too, as were leprosy, epilepsy, and AIDS.

Removing stigma is not only good for public health; it is also a smart fiscal policy. Psychiatric illnesses are expensive. Ten years ago, the financial toll of mental illnesses was already $16 billion a year to Canada, 14% of the net operating revenue of all Canadian business, making mental health problems among the costliest conditions in Canada and the number one cause of disability. Mental illnesses lead not only to time off work but also to the loss of productivity while at work. Dewa and Lin (see Further Reading) estimate that 8% of the working population suffers from a diagnosable disorder but that two thirds of Canadians with a mental health problem do not seek help for it (Statistics Canada 2003) http://www.statcan.ca/Daily/English/030903/d030903a.htm

What needs to be done? In order to reduce the emotional and financial toll of psychiatric disease, the fostering of research must take high priority. The researchers profiled in this book are among the most highly respected in Canada but one seldom hears from them in public policy debates about priority setting. Scientific authority has had little voice in setting policy. According to our own multi-year searches of the Scientific Citation Index and the largest media databases, the Canadian scientists most cited in journal articles – the ones whom their peers deem most knowledgeable in their specific area of expertise – are virtually never interviewed in the mainstream Canadian media. And yet, expert professional and epidemiological advice to government and to the lay public is essential if stigma is to be extinguished, and if mental health policy is to be based on evidence of population needs, identifiable risk factors, effectiveness of treatments and services, and measurable outcomes. As a corollary, it is important to develop the capacity for policy work in the mental health professions by encouraging not only research but also public health, epidemiology, and policy placements for young psychiatrists and psychologists.

While most would agree that more dollars are needed for research, the actual apportioning of research funds, both public and private, is a thorny issue. The funding pie is difficult to slice equitably. Mental Health receives 5% of Canada's medical research funding. This percentage, by any rational measure of equity or cost-benefit analysis, seems too low. A scientific method of apportioning funds would be to take the important components of illness into account: prevalence, distress, disability, mortality and economic burden and to preferentially fund those illnesses that score highest on a composite measure of these factors. At the same time, funders need to be sensitive to the scientific merit of any proposed project and its chances of leading to successful discovery. It is usually because the field is deemed not ripe for discovery that funds are directed elsewhere. In this, Canada is influenced by events in the United States where many new scientific fields initially reach maturity, the maturity to subsequently materialize into relevant breakthrough. Should Canada continue to copy the United States or should priority setting be a more Canadian enterprise? As described by Martin Alda and Rémi Quirion (please see Chapters 4 and 12), neuroscience is especially strong in Canada, and large families in some parts of the country make Canada a geneticist's paradise. Canada has been particularly successful at integrating psychological and biological approaches to psychiatric illnesses. We are known throughout the world as good collaborators, an essential skill in today's research world. We need to recognize our unique needs (regional epidemics of suicide are an example) and take advantage of our strengths (a tradition of neuroscience excellence and large, ethnically diverse pedigrees for genetic studies).

Still on the question of apportioning funds, Kathy Hegadoren raises an important issue (Chapter 15): Is it advantageous to mental health and addictions to be grouped with neuroscience in Canadian Institutes of Health Research (CIHR) competitions? Should there be an Institute specifically for mental health and addictions, separate from the broader field of neuroscience? CIHR, through the Institute of Neurosciences, Mental Health and Addictions (INMHA) is the primary federal funding agency for research into mental health, mental illness and addiction. For the fiscal year 2004-2005, CIHR allocated $150 million to INMHA from its total base budget of 619 million. From the INMHA portion of the budget, $40 million went to mental health and $13 million to addiction research. The rest went to basic neuroscience, which, it can be argued, is inseparable from mental health and addiction. Nevertheless, the $53 million (for mental health and addiction) seems too small a sum, one that does not reflect the immensity of the toll of mental illness. The proportion of the total health research budget that goes to mental health and addiction is approximately the same in Canada as in the United Kingdom but it is higher in the U.S., a reflection of the U.S. war on drugs, which has markedly enhanced mental health research funding in that country.

A fine-grained analysis of this issue was conducted for fiscal year 1990–91. There were 48 funding agencies for psychiatric research in Canada that year. Together, they disbursed $16,406,300, only 3.7% that year of the funds that were awarded to all health research. But the direct cost of mental health care that year was approximately 11–14% of the cost of health care (Health Canada, 1997). The $16.4 million came mostly from the federal government where it represented only 3.3% of federal funds for all health research. Thirty-nine percent came from the provinces; here it represented 8.7% of health funding. Private and non-profit agencies and foundations together accounted for 7.6% of psychiatric research funding. The Canadian Psychiatric Research Foundation that year provided $341,000. Funding (from all sources) was distributed in the following way: dementia research (19%), mood disorders (17%), schizophrenic psychoses (10%), alcohol/drug dependence (7%), and anxiety disorders (5%). These percentages roughly parallel the rates of hospitalizations for the respective disorders.

Substantial resources must be directed toward psychiatric research because understanding causation and evolution of illness will result in improved prevention and treatment. Improved funding will attract young researchers to the area of mental illness throughout Canada. Appropriately, CIHR awards are spread over all Canadian universities even though, traditionally, the largest universities receive the largest grants. McGill University, for instance, has always been a front-runner.

2001–2002 CIHR Awards (in millions $Can)	
1. McGill University	40.9
2. University of British Columbia	36.2
3. University of Toronto	35.2
4. University of Alberta	29.2
5. University of Calgary	25.0
6. McMaster University	22.1
7. Université Laval	20.2
8. Université de Montréal	19.2
9. Hospital for Sick Children	18.5
10. University of Ottawa	16.9
Source: The Scientist 2003; 17: #3 14	

The smaller universities are often, however, judged as better places in which to do science. Dalhousie University has ranked high as a place to work, as have the University of Alberta and McMaster University, suggesting that the CIHR policy of awarding all Universities, large or small, is manifestly correct.

Attracting scientists requires more than good funding (although that is vital). Also important are adequate laboratory and research facilities, incentives for new faculty members, a research infrastructure, good library facilities, opportunities for collabo-

Best Places to Work in Academia, Outside the U.S.
1. Dalhousie University (Canada)
2. INRA Research Center at Versailles-Grignon (France)
3. University of Dundee (Scotland)
4. University of Alberta (Canada)
5. McMaster University, Hamilton (Canada)
6. Hebrew University, Jerusalem (Israel)
7. University of Manchester (England)
8. University of Toronto (Canada)
9. Ghent University (Belgium)
10. Catholic University of Leuven (Belgium)
Source: The Scientist 2003; 17: #20, 19.

ration (mentioned by many of our interviewees), the academic quality of colleagues, effective and supportive management, a flexible balance between research and teaching duties (mentioned by Cheryl Grady and Harvey Chochinov – please see Chapters 7 and 11), a clear and supportive policy about commercialization of research (an emerging issue), and a geographic location that allows for a good quality of life.

Research areas that are today attracting the most attention in the brain sciences are neuroimaging and genetic studies. Neuroimaging (functional MRI, PET, MR spectroscopy, and SPECT) promises to yield ever-increasing amounts of information about the brain in health and disease. In this book, the chapters on memory, mood, schizophrenia and stress best illustrate the potential of neuroimaging techniques. With respect to genetic studies, it has proven difficult to identify the genes that contribute to illnesses of complex traits, e.g., most psychiatric illnesses, although some genes for Alzheimer's disease have been isolated (see Chapters 1 and 4). By applying knowledge gained from the Human Genome Project, the Haplotype Project, and from animal models, and from a greater appreciation of epigenetics (the study of heritable changes in gene function that occur without a change in the sequence of nuclear DNA), psychiatric genetics, it is predicted, will soon undergo a period of unprecedented discovery. On the other hand, some researchers believe that too much money is being spent on molecular genetics, a field that has not yet produced demonstrable dividends in psychiatry. Several chapters, however, illustrate promising approaches to candidate genes for psychiatric illness or describe research on biological markers that could eventually lead back to the relevant genes.

In terms of populations, Chapters 5, 6, and 12 exemplify the ability of epidemiology, health policy and health services research to improve the health of Canadians. Demographic studies and clinical trials translate laboratory findings into interventions whose outcomes can subsequently be compared with respect to efficacy, safety, and cost. Translational studies (i.e., from laboratory to clinic) are described in the chapters about anxiety disorders, mood disorders, personality disorders, and substance abuse disorders although Ray Lam (Chapter 8) points out that it takes too long a time before the results of research are translated into service provision.

The Business Equation

Major depression results in poor productivity and sick leave from the workplace (Please see Chapter 19). The workplace, therefore, is an important focal point for addressing mental health issues. As the Institute of Neurosciences, Mental Health and Addiction has understood, it is critical to support the development of healthy work environments, to educate employers and employees in the area of mental health, and to provide supportive reintegration into the work environment for those experiencing mental illness. Mental illness currently accounts for 30% of disability claims (with costs of $15 to $33 billion to the employer annually in Canada (Please see Srouijan in Further Reading). A recent UK study of 610 respondents with chronic illnesses including arthritis, musculoskeletal pain, diabetes, asthma, migraine, heart disease, irritable bowel syndrome, and depression found that depression, among all these illnesses, was most debilitating to one's capacity to work. Employer work adjustments were available to those with illnesses that required a *physical* work adjustment and, for most illnesses, work adjustments were made and social supports provided. And yet, those with depression were least likely to receive a work adjustment, indicating either that they had failed to disclose their depression or that the employers felt no adjustments were necessary (or did not know what kind of adjustments to make). In Canada, the consulting firm Watson Wyatt Canada reported in 2000 that only 35% of the organizations they polled had return-to-work practices in place that were specific to mental health claims. A 2005 survey by the same organization showed that only five per cent of Canadian companies had any proactive plans or awareness policies to deal with the social stigma of mental illness, which may keep sufferers from being open about the cause of their time off work.

Philanthropy Matters

Many of the chapters in this book are narratives of philanthropy. What seems to be new about today's philanthropists is that they want to make a personal difference in their world. They are younger and more energetic than benefactors of old and they have the means to indulge their personal interests. They are tackling large issues such as poverty, education, and health. While the motive for earlier generations was to leave behind family fortunes, many prosperous people today expressly do not want to leave excessive wealth to their children, aware of the psychological problems that can sometimes accompany affluence. Some give anonymously, achieving the seventh level of *tzedaka* identified by Maimonides (please see Chapter 26). They are grateful for having been blessed with wealth and feel that they are obligated to give back in return. They don't require recognition. The knowledge that they have contributed to something of significance is reward enough. Instead of waiting until they die, many of today's philanthropists want to donate while they can still direct how the funds will be spent.

Philanthropists do receive tax benefits when they contribute to charity. This is the way governments encourage philanthropy; yet Canada could clearly offer greater donation deductibility and flexibility and thereby ensure greater giving. As Michael Wilson notes in Chapter 24, the tax burden and underlying wealth base are variables that figure prominently in aggregate donor calculations. Accordingly, the federal government needs to recognize that incentives matter in the crafting of philanthropic policy in Canada. Currently, much of the money for health-related charity goes to organizations that are poorly financed, poorly staffed, and poorly managed, and that continue to ask for additional donations every year. In contrast, a better investment vehicle for charitable dollars is an organizational infrastructure that can eventually become self-supporting. A relatively new phenomenon has been active partnering among governments, corporations, individual donors, and private foundations, so called public-private partnerships. Sandra Schulze (see Chapter 28) advocates an organized, interlocking network model for charitable giving on a national basis.

Interestingly, the people who give the most to charity in Canada may be the ones who make the least. This phenomenon is exemplified in our book by the story of Marier in Chapter 27. In 1994, the average Canadian claimed charitable donations totaling $586, up from $567 in 1991. Households earning under $10,000 give 5.2% of their income to charity – a larger percentage of their money than any other income group.

And yet, there are sufficient numbers of wealthy people in Canada that some well-attended charity events cost $100,000 a table. The tradition of philanthropy needs to grow in Canada and this can be aided by a tax structure that promotes it.

Canadian Millionaires (Merrill Lynch and Cap Gemini Ernst & Young, 2003)	
450,000	$1 million in assets
54,000	over $5 million
7,000	over $20 million
500	$50–$100 million
13	over $100 million

We have tried in this book to solicit the viewpoints not only of objective researchers but also of subjective sufferers. Chapter 21 asks the question whether psychological illness is best understood from the inside, the sufferer's view, or from the outside, the view of the neutral observing professional. In Bruno Cormier's terms (Chapter 6), this encompasses "the watchers and the watched." Both perspectives are needed – the entire enterprise of psychiatric research would fail without research volunteers who report their experience and agree to be studied. It is critical to address the needs of patients, to ask for their input and to provide them with timely feedback when they participate in research.

Researchers are not alone in seeking and producing new information. The stream of expertise needs to flow back and forth between researchers and stakeholders (please see Lomas, 2003 in Further Reading). Those who have experienced mental illness or who have lost loved ones to suicide have shown us new ways by which grief and suffering can be overcome – through creative pursuits or through helping others, or through the growth of wisdom. As we were writing this book, it quickly became evident that scientists, philanthropists and sufferers, working together, constitute Canada's hope for the future. The book itself illustrates how much the private and the academic, the medical and the professional, the family and the individual sector of a community can accomplish when they work together – and how critical it is that they do so. This is perhaps the most important message of *Psyche in the Lab*, which, while starting out as a book about psychiatric research, spontaneously evolved into a testament to human resilience.

Further Reading

Anderson MW. The Scientist. 2004;18:21,46.

Canadian Community Health Survey: Mental health and well-being; 2002. Available at: www.statcan.ca

Canadian Health Services Research Foundation. Available at: http://www.chsrf.ca/home_e.php

Canadian Institute for Health Information. Available at: http://secure.cihi.ca/cihiweb/dispPage.jsp?cw_page=home_e

Canadian Mental Health Association. Available at: http://www.cmha.ca/bins/index.asp

Canadian Psychiatric Research Foundation. Available at: http://www.cprf.ca/

Corrigan PW. Target-specific stigma change: a strategy for impacting mental illness stigma. Psychiatr Rehabil J. 2004;28:113–121.

Corrigan PW, Markowitz FE, Watson AC. Structural levels of mental illness stigma and discrimination. Schizophr Bull. 2004;30:481–491.

Crisp AH, editor. Every family in the land: understanding prejudice and discrimination against people with mental illness. London. Royal Society of Medicine Press. (2004).

Crowther RE, Marshall M, Bond GR, Huxley P. Helping people with severe mental illness to obtain work: A systematic review. Br Med J. 2001;322:204–208.

Dewa CS, Lin E. Chronic physical illness, psychiatric disorder and disability in the workplace. Soc Sci Med, 2000;51:41–50.

Dewa CS, Lesage A, Goering P, Caveen M. Nature and prevalence of mental illness in the workplace. Healthcare Papers. 2004;5:12–25.

Estroff SE, Penn DL, Toporek JR. From stigma to discrimination: an analysis of community efforts to reduce the negative consequences of having a psychiatric disorder and label. Schizophr Bull. 2004;30:493–509.

Falk G. How we treat outsiders. New York, Prometheus Books (2001).

Jenkins R. Making psychiatric epidemiology useful: the contribution of epidemiology to government policy. Acta Psychiatr Scand. 2001;103:2–14.

Lavis JN, Robertson D, Woodside JM, McLeod CB, Abelson J. Knowledge Transfer Study Group. How can research organizations more effectively transfer research knowledge to decision-makers? Milbank Q. 2003;81:221–248.

Lavis JN, Posada FB, Haines A, Osei E. Use of research to inform public policymaking. Lancet. 2004;364:1615–1621.

Lim D, Sanderson K, Andrews G. Lost productivity among full-time workers with mental disorders. J Mental Health Policy Economics. 2000;3:139–146.

Lomas J. Using "linkage and exchange" to move research into policy at a Canadian Foundation. Health Affairs. 2000;19:236–240.

Lomas JN, Fulop N, Gagnon D, Allen P. On being a good listener: setting priorities for applied health services research. Milbank Q. 2003;81:363–368.

Merrill Lynch and Cap Gemini Ernst & Young. World Wealth Report, 2003.

Munir F, Jones D, Leka S, Griffiths A. Work limitations and employer adjustments for employees with chronic illness. Int J Rehabil Res. 2005;28:111–117.

Rochefort DA. More lessons, of a different kind: Canadian mental health policy in comparative perspective. Hosp Community Psychiatry. 1992;43:1083–1090.

Sackett DL, Straus SE, Richardson WS, Rosenberg W, Haynes RB. Evidence-based medicine: how to practice and teach EBM. New York: Churchill Livingstone; 2000.

Stephens T, Joubert N. The economic burden of mental health problems in Canada. Chronic Diseases in Canada. 2001;22:18–23.

Sroujian C. Mental Health is the number one cause of disability in Canada. Insurance J. 2003;8.

Stuart H. Stigma and the Daily News. Evaluation of a newspaper intervention. Can J Psychiatry. 2003;48:301–306.

Stuart H. Stigma and work. Healthcare Papers. 2004; 5:100–111.

Townsend C, Whiteford H, Baingana F, Gulbinat W, Jenkins R, Baba A, Lieh Mak F, Manderscheid R, Mayeya J, Minoletti A, Mubbashar MH, Khandelwal S, Schilder K, Tomov T, Parameshvara Deva M. The mental health policy template: domains and elements for mental health policy formulation. Int Rev Psychiatry. 2004;16:18–23.

Ustun TB, Chisholm D. Global "burden of disease" study for psychiatric disorders. Psychiatr Prax. 2001;28 Suppl 1:S7–11.

Watson Wyatt Worldwide. The dollars and sense of effective disability management. Catalogue # W-377. Vancouver, Watson Wyatt Worldwide; 2000.

Watson Wyatt Worldwide. Staying@Work™ 2005 – Making the connection to a healthy organization. Available at: https://www.watsonwyatt.com/canada-english/research/resrender. asp?id=W-860&page=1

Appendix I:
List of Interviewees

Martin Alda
Michael Alzamora
Jack Barr
Keri-Leigh Cassidy
Harvey Max Chochinov
Ruby Cormier
Beva Dudiak
Earla Dunbar
Paula Goering
Cheryl Grady
Cyril Greenland
Herta Guttman
Katherine Hegadoren
Judy Hills
Jeanette Holden
Henderika Holden
Jim Holden
Raymond Lam
Ellen Lipman
Ana Lopes
Alex Lowy
Renee Marier
Patrick McGeer
Edith McGeer
Rachel Morehouse
Juan Carlos Negrete
Margaret Offord
Rémi Quirion
Sandra Schulze
Philip Seeman
Zindel Segal
Sandra Sharwood
Doris Sommer-Rotenberg
Richard Swinson
Joseph Tanenbaum
Don Tapscott
Ross Taylor
Diana Tremain
Edward Tremain
Michael Wilson

Appendix II:
Canadian Psychiatric Research Foundation

Board of Directors

President: Frank C. Buckley	1980–1985
President: Robert C. Paterson	1986–1991
President: John S. Lane	1992–1993
President: John S. Hunkin	1994–1995
Chair: Stanley H. Hartt	1996–1999
Chair: Gordon J. Feeney	2000–2002
Chair: Paul K. Bates	2003–2005
Chair: Kevin McNeill	2005–

Professional Advisory Board

Chair: Dr. Harvey Stancer	1980–1982
Chair: Dr. Quentin Rae-Grant	1982–1986
Chair: Dr. Paul Garfinkel	1986–1990
Chair: Dr. A. George Awad	1990–1993
Chair: Dr. Stan Kutcher	1994–1995
Chair: Dr. Sidney H. Kennedy	1996–1997
Chair: Dr. Trevor Young	1998–2003
Chair: Dr. Robert Zipursky	2003–2005
Chair: Dr. Richard Swinson	2005–

PAC Chair

Mary Early	1984–1988
Inta Kierans	1988–1994
Sandra Sharwood	1994–2000
Jane Drynan	2000–2003
Alex Lowy	2003–

Executive Directors

Manuel Zack	1984–1989
Ron Rea	1989–1988
Judy Hills	1998–2006
Joan Montgomery	2006–

Grants Administrator

Monica Vaus	1990–2005

Subject Index

Name Index